Advance Praise for
ROI of Social Media
How to Improve the Return on Your Social Marketing Investment

The biggest shift in today's marketing world isn't the much-discussed declining effectiveness of television advertising but the changes in how consumers research and buy products—and social media is at the heart of this structural dynamic. Simply measuring ROMI will not improve performance since marketing strategies are often flawed and their spending is inefficient. Indeed, we need to go beyond metrics and take a hard look at why the numbers are so bad! Groves, Powell and Dimos provide a timely and accessible text to allow a new and less controllable brand communications channel be managed within a holistic framework. Full of practical gems, it will stimulate your thinking and help you make better decisions.

Chris D. Beaumont
Professor, Tokyo University, Global Center of Excellence
Director, North Asia, Results International

If you've ever tried to integrate social media into your marketing planning, and especially if you've tried to measure its impact, The *ROI of Social Media* is a must-read. The authors bring decades of experience and a wealth of insight to anyone who is trying to plug into this elusive media channel and determine its value to your organization. The depth of discussion on ROI provided in this book addresses the glaring void in evaluating social marketing—its effect on my income statement. You need to read this book.

Dominic "Nick" Popielski
Director, Marketing Analysis Sales & Marketing
AGL Resources, Inc.

Before you spend another second on your latest social media marketing campaign you should read this book! Doing so will be the first step in improving your ROI for all your media investments. Congratulations to Steven, Guy and Jerry for showing the way in developing a strategy that actually works for businesses wanting to harness the power of social marketing.

Bill Jula
CEO & Co-Founder
Fast Pitch!

I would like to congratulate the writers for their great initiative and achievement in putting such a comprehensive and knowledgeable book together which would be a vital asset to the Chief Marketing Officers, Chief Executive Officers and Chief Financial Officers. The growth in popularity of Social Media and ROI has created a vacuum and necessity for a credible, leading material— *ROI of Social Media* fulfills it.

Nisar Butt
President and Chief Executive Officer
International Institute of Marketing Professionals

ROI of Social Media

ROI of $ocial Media

HOW TO IMPROVE THE RETURN ON YOUR SOCIAL MARKETING INVESTMENT

Guy Powell | Steven Groves | Jerry Dimos

WILEY

John Wiley & Sons (Asia) Pte. Ltd.

Other Wiley Editorial Offices

John Wiley & Sons, 111 River Street, Hoboken, NJ 07030, USA
John Wiley & Sons, The Atrium, Southern Gate, Chichester, West Sussex, P019 8SQ, United Kingdom
John Wiley & Sons (Canada) Ltd., 5353 Dundas Street West, Suite 400, Toronto, Ontario, M9B 6HB, Canada
John Wiley & Sons Australia Ltd., 42 McDougall Street, Milton, Queensland 4064, Australia
Wiley-VCH, Boschstrasse 12, D-69469 Weinheim, Germany

Library of Congress Cataloging-in-Publication Data
ISBN 978-0-470-82741-3 (Hardback)
ISBN 978-0-470-82743-7 (ePDF)
ISBN 978-0-470-82742-0 (Mobi)
ISBN 978-0-470-82744-4 (ePub)

Typeset in 10.5/11.5pt ITC Garamond by MPS Limited, a Macmillan Company, Chennai
Printed in Singapore by Saik Wah Press Pte. Ltd.
10 9 8 7 6 5 4 3 2 1

DEDICATION

From Guy

To my wife, Karen, for putting up with all the time it took to write this book.

To Robert, Collin and Kristin.

To the children of the United Methodist Children's Home. The mission of the United Methodist Children's Home is to serve the needs of children and their families in crisis. Ten percent of the royalties derived by Guy from the sale of this book will be contributed to this worthy charity. If you would like to learn more about the United Methodist Children's Home, please contact them directly at 500 S. Columbia Drive, Decatur, GA 30030, or www.umch.com.

From Steven

To my Sister Stephanie and partner Cynthia for believing in me, to Parker and Megan for inspiring me and to my co-authors Guy and Jerry for being supportive in the process and nurturing a deeper understanding of traditional marketing in me.

To my son Steven II and my parents Gerry and Betty who are always in my thoughts and prayers. There have been so many people that have meant a lot as this project has unfolded, they all deserve a thought and consideration.

Finally, to all the people in my life that make it rich and rewarding and just the most wonderful place to be—keep on being social!

From Jerry

To my wife, Megan, for her support even though she knew that this book would consume all my time and generally make me a less enjoyable person to be around.

Contents

Foreword .... **xvii**

Preface .... **xix**

Acknowledgments .... **xxvii**

Introduction **1**

SECTION 1—Getting Started with Social Media ROI **5**

**Chapter 1—Getting Started with Social
Media ROI** **7**
What is social media ROI? 7
Social marketing is measurable: The marketing
process model applied to social marketing 8
The Media Engagement Framework introduced 9
Make better strategic and tactical marketing decisions 11
Value for social media infrastructure providers 13
*Case Study: Viral videos provide serious ROI: $50
Budget = two million hits on YouTube* *13*
Blendtec *13*
A (short) history of social marketing ROI 15
Discussion forums 16
Ratings and reviews 17
Proprietary branded communities 18
Blogging 18
Micro-blogging 19
Social networks 19
Paid word-of-mouth advertising networks 20
Obstacles in determining social marketing ROI 21
The definition of ROI 21
Calculating costs 22
Losing control of your brand 22
Separating buzz into its component parts 23
Traditional media versus social media 23
Case Study: Social media and customer support *24*
Comcast *24*
Engagement is the key 26
Measuring traditional media 28
*Case Study: Making social media a part of your
company's DNA* *29*

Bravo Networks.. *29*
Social marketing strategy 32
   Influencers..32
   Individuals 33
   Consumers...34
     Case Study: Metrics for social media resemble
      those for traditional media *35*
      Edelman Digital *35*
Measuring social marketing 37
   Social media measurement tools 37
   A process to social marketing ROI..........................37
The future of social media and ROI 37
Let's get started. 38

Chapter 2—Social Media Motivations
and Behaviors **41**
Motivations for participating in social media..............42
   Individuals—social media participant hierarchy 42
   Conversation hierarchy..44
The three tiers of social media strategy 45
   Influencers..45
   Consumers...46
   Individuals 47
Motivators 48
   Motivators for individuals 49
   Motivators for influencers.......................................57
Behaviors...61
     Case Study: Segmenting messages by
      social community *62*
      Sessions College for Professional Design *62*
Social media segmentation model...............................63
   Behavioral targeting...65
   Social Web-Reputation Management Cycles 73
Conclusion 74

SECTION 2—The Media Engagement Framework............77

Chapter 3—Introduction to the Media
Engagement Framework..**79**
     Case Study: Stratification of engagement *80*
     PitneyBowes *81*
Applying the Media Engagement Framework 83
   Media channel agnostic 84

The personas of the media engagement framework....................84
  Influencers..84
    Case Study: Co-creating a brand with the customer... 87
      Delta Airlines.. 87
  Consumers..88
  Individuals 89
Brand imagery 90
Competitive set..92
  Influencer: Endorsement share 92
  Consumer: Brands 92
  Individual: Time 92
Measurement set 92
  Influencer endorsement funnel 93
  Consumer purchase funnel.......................................93
  Community engagement funnel 93
Conclusion 93

Chapter 4—Influencer Persona in the
Media Engagement Framework 95
The influencer and the Media Engagement Framework 95
  Case Study: The three pillars of marketing 96
    Microsoft, Southeast Asia.............................. 96
  Evaluating Influence 99
  Influencer segmentation...100
  Influence measurement tools 105
  Compensating influencers.......................................106
  Influencer communities..106
  Influencer marketing agencies.................................108
  Influencer stratification..108
  Other influencer segmentation dimensions 110
  The influencer endorsement funnel........................110
Conclusion 114

Chapter 5—Consumer Persona in the
Media Engagement Framework 117
  Case Study: Amplifying the effect of offline with
    online social media...120
    Guinness Anchor Berhad..............................120
The consumer and the MEF 123
  Consumers as a subset of individuals 123
  Consumer purchase funnel.......................................124
Social media and B2B marketing and selling.............................133
  The purchase committee..134

Messages moving B2B consumers down the
consumer purchase funnel..135
Case Study: Marketing is the new finance....................*136*
Dell Computers, Inc., EMEA...*136*
Conclusion 139

**Chapter 6—Individual Persona in the
Media Engagement Framework 141**
The individual and the MEF 141
*Case Study: Driving value and users in the
community engagement funnel—Twitter
versus F150online*..*142*
Twitter...*143*
F150online...*144*
The community engagement funnel.......................................146
Conclusion 166

**Chapter 7—The Competitive Set—Vying
for Attention..169**
Endorsement share as the competitive
set for influencers...169
Brand as the competitive set for consumers............................171
*Case Study: Competing demands for time—
how much zoo can you use?*...*171*
*The world-famous San Diego Zoo and
the San Diego Zoo's Wild Animal Park*.......................*172*
Time as the competitive set 174
Conclusion 175

Chapter 8—The Brand Image..177
Brand image across the MEF 177
Brand imagery..177
Brand preferences..179
Case Study: Audience segmentation around a topic...180
Joan Koerber-Walker—CorePurpose.......................*180*
Influencers and the brand...182
Consumers and the brand...182
Individuals and the brand 183
Tracking attribute scores in social media 183
Conclusion 183

Chapter 9— Search-Being Found in Social Media 185
Being visible in social media 185
Social media and search...186

Organic search 187
Paid ads on the search pages 188
Social marketing and the impact on SEM 188
The "memory" of the web 189
Web page archiving and storage 190
Conclusion 190

**SECTION 3—Practical Applications of
Social Media ROI** **193**

**Chapter 10—Putting Values to the "R" and "I"
of ROI in Social Media** **195**
Why ROI? 195
Put marketing in the critical path to
corporate success 196
Marketing ROI for the short and long term 196
Revenue, profit, brand and share 196
Optimization: Approachable through
continuous improvement 197
*Case Study: Social marketing ROI: A focal point
for the financial services industry* *198*
First Tennessee Bank *198*
Introduction to ROI 200
The "I" side of the ROI equation 202
The cost of a CEO blog 205
*Case Study: Stratifying response to
determine effectiveness* *205*
1800Flowers.com *205*
Measuring the "R" of ROI 208
Conclusion: The ROI of ROI 212

**Chapter 11—Eight-Step Process to Measuring
Social Marketing Strategy and ROI** **215**
Building a culture of metrics in social media 215
Social marketing metrics infrastructure 216
Corporate and marketing infrastructure 216
Social media channel 217
Campaign 218
Ongoing metrics and flighting of messages 218
Eight-Step process to measure social marketing
strategy and ROI 219
1. Develop strategy and set goals 220
2. Identifying target audiences 221

3. Developing the campaign message and monitoring conversation content...223
4. Executing social marketing campaign tactics.....................224
5. Defining, monitoring and evaluating interim and success metrics; choosing the analytical methodology...226
6. Monitoring and managing the execution of social marketing campaigns...228
7. Measuring and tracking actual costs, calculating ROI...229
8. Reviewing success or failure and iterating........................231
Conclusion...232

Chapter 12—Social Media Metrics Tools Providers......233
Evaluating metrics tools and how to survey tool capabilities..233
Monitoring versus metrics versus influence.............................234
A framework for evaluating tools...234
Tool pricing...235
Tool assessment characteristics...236
Type of tool...236
Listening capabilities..236
The metric of tone and sentiment...237
Platform orientation...238
Scalability..238
Metrics provided..238
Examples using the ROI of social media tool analysis framework...239
Tool evaluation summary..239
Vendor Interviews...239
Case Study: Answering the (social) phone.................240
Radian6..240
Case Study: Measurement makes sense when social media has a clearly defined strategy...........245
Alterian..245
Case Study: Twitter can be analyzed..............................248
Twitalyzer...248
Case Study: Check the clout of influencers in your market..249
Klout...250
Conclusion...252

**SECTION 4—Where Does Social Media
Go from Here?** **253**

Chapter 13—The Future of Social Media and ROI.......**255**
   *Case Study: Being social before the advent
      of social media*..*256*
      Allrecipes.com *256*
  Greatly expanded business adoption of social media................258
  The death of social media and the emergence of a
    new social paradigm...258
  Noise 259
  Consumer expectations of understanding who they are...........260
  A global market that never closes 261
  Consumer privacy, identity, location and portability.................261
    Privacy and identity in social media 262
    Physical location in a virtual world......................................263
    Single sign-on..263
  Trust and reputation-based economy..264
  Semantics 264
    Semantic engines get smarter...265
    Semantic analysis of consumer generated content................265
  Network access and mobile 267
  The micro scale economics of social media 268
  The social media bubble and global
    platform consolidation...269
  China and social media 269
  Unforeseen applications of social technology 270
  Conclusion 270

Afterword...**273**

Appendix **275**

Bibliography **279**

Index..**281**

PREFACE

As recently as early 2010, many social marketers would have claimed that social media couldn't be measured, it shouldn't be measured or that businesses should be content with the new interpersonal engagement provided by social media, regardless of cost. It's easy to draw comparisons to the 80s when computers would enable the paperless office and the 90s when the Internet would make bricks and mortar commerce obsolete. Predictably this has changed and many marketers are seeing the need to measure their success in social media because costs need to be accounted for, and incremental earnings are what really matters. Social media is not just about engaging potential customers, but it is about promoting the brand to drive increased revenue, profit, brand and market share with an acceptable level of cost and risk. Over the past few months, a few good books have been published that talk about social media and social media metrics, but they only tell a partial story. The complete story is that in order to determine whether social media is driving incremental sales volume and earnings, it must be considered a part of the entire marketing mix. Social media marketing can only be measured in the context of the entire marketing mix, including both traditional and social media. With that in mind, we need to understand what the drivers of value are for a brand and how a message in social media differs from, or is similar to, a message in traditional media. With that in mind, we have developed the concepts presented in this book and a practical model for business. If marketers can take these concepts to heart, they will not only be better social marketers but they will be better marketers overall.

IT ISN'T SIMPLY SOCIAL MEDIA.
IT IS MEDIA THAT IS SOCIAL!

Social media is also not just one big monolithic channel. It is made up of many different types of channels, each with its own nuances. Just as newspaper advertising is different from trade publication advertising, which is different from TV advertising, which is also different from out-of-home subway advertising, so too is Twitter different from Facebook and MySpace. Also, traditional media doesn't need to be just a silo of messages being broadcast out to the nameless masses. It can be shaped by the give and take of social media. It can be used to support social media marketing campaigns and social media can be used to support traditional marketing campaigns. Traditional media is no longer just traditional. Social media is no longer just social. It is media overall that is social. In that light, we have chosen to use the term *social marketing* when referring to social media marketing.

SOCIAL MARKETING IS ANOTHER MEDIA CHANNEL SITTING EQUALLY ALONGSIDE ALL OTHERS

In this book, we aren't just talking about social media marketing. We are talking about combining in an integrated fashion any and all media to deliver the best results for the least investment and least risk, but with the primary focus on social marketing. Just as integrated marketing communications became popular about a decade ago, we now see the same integration taking place with the addition of a new media channel to the marketing mix. All media must act in concert to deliver the best results for the company and with that we need to think about marketing in social media as simply social marketing—one component alongside mass media, direct media and one-to-one media. Social marketing won't replace traditional media. It will just be another media channel that marketers can use to engage with their customers. With social marketing, marketers will be able to engage with certain groups of individuals to deliver certain types of messages to certain types of audiences that are more effectively delivered than through other traditional media channels.

ROI OF SOCIAL MEDIA HAS MANY TARGET AUDIENCES

This book was written for a number of groups and individuals in the organization. Certainly, anyone in marketing is a primary target audience for this book. Marketers must not only understand how messages from any source impinge on their consumers, but how messages must now be targeted to individuals in general—and influencers pertinent to the brand—as well as to their consumers. Business managers, entrepreneurs, CEOs and CFOs are also targets for this book. Other groups in the organization also benefit from social media, including customer service, operations, market research, product development, investor relations and human resources. All of these functions have a stake in social media and they need to know how they, too, can take advantage of social media and measure its impact on their business functions. In addition, many of these business functions need to understand how they can support the marketing team in developing a metrics infrastructure to measure the results from marketing in general and social marketing specifically.

THE TOP LEVEL TAKEAWAY

Overall, we see this book helping the CMO to answer that nagging question from the CEO and CFO about social media and its value to the firm:

> "How can the company use this new media channel most effectively to drive more revenue, profit, brand and share with the highest ROI and least risk?"

Whether the company is a multinational fast moving consumer goods (FMCG) or consumer packaged goods (CPG) company, needing to justify its investments in social media, a small 10-man firm looking to find inexpensive ways to grow its niche business, or a mid-sized organization needing to determine the best allocation of its limited marketing resources, this book will provide clear guidelines on how this can be done. In order for these organizations to fully understand social marketing metrics and ROI, a discussion of how to develop successful social marketing strategies and tactics is also included. Only with a clear understanding of the fundamentals of social marketing strategy will the ROI and metrics concepts be able to be fully applied. For marketers looking to explain, improve and get approval for social marketing in their organizations, this book provides a strategic and tactical overview of social marketing and how it can deliver greater ROI. It differs from other social marketing books because it has ROI—the language of business—as the primary focus. With ROI as the primary focus, businesses will learn from their mistakes more quickly and understand precisely how to adjust their social go-to-market model. They will need to spend less time and effort experimenting with arbitrary tactics and more time executing tactics that provide results. Our guiding philosophy for return on marketing investment is based on the concepts of ROI developed in *Marketing Calculator: Measuring and Managing Your Return on Marketing Investment:*[1,2]

> "The purpose of return on marketing investment (ROMI) is to optimize marketing spend for the short and long term in support of the brand strategy by building a market model using valid and objective marketing metrics and analytics."

Many industries will differ in how social marketing will apply. Some industries are highly regulated—such as financial and pharmaceuticals—and they will need to apply some of the concepts in this book differently from marketers in those industries where there is less regulation. Businesses that are already spending heavily on traditional media—such as large consumer marketing companies—will find that social media will make up only a small component of the overall volume of messages inserted into the marketplace, but that proportion of messages can provide high leverage (i.e. bang for buck). Other industries where their customer base is primarily Internet and social media savvy—such as, high tech—will need a highly sophisticated implementation of social marketing metrics in order to stay ahead of the competition and reap the full measure of rewards from social marketing. Yet other industries where the purchase is highly considered—such as higher value consumer electronics where ratings and reviews play a key role in the consumer choice—will have other requirements in how they'll need to implement social marketing strategy and optimize their marketing spend. We have also included many references to social marketing cases from around the world. These case studies illustrate some of the nuances of building a social marketing strategy in different countries and what it takes to measure their success.

SOCIAL MEDIA SUPPORTS MANY BUSINESS FUNCTIONS

Social media isn't just for marketing. It also supports many other business functions. The king above all else must be that of customer discovery. The ability to gain customer insights is a competitive differentiator that generates momentum for the brand. The momentum effect,[3] which is based on the 20 year study by Jean-Claude Larreche, enables firms to grow faster than the competition—outperforming the Dow Jones average by up to 80 percent. Social media marketing can generate a two-way exchange that reveals valuable customer insights beneficial to firms implementing business structures based on the concepts of the momentum effect.

Many industries augment their customer service functions through social media and don't yet invest in social marketing. Others have fully operationalized the use of social media and have made it into a core component of their business processes. Even in these cases, social media has a strong impact on how marketing can take advantage of these functions to drive the most value for their brands. As we will see from the case studies, Dell Computer and Comcast have been able to fully internalize social media into their customer service operations to drive a competitive advantage in their categories. Social media can also be used: for product development and innovation by listening to the needs of their customers in their own voices; for market research in order to understand specific trends affecting their brands; and for lead generation for business-to-business marketers.

SOCIAL MEDIA REQUIRES CEO INVOLVEMENT

Social media shouldn't be just a low-level function within the organization or delegated to the person with nothing to do. The CEO now needs to be concerned and involved to make certain that the individuals on the front lines participating in social media are portraying the brands as they should be and not exposing the company to undue risk. Social media provides bi-directional connections between the brand and the consumer, and consumer-to-consumer. It opens up new opportunities and new risks that the company must be ready for. Social media will become a highly important channel for the company to convey its brand messages and the CEO must understand how it works and how it can augment and drive the value of all media for the company's brands. Social media is something that must be executed earlier rather than later. The brand that has the first, best social media presence will quickly achieve a critical mass that will be difficult for its competitor's brands to beat. This competitive advantage can be long-lived if it is given the proper support at all levels in the organization.

BOOK OUTLINE

This book is broken down into four sections. The first section describes the development of the core concept: the media engagement framework. This concept has three pillars to it and describes each of the personas (influencers, individuals and consumers) that are important to the development and measurement of a successful social marketing strategy. This framework can be used by any organization at any stage in their use of social media. Whether they are just developing their first social marketing plan or have developed many in the past, this framework will help all marketers develop and measure their strategies to provide the most value for the organization.

The second section builds out in detail each of the elements of the media engagement framework, and looks at how a social marketing strategy can be measured at each level in the framework. The media engagement framework provides a comprehensive view into the requirements of developing, measuring and evaluating a successful social marketing strategy. It is made up of much more than just a few disparate metrics. Instead, the required metrics are described along each of the critical dimensions in the framework so that social marketers can deliver a fully comprehensive social marketing strategy. Because data is one of the key limitations in any measurement framework, methodologies are presented that can support the marketer in defining the right data sets that accurately and reliably go into the calculation of the ROI of social marketing. With accurate and reliable data, social marketing risks can be reduced because the right activities will be done at the right time, in the right way with the right messages. In an ideal world, perfect data would be available in a timely manner at no cost. In reality, there are compromises that need to be made and these will be discussed so that the ROI of ROI—that is the return on investment from measuring the ROI of social marketing—can deliver a high value for the investment in the associated manpower and costs in implementing a successful social marketing ROI function, which is made up of the right management, staff, technology and workflow.

The third section looks at how other organizations have begun to implement some of the concepts and what they have learned in the process. It includes a discussion on how the "R" and "I" of ROI can be measured and properly evaluated. It also includes an eight-step process for the implementation of these concepts in any organization.

Lastly, the fourth section provides a view of the future and how the media engagement framework can be applied as social media technologies evolve and grow.

This book provides a foundation for all marketers to be successful with social marketing. We believe we have brought together a mix of:

- valuable case studies to see how other companies have tackled the implementation and execution of social marketing and social marketing metrics and ROI
- a comprehensive media engagement framework to make certain the concepts fit together in a logical and executable fashion representing the real world
- a unique blend of social media strategy savvy, marketing ROI expertise and marketing strategy to make certain the presented concepts can truly drive value for the brand
- a short- and long-term view of the critical drivers of marketing excellence and brand value.

The concepts contained in this book also don't end with the reading of all the chapters in the printed book. We have put together a group of social media properties on Facebook (http://www.facebook.com/ROIofSocialMedia), LinkedIn (www.TheROIofSocialMedia.com will get you there), and Twitter (@ROISocialMedia) to provide a source of conversation and ongoing value as the technologies and markets evolve and change.

We hope you will join the conversation.

ENDNOTES

1. Yes, this is a blatant plug—more to follow. Nevertheless a worthwhile read, especially if you are serious about marketing ROI.

2. Guy R. Powell, *Marketing Calculator: Measuring and Managing Your Return on Marketing Investment.* (Singapore: John Wiley & Sons (Asia), 2008).

3. J.C. Larreche, *The Momentum Effect: How to Ignite Exceptional Growth* (New Jersey: Wharton School Publishing, 2009).

ACKNOWLEDGMENTS

Our greatest thanks and appreciation go out to the many marketers who have helped us to write this book. Some of them helped directly—many indirectly. Having worked with and trained many marketers in workshops around the world, each of their questions and concerns helped us to keep searching for new ways to explain the concepts of social media and marketing effectiveness. These comments and inputs have now been used to put together this book on social media ROI. Each of us would also like to thank each of our interview participants in providing us great material for the case studies used and referenced throughout the book. They provided us input that we would have never been able to acquire and helped us to hone our thinking in putting this book together. Special thanks go to Peter Storer, with whom we've worked before and he is great at what he does. Thanks also go to Joel Balbin and Nick Melchior for keeping us on track and delivering a great manuscript.

FOREWORD

Placing the user at the center of our thinking—whether in the way in which we design our software or the sales, marketing and services strategies we use—has always been of paramount importance at Microsoft. Indeed, empowering users with access to "information at their fingertips" was at the heart of the company's original philosophy when it was created 35 years ago.

Today, with over 90 percent of users choosing Windows for their computing needs, and the majority of these using their computer to connect to the Internet, social media is both a highly relevant and important marketing communication channel for us. What's more, we are also a significant digital media owner in our own right, providing our advertising clients with access to over 650 million Internet users a month through properties such as Windows Live, Hotmail, MSN, Bing and others.

So, at Microsoft, we are not just *consumers* of digital marketing and social media, but also major *suppliers* of solutions in this area as well. With this in mind, the ROI of social media is of great interest to us and we are an active and vocal contributor to this growing debate.

Recently though, it seems more and more business books are drawing conclusions that aren't completely fact-based. They analyze various successful companies and then find some nugget that seems to be the "one thing" that correlates with success and yet, after the book is published, those companies end up losing their ability to sustain success. More often than not, nothing's changed in the organization and yet success eludes them. This is not the case with the *ROI of Social Media*. This book puts forth a solid ROI methodology supported by an analytical model that is brought to life by relevant case studies.

In doing so, the authors make a great team. Guy brings his experience as an ROI expert, Steve his strong social media strategy skills and Jerry his consulting and marketing strategy expertise. It is the only way that this topic could be fully covered. So many social media books tend to only a one-sided view to ROI, and without the practical recommendations to making better marketing decision. Because they actually work day to day in their respective areas, the authors' capabilities are truly tried and tested.

The *ROI of Social Media* is a must read. It starts with a clear foundation of marketing strategy. It takes that strategy and applies social media and social media marketing—social marketing—to it. There is no question that this team of authors has real world experience and made it accessible to brand managers everywhere. There is good, actionable content in each and every chapter.

This book is also one of the first global books with numerous case studies spanning three continents—North America, Europe and Asia. With the rise of Asia, and specifically China, in social media, it will be critical for global marketers to understand how to put their social marketing strategies together for each of the top countries in each region.

Some marketers think social media will replace all other media. This may happen at some point far, far off in the future, but for all practical purposes social media will simply be another media channel standing alongside other traditional media channels. Nevertheless, for some businesses, social media will be the primary media to make their businesses grow. For others, social media will simply leverage traditional media and delivering incredible value for their efforts. Then there are yet others where their traditional media presence is so strong that social media may never catch up.

Regardless of your business type, where your brand is in its lifecycle, or where your marketing team is in its sophistication using social media, this book will help you strategize it, measure it, value it and make it better.

Andrew Pickup
General Manager, Marketing & Business Operations
Microsoft Asia Pacific

INTRODUCTION

Social media is exploding as a new media channel. It differs from other advertising media channels because messages are multi-directional and generated by many parties: the marketer, influencers, individuals and consumers. Social media isn't a one-way broadcast of messages to the masses, but a conversation taking place between many individuals and which, unlike the real world, can have many others observing and consuming the content, not just during the conversation but practically forever into the future. Social media marketing has an easily accessible and long memory.

With multiple parties publishing brand-related messages for their own circle of friends and followers, the marketer is no longer in complete control of the message. Because everyone can play a role in what gets said about a brand, a competitor or the category, social media allows a high level of engagement with consumers compared with other "traditional" one-way media channels. Not only can the brand engage directly in a one-to-one conversation, but the conversation itself can provide value to those consumers passively observing it. By using search and the various conversation threads, individuals can read what others say and, in the process, gather both positive and negative brand impressions.

As social media marketers, we need to understand how to engage with these different types of individuals and their behaviors in order to deliver the most value for the brand and to mitigate the risk and impact of the potential negative word of mouth that might take place. The goal of this book is to help corporate marketers to understand these processes and the motivations and behaviors of these groups so that marketers can make better decisions about their use of social media, how it's measured and how it's managed.

SOCIAL MARKETING INVESTMENTS ARE RISKY AND MUST BE MEASURED

But, as with any investment in time and money, top management wants to see what the returns were in the past for that investment and what they could be in the future. This is doubly true when there is a certain level of risk involved in a particular investment. Social media is the one medium where both positive and negative comments can be made about the brand. The marketer is potentially delivering a message that can be amplified to many additional followers at very low cost, but that amplification may not always be positive. With social media, individuals can and will simply talk about their brand perceptions and experiences, whether they are positive or negative. At the other extreme, individuals can purposely try to sabotage a brand by becoming activists for or against some brand-related cause. Regardless of whether the marketer participates or not, individuals are probably already talking both positively and negatively about the brand. With these extremes in mind, marketers need to understand the potential risks versus the rewards of participating.

Not participating may also be risky. By not entering the conversation early, a competitor's brand may reach critical mass, making it difficult or expensive for a late entrant to catch up. Future marketing opportunities may be lost, without any hope of recovery.

Once a social marketing campaign has begun, the marketer must then monitor and measure the response in order to determine its effectiveness, diagnose potential problems and adjust and re-allocate investments accordingly. Top management demands that any investment, whether it's small or large, produces a return higher than a return that could be garnered elsewhere given the level of risk associated with that investment. Section 1 will discuss how to develop and define a social marketing strategy that can deliver the needed metrics in order to determine its success and validate that marketing is investing corporate funds wisely and delivering on the promised value for the brand.

SOCIAL MEDIA IS ONE COMPONENT OF WORD OF MOUTH

Social media is really just a subset of all word of mouth. Word of mouth (WOM) conversation takes place both offline between friends, family and others or it takes place online. According to a recent study, 90 percent of all word of mouth conversations about a brand still take place offline.[1] Nevertheless, this proportion of offline WOM will decline as the speed, reach and quality of online word of mouth—social media—continues to grow and become a larger part of daily living. For the purposes of this book, we are limiting the definition of social media in this book to mean the online conversation about brands.

SOCIAL MEDIA WILL STAND ALONGSIDE OTHER TRADITIONAL MEDIA

This book differs from others on the topic of social media metrics and ROI in that social media is not looked at in isolation. It is not the media that will replace all others. The traditional media will still have a long and fruitful life, yet marketers realize that messages about their brands are reaching their audiences from this new channel. Indeed, certain market segments prefer to receive information through this channel. Social media is an important research tool for some products and a source of spontaneous retail therapy for others. Just as integrated traditional marketing campaigns were in vogue only a handful of years ago, so, too, must integrated marketing campaigns now include this new media channel in the integrated marketing communications plan. Social media must now be fully linked with all other media when building and measuring a successful marketing strategy.

GROWTH IN SOCIAL MEDIA DRIVEN BY HUMAN NEEDS

The phenomenon of social networking, the growth of Facebook and the proliferation of social network platforms are a testament to how well social media is addressing the needs expressed in Maslow's hierarchy of needs at a level beyond food and shelter. Social media is technology applied to support a basic human need: the need for belonging and connecting with others.[2]

THE NEED FOR A SOCIAL MEDIA MEASUREMENT FRAMEWORK

Marketers need to fit social media measurement into a framework that includes the elements unique to social media in order to build a successful strategy, to monitor execution of that strategy, to prove that that strategy actually works and to improve that strategy where necessary. It must be designed with a high degree of financial and conceptual rigor. With this framework, a marketer can make better investments in social media that can deliver increased on revenue, profit, brand value[3] and market share for the short and long term, given the level of risk associated with that investment.

ENDNOTES

1. Keller Fay Group; WOMMA website; http://buyers.womma.org/companies/keller-fay-group/; collected May 27, 2010

2. Maslow hierarchy of needs: http://www.edpsycinteractive.org/topics/regsys/maslow.html

3. Brand value and brand in this context are often used synonymously. As opposed to revenue and profit, which are more short-term metrics, brand value and market share are often considered more as long-term metrics and must be considered part of the objectives for a marketer as they endeavor to deliver the most revenue, profit, brand and share for the both the short and long term.

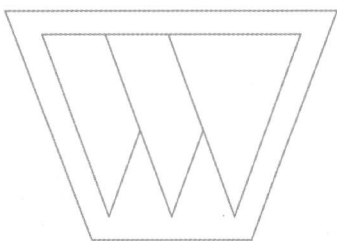

SECTION 1
GETTING STARTED WITH SOCIAL MEDIA ROI

Getting Started with Social Media ROI

What is social media ROI?

The future of social media and the ability to measure its return on investment (ROI) are being hotly debated. Regardless of which side of the debate you come down on, the need to demonstrate the ROI of a social media investment is becoming more urgent. With the advent of consumers now expecting to participate in a two-way conversation with your brand in a genuine manner, the role of marketers in organizations has changed forever. Marketers must now build their strategies incorporating this two-way dialog and they must measure the impact on their brands in order to make the right strategic and tactical decisions. Marketers can no longer gloss over the importance of measuring the impact of social media without endangering the health of their brands—and their careers.

In the coming chapters, we will introduce the media engagement framework. This concept will finally put in context the key elements of measuring the right things in social media to prove the value of social marketing and to finally compare that value to the value of a similar investment in traditional media. In this way, marketers can make better strategic and tactical decisions about where and how they allocate and invest their precious budget dollars, Chinese yuan, euros and yen.

This book was written to cover the role the marketing function plays in social media as it relates to marketers' ability to reap positive short- and long-term value for the organization from their social media marketing activities. It will cover all of the popular types of social media from blogging and micro-blogging to social communities. It will cover the popular social marketing sites such as Facebook, Linkedin, Twitter and YouTube, as well as a few from around the world, such as Orkut, Tencent and Cyworld. In order to limit the scope of this book, it will be confined to the ROI generated by marketing (and selling) activities that are driven through social media. Other business functions, such as customer service, operations and product development also generate ROI, but they will only be touched on because they influence the ROI of marketing investments made to support a brand.

SOCIAL MARKETING IS MEASURABLE: THE MARKETING PROCESS MODEL APPLIED TO SOCIAL MARKETING

In the past, even the recent past, marketing was a process thought to be nearly unmeasurable. Marketing leadership would invest in marketing communications with little to no certainty of the successful outcome of a campaign or branding effort. This has changed significantly over the last decade and, with the advent of social media, marketers can now apply many of the lessons learned from measuring traditional media to measuring social media. John Wanamaker said, "I know half the money I spend on advertising is wasted, but I can never find out which half."[1] Recent surveys (see *What Sticks* by Briggs and Stuart) now suggest that only 37 percent of the marketing budget isn't functioning.[2] Now marketers need to move to measuring the effectiveness of their social marketing investments.

Just as a website became *de rigueur* over 10 years ago, so too will social media become a required component of all brands' marketing activities. As this trend progresses, marketers will need to make the right decisions concerning the key aspects of social media and determine how to measure its effectiveness in the context of all other marketing activities. They will need to make certain that the brand is allocating its marketing investments optimally across all media channels, including social media.

Smart marketers have built and tested many techniques to measure marketing effectiveness for traditional marketing. They invented redemption codes for coupons, built a science around marketing mix modeling using least squared regression analysis and have designed market research methods around choice, brand tracking and many other tools. All this was done to understand how consumers make product choices in order to understand the linkage between those choices and their marketing actions. A clear framework of marketing analytics and data gathering has evolved and been defined for many organizations to support strategic and tactical marketing decisions.

THE MEDIA ENGAGEMENT FRAMEWORK INTRODUCED

This book presents a comprehensive framework to develop metrics and calculate ROI for social marketing activities. It can be applied against all currently known social media channels and we believe it will easily be applicable to other future social media types. It describes how to measure the value of a single social marketing channel, such as Twitter, an integrated social marketing campaign combining, such as Facebook, Twitter and YouTube, and an integrated marketing campaign combining, such as TV advertising, price changes and a branded social media community. In Section 3, the link between incremental value and ROI is then described.

Marketing begins by developing a strategy based on the financial and corporate strategy for the brand, focusing on the customer, competitors, external factors and the resources of the company. Once the marketing strategy has been determined, tactics are defined and specified within a framework, such as the 4Ps: product, price, place and promotion.[3] With these tactics now in place, traditional marketers determine how they want to measure the success of these tactics through the definition of appropriate metrics. Some of these are interim metrics such as awareness and purchase intent; others are outcomes metrics such as unit volume and revenue. Once these metrics are in place—depending on the business question—financial values can be determined and a return on investment (ROI) can be calculated. With the ROI known for the various marketing tactics, the marketing strategy can be refined, budget allocations can be adjusted, problems diagnosed and the cycle repeated. This cycle is illustrated in the marketing process diagram in Figure 1.1. It is comprised of the four elements surrounding a central element defined here as the media engagement framework.

The media engagement framework is made up of three distinct personas: the influencer, the individual, and the consumer. For social marketing specifically and traditional media more generally, marketing strategy, tactics, metrics and ROI can be determined by the level of engagement a particular marketing activity has with these three

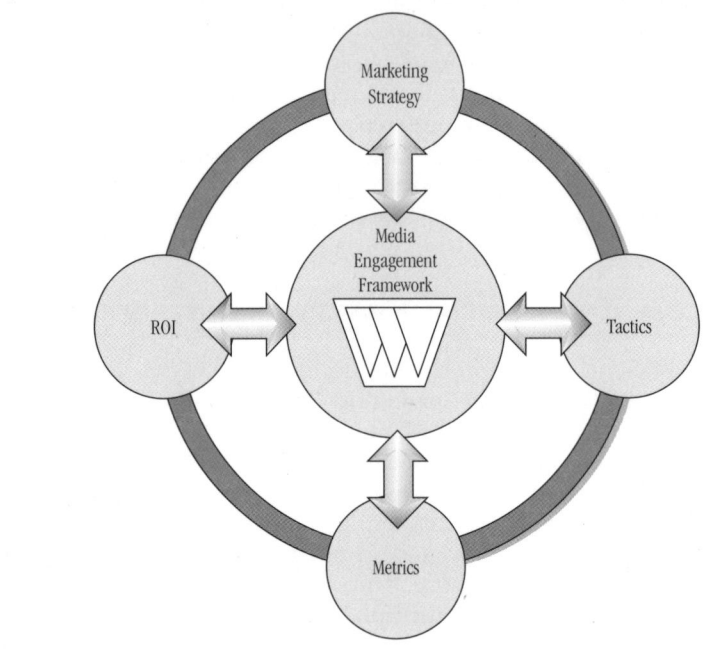

Figure 1.1   Marketing process diagram

personas in the marketplace. Social marketing strategies are built by first listening and then engaging with influencers, individuals and consumers in order to move consumers down the consumer purchase funnel to stimulate product purchase and later to create loyalty for repeat purchase.

On the other hand, with traditional media, Oprah Winfrey, for example, would be considered an influencer and the marketing team may seek sponsorship to promote their brand to her audience. Television advertising may be targeted to individuals hoping to convert them to consumers. Consumers may receive a Valpak[4] coupon to drive them down the consumer purchase funnel to purchase a promoted product. The media engagement framework describes in detail how marketing actions drive engagement with each of these targets and this book will discuss how it applies specifically to social marketing activities.

In order to develop a specific social marketing strategy, it is important to realize that social media makes up only one facet of a marketing strategy. Because no single marketing channel can be considered in isolation, we must make certain that all marketing channels, including each type of social media channel, are considered in the context of all other marketing actions being taken. For example, will a temporary price reduction increase response to a Twitter campaign? Will a new competitive TV advertising campaign affect the fan engagement on Facebook? What are the synergy effects between TV advertising and a YouTube channel? Similar types of questions relating to integrated marketing campaigns were solved for traditional media and they must now also be considered when capturing and calculating the ROI on social media. With the right framework in place, we can not only measure the impact of each of the social media channels but also their combined impact for integrated social marketing campaigns and integrated marketing campaigns in general.

In our model, there is much more to be considered when leveraging social media as a means of presenting a marketing message to drive increased engagement and, finally, increase revenue.

MAKE BETTER STRATEGIC AND TACTICAL MARKETING DECISIONS

As marketing moves to fulfill this trend, new methods will be required to understand the relative impact of each of their brands' social marketing tactics. They will be required to measure their ability to influence the bottom line—the truest measure of ROI across all media channels. This book was written to help marketers in two ways:

- to help marketers make better strategic and tactical social marketing decisions to drive increased revenue, profit, brand and share for the short and long term
- to help social marketers communicate their results to the rest of the organization in a language they understand: ROI.

With their ability to make better decisions, marketers will be able to improve the bottom line driving valuable corporate profit for both the short and long term. With their ability to communicate their results back to the rest of the organization, they will be able to build, defend and grow their budgets.

To that end, we put forth a series of concepts, methods and techniques that will help the marketer make significantly better strategic and tactical decisions. Marketers need to make better allocation decisions between investments in traditional media (defined here, and throughout the book, as all other non-social media channels) and in social media. They need to make certain that they invest in the right social media tactics, others are improved and the wrong ones are discontinued or reduced. This book will look at each of these dimensions of decision making:

- diagnosing unsuccessful tactics to determine whether their execution can be improved
- reducing or discontinuing those tactics that aren't delivering value for the brand
- allocations between traditional media and social media—investing more in the best tactics
- choosing successful tactics to drive social media effectiveness and making them even better
- understanding how social media tactics deliver synergies for traditional media and vice versa
- understanding how social media tactics build on each other to deliver overall success.

Generally, we see that executives want to use social media to promote the brand, but they do so in a mindset that has social media as just another channel to put the same message "out there." They see it as relatively inexpensive compared with traditional media. They see social media as a much higher risk platform. Nevertheless, social media is a much richer method than other traditional media to deliver a message to the marketplace. For that reason, it requires a higher level of finesse in order to make it work properly. It requires a clear understanding of consumer behavior and response in order to determine whether the marketer's actions are working, compared with other potential marketing investments.

We acknowledge that some social media purists have come out in opposition to measuring ROI in social media, because it dilutes the purported "transparency" of social media. In some cases, we've seen the bending of the definition of ROI to mean "return-on-influence" and there have been put forth many other reasons to avoid measuring the ROI of social media in financial terms. (See box: False measures of ROI.)

With this book, we will give marketers a pathway to start to develop data, statistics and analytics to clearly identify the incremental impact on revenue, profit, brand and share that social marketing investments can deliver. In so doing, they will also be better able to develop social marketing strategies and tactics that can deliver significantly better results for their brands. Our encouragement to the reader is to not be sidetracked by non-financial ROI arguments; social media can be, and should be, put in a similar framework as traditional media and the ROI can, and should, be assessed.

VALUE FOR SOCIAL MEDIA INFRASTRUCTURE PROVIDERS

As social marketers get more sophisticated, they will demand better and more pertinent information and measurements from the public social network platforms—Facebook, QQ and Twitter—in order to improve their use of these communities. This will help them to drive more activity with their target audiences and more targeted activity for their brands leading to more revenue and opportunity for the public social network platforms. In this way, community participants, the brands and the communities can gain more value. The media engagement framework

---

CASE STUDY

VIRAL VIDEOS PROVIDE SERIOUS ROI: $50 BUDGET = TWO MILLION HITS ON YOUTUBE

Getting a video to go viral is as much alchemy as it is talent and creative content. Imagine going to market with $50 and producing two million hits on YouTube and getting the reputation as the toughest kitchen appliance on the planet.

Blendtec

At age 63, Tom Dickson is the elder celebrity in the YouTube universe. Tom grew up in the San Francisco Bay Area building and loved riding motorcycles as fast as he could. He had no idea that his interests as a mechanic and engineer would lead him to build a grain mill that would drive 40 of his competitors out of business. Eventually, it would pit him against a global competitor, Bosch, when he engineered the Blendtec household blender to provide superior performance yet again; in the process, Tom became an international social media celebrity.

Build the best machine in the world, and they'll beat a path to your door

Tom and his team realized that the adage wasn't true that if you "build a better mousetrap, the world will beat a path to your door."

(continued)

With the most powerful blender on the market, they needed to find a way to create awareness and get attention from consumers. The first challenge to overcome was that they had no money budgeted for marketing.

The Blendtec WillitBlend.com legacy was initiated by their then marketing director, George Wright, when he asked for a marketing budget and was handed $50 and told to "do something with this". They spent the $50 on a variety of items at the local supermarket that fitted in a blender, but were not supposed to be in a blender. They produced five videos of the Blendtec machine tearing through happy meals and whatever they could fit in the machine and posted them on YouTube. Within a week, they realized they had something—they racked up over 2 million views and the brand began its love affair of blending stuff to smithereens. When Tom was told of the success of the videos on YouTube, his response was "Who-tube?".

The Blendtec brand has since become well entrenched as the most powerful device in its category and revenues increased five-fold in its last few years. WillitBlend.com shows the robustness of the product by blending whatever is put into the blender into a pile of sometimes toxic dust. Golf balls, hockey pucks, glow sticks and butane lighters have all seen the inside of a Blendtec blender and, depending what goes into the blender, a different type of consumer has come to see the video—golfers came in droves to see a golf ball blended and hockey fans couldn't get enough of the hockey puck episode. Each view represents an incremental lift in awareness that has translated into their phenomenal increase in sales over the last few years.

The big hits came from the times they blended something popular or fantastic—the iPad session drew 6.5 million viewers and blending an iPhone has drawn over 8.8 million views. When they get one of these devices, they attain the number one position for the week or the month out of all YouTube viewers—not too bad for a couple of twenties and a sawbuck.

Initially, the viewing audience was 16-year-old males, fascinated by the destruction. Now the demographic has evolved to 35-year-old men, but it turns out that kids can still have an impact on buying decisions. Tom was in a local store, watching his staff demonstrate the Blendtec product, live. When a mother suggested to her son that the Blendtec blender wasn't the one they wanted, he told her about the power and capability of the machine he had seen on the YouTube video: it was the one she wanted.

Tom and VP of Marketing, Jeff Robe, share in our podcast of the time they had to defend themselves against a German TV company's accusations that Blendtec was making up the videos or editing them to be misleading. A film crew was dispatched from Germany and, in the end, Blendtec easily withstood the tests they put the device through—proving the strength of their engineering and the truth of the videos. Similar proof cases were requested by the Discovery Channel and the History Channel, and each time Tom and the Blendtec products came through as authentic.

Social media is something that will continue to grow with Blendtec. This is a great example of how creative drive and a successful viral effort can make the public aware of your product in ways that exceed what could ever be purchased in terms of traditional advertising. It's the ability of social media to create a buzz and visibility that cannot be purchased at any price.

Source: Interview with Jeff Robe, VP Marketing, BlendTec, Inc. on April 21, 2010. Published with permission. All rights reserved.

applied to social media will help these public social network platforms provide the right type of information for their customers—the marketers—further accelerating growth and profits.

A (SHORT) HISTORY OF SOCIAL MARKETING ROI

The history of measuring ROI in social media has not always been clear-cut. In the early years, there have been many smart marketers contending that there was no real way to measure ROI in social media. They were wrong. To them, the tools were rudimentary, the tactics undeveloped and they felt there was no clear way to collect and apply financial data to the equation. For those of us in the marketing measurement and analytics space, this hasn't been the case. The authors have been successfully measuring the ROI of social marketing activities over the past five years. At the time, social marketing tactics were rudimentary and there were challenges with the data, but these experiences helped the authors to develop techniques that clearly led to determining the impact of social marketing activities on key business objectives. Clients were able to make better informed decisions and were able to justify to the rest of the company that their efforts had indeed moved the needle in driving incremental revenue and profit.

Early on, communities were proprietary. Facebook and Twitter didn't even exist, yet marketers wanted to support a community through the sharing of discussions about issues concerning their brands. If they sought any consumer input at all, they used proprietary, branded discussion forums. Some included voting and rating capabilities and other consumer-generated input options. They allowed their customers to support the brand through the posting of valuable content to all members of the community. Prospective customers asked questions of the community and received answers from other members. The marketer was primarily a passive observer of the conversations taking place in their branded community. Below are a few brief introductions to the dominant social media channels that marketers have begun to apply to their businesses and how they have been able to measure the effectiveness of their actions. There are many other social media technologies that can also provide metrics and increased engagement for use by marketers to deliver their messages to the market.

In later chapters, the media engagement framework will be applied against each of these social media channels in order to determine how they can be best measured to deliver increased ROI and improved marketing investment allocations.

Discussion forums

Intuit, Microsoft and others were key movers in providing their customers discussion forums to help their customers make the best use of their products and services, and consequently reduce the company's pre-sales customer service and post-sales technical support costs. These forums became key differentiators against competitors in their categories. The brand that had the strongest community following was able to build a differentiator that was hard for their competitors to match. Once the community reached critical mass, it drew key influencers to provide highly valuable content at a low incremental cost to the brand. Occasional users were able to get their questions answered and were able to more fully gain the value of the product they purchased. Instead of having to wait on a telephone customer support line, answers were available in seconds.

ROI from discussion forums had more to do with call center load reduction and less with improved marketing, although search results are clearly improved through the use of social media. High-quality discussion forums delivered high marks for the customer service brand attribute and increased loyalty.

RATINGS AND REVIEWS

One of the earliest areas of social media utilized by marketers was the use of voting and ratings and reviews applications. Through this process, online and brick-and-mortar retailers were able to solicit and receive ratings from their customers about their experiences with specific products. Consumers could become reviewers and post comments about a particular product and give it a rating by voting on it (Figure 1.2). Some applications even allowed the reviewers to be rated, helping consumers to determine the perceived quality of the reviewer and the review. In this way, the retailer was providing highly valuable, independent input on popular products. Consumers now felt confident that the purchase decision they were making was truly the right one for them and their circumstance. These same ratings and reviews provided valuable information that retailers and brands could use to improve their offerings and their marketing. Retailers could even start to adjust their stocking policies to make certain they had more of the best-rated products in stock. Marketers gained valuable customer feedback and could use it to enhance their messaging and adjust their product development.

Because ratings and reviews take place very near the point of purchase, marketers could use ratings and reviews to drive ROI by soliciting more, higher-quality reviews from product-savvy enthusiasts.

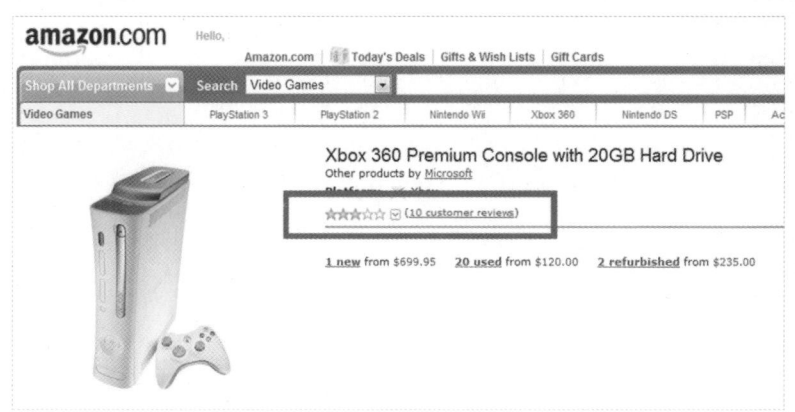

Figure 1.2 Review on Amazon.com

PROPRIETARY BRANDED COMMUNITIES

Marketers also used the available social media tools to support their messages in the marketplace by building a proprietary-branded community. Some of the top consumer brands, such as Dove, were supported through these tools to build a following among their target consumer groups. When Dove launched their "campaign for real beauty," they were able to combine traditional media and online media to build a significant community of teenage girls to help them thrive in a market of artificial beauty. This community exists today, but continues to evolve in many ways and now has migrated a large component of their following over to Facebook.

Marketers could realize increased ROI through the high level of engagement their target audience has with the brand when visiting the branded community. Not only can the marketers closely monitor the conversation but they can insert high-value, highly targeted messages to the members of the community. In this way, proprietary-branded communities are one of the top channels for marketers. As these communities are migrated to Facebook, it will be imperative that these monitoring functions also be built into the Facebook pages and the Facebook platform in order to support the highly targeted decision making of the marketers.

BLOGGING

Originally, blogging was the first significant social media tool available to marketers. CEOs were encouraged to write posts about their thoughts and brands. Key influencers were writing their own thoughts, and the blogosphere was born. Since 2002, the blogging search engine Technorati has indexed over 133,000,000 blogs,[5] and 77 percent of Internet users now read them.[6] Individuals use these blogs to write their opinions on anything and everything and, every once in a while, a blogger will make a post about a brand in either a positive or negative tone. These posts are picked up by consumers and often develop some level of authority, credibility and popularity and can deliver a positive or negative value for the brand. PR professionals have generally learned that bloggers are different from traditional media editors and they now work very hard to interface and engage with them to mitigate negative messages and promote more positive messages. Some brands have even tried too hard to influence key bloggers and learned new lessons the hard way about the differences between bloggers and editors.

As the use of blogging tools expanded, creative users began adding rich content to their blogs—first pictures were scanned and included;

audio recordings were converted to MP3 files and added; and video clips were digitized and added. These content types are referred to as "rich media" for a posting and they help create a more compelling reason for individuals to visit a blog and "consume" the post's content (aka—read the post, listen to the audio or view the picture or video).

Blogs helped deliver value for the brand by focusing the message, increasing the visitor counts to, and engagement with, all branded properties, and providing further links to other high-value components of the corporate website.

MICRO-BLOGGING

Blog posts can be long though and, because the content isn't edited by any standard, the blog writer can wander and delay in making a point. The opportunity to provide a smaller, more easily consumed post was taken up by Evan Williams, Jack Dorsey and Biz Stone. They developed a service that constrained the writer to 140 *characters*, not words. What could you possibly say in 140 characters that would be even remotely engaging? Apparently a lot, because the service is called Twitter and, as of December 2009, they had raised $155M in capital, without making a dime of revenue and at last report they had over 75,000,000 users.[7]

Twitter offered a number of valuable functions that were not available through other channels. Marketers could increase the number of messages and the number of followers with low investment, thereby increasing engagement and delivering targeted, incremental sales, just as Dell[8] claims to have done. They could quickly and easily set up multiple Twitter accounts, each acting as a conduit for one target consumer set or one targeted message. In doing so, they could further refine their messages in a cost-effective way to provide even higher value to their target audiences.

SOCIAL NETWORKS

Social networks round out the most popular category of social media tools, with Facebook being the elephant in the room, boasting an ever-growing membership of over 500 million members[9] in over 180 countries worldwide. Facebook is not the only social network. MySpace, FastPitchNetwork.com, Orkut, Cyworld (Korea) and QZone (in China) are all social networks, each with some feature or characteristic that differentiates it from another. If there is a topic not already covered in a given social network, you can start your own social network by installing software from vendors such as Jive, Telligent Systems or Mzinga on

THE POWER OF SOCIAL MEDIA:
UNITED AIRLINES AND THE
DAMAGED GUITAR

United Airlines has experienced the power of social media and, at least once, been unable to manage the message the market was getting in regard to their brand. It began with a group of musicians traveling to their next performance. En route, one of the instruments became damaged by a baggage handler. The story goes that the musician made several polite inquiries to resolve the situation and only after repeated failure to either recognize their fault or to provide adequate compensation did the musician take matters into his own hands and carry his plight to the public.

He produced a series of short videos and posted them on YouTube on July 6, 2009. Within two days, there were over 125,000 views, and by December, views exceeded six million. For several weeks, as the video caught people's attention, when "United Airlines" was searched for, the video came up as the first listing on the first page in Google over and above all other more-commercial references for the term.

a server of your own or by signing up with a service such as KickApps. com or Ning.com. Ning already boasts hosting over 4,000 special purpose social networks with the ability to customize the site to just about any purpose. If you want to connect on almost any topic, there is a place, or there can be a place, for you.

Although metrics from these networks are sometimes rudimentary, or are restricted through privacy policies, they are starting to become more transparent. Also, third-party web metrics providers are beginning to measure engagement and visitor counts as an interim metric in determining marketing effectiveness.

PAID WORD-OF-MOUTH ADVERTISING NETWORKS

An emerging category of tools and technology for the social media marketer is the online panel that leverages social media as a marketing media channel—a category of tool that includes Tremor (primarily focused on consumer packaged goods) and BzzAgent. For example,

BzzAgent is a word-of-mouth marketing company made up of a diverse group of individuals building a selectable demographic panel of over 600,000 volunteers, who can be recruited to use personal, face-to-face conversation, Facebook, Twitter and other tools to tell their friends and acquaintances about what they think of a brand or product.

These paid word-of-mouth advertising networks offer an interesting approach to social marketing. Because of the design of their system, they can provide highly valuable metrics on the success of their marketing campaigns.

Obstacles in determining social marketing ROI

We've found a number of obstacles to measuring the ROI of social marketing. Even sophisticated marketers investing heavily in social marketing to drive their brands are only partially measuring rudimentary metrics of success. This will change as the social media channel matures and starts moving from experimentation into the mainstream. This will especially change as marketers see competitors thriving in the social media space.[10]

The definition of ROI

The first, primary obstacle that many traditional marketers have in trying social marketing is that they don't believe there is a measureable ROI in it. They understand that there probably is some value, but don't know how to relate it to their businesses. Anecdotally, we've found that most firms simply don't understand the entire concept of marketing ROI—even for traditional media, let alone for social media. Calculating the ROI from traditional media has been a challenge for them, let alone calculating the ROI for this new-fangled "social media". This is further exacerbated by the fact that many non-marketing executives also don't understand or apply the concept of ROI as it pertains to marketing. This book will be valuable for them because they will learn how to measure the ROI of social marketing and marketing in general.

We believe that once you've read this book, you will have a belief that it is worth investing in social media activities and you will be able to measure the ROI of those social media activities. We will answer the question of how to best measure ROI and show that marketers are able to make significantly better decisions to drive more revenue, profit, brand and share through the use of critical measurement and analytic techniques. To that end, the media engagement framework focuses primarily on the sales and outcome side of the equation. Then in Section 3, we focus on the evaluation in dollars and sense of the outcomes—the "R" of ROI—and the investment—the "I" of ROI.

CALCULATING COSTS

Marketers also find obstacles in the measurement and calculation of costs and returns. Some of the costs are personnel costs and are allegedly difficult to allocate to a specific social marketing activity. Determining the true incremental costs from personnel and other sources to drive the social marketing activity is critical to measuring the investment element of the ROI equation. Sometimes, these costs are confidential and are kept hidden from the marketing team. In other cases, a determination of the fixed and variable costs associated with these personnel may need to be ascertained. In order to effectively determine ROI for social marketing, it is often imperative to work with the finance team to properly measure and allocate the true costs associated with social marketing and apply them correctly to the business question at hand.

LOSING CONTROL OF YOUR BRAND

Another and potentially higher barrier for many marketers is the risk they perceive in losing control of their brand in a very negative way. There are many horror stories of brand reputations that escaped the control of the marketing effort and went awry. Historically, brands have been handled by brand managers who worked hard to make sure the market perception of the brand was precisely what they wished it to be. With the advent of social media and its ever-increasing influence over messages in the marketplace, the brand manager is no longer the only talker. Instead, in the social media channel, marketers become active listeners of conversations between consumers. Now, it is the consumer that has taken over partial control of the brand's messages and, in so doing, has modified the brand perception for social media-active individuals. In the social media model, the consumer can wield a great deal of power in what gets talked about over the water cooler and on the various social media sites. Smart marketers have begun to participate in these conversations. Others have ignored these interactions and have had to learn the hard way the power of social media.

From an ROI perspective, the potential impact of this loss of control increases the risk marketers are faced with when using social marketing channels. Compared with traditional media channels, the potentially higher ROI of social marketing channels must be offset with the risks associated with the potential negative impact on the brand reputation.

SEPARATING BUZZ INTO ITS COMPONENT PARTS

A further obstacle has to do with the background level of social media activity that takes place whether the company is doing any marketing or not. Some marketers find it difficult to separate out the background buzz, or baseline, of social media activity from that generated by their marketing actions. As in any industry, there is always a background noise level of activity. Sales don't go to zero when advertising stops, nor does social media activity. In order to determine the incremental impact from a social marketing activity, this baseline of activity needs to be separated out from the incremental amount generated by any marketing activity—whether it's traditional or social—in order to determine the true incremental effect from social marketing.

Also, this baseline of buzz is driven in the long term by the overall value of the brand and past marketing activities. As the brand grows over time, the level of baseline buzz will also grow correspondingly.

TRADITIONAL MEDIA VERSUS SOCIAL MEDIA

There is probably no single definition of social media that will satisfy everyone. For simplicity, we will use the definition put forth by *The Social Media Bible*:[11]

> "Social media" refers to the activities, practices and behavior among communities of people who gather online to share information, knowledge and opinions using conversational media. Conversational media are web-based applications that make it possible to create and easily transmit content in the form of words, pictures, videos and audios.

Social media differs from traditional media on a number of levels, but mostly because of its multi-path, multi-directional dialog between individuals (person-to-person), influencers and companies.

Social media is similar to traditional media in that social media messages can be evaluated along similar dimensions as those messages received through traditional media. They have some level of authority and persuasiveness—they are read by a certain number of individuals, this reading takes place at certain points in time and they support the brand image in a particular way. These messages affect consumer behavior directly concerning the specific brand or indirectly through comments about competitive brands or about the category.

The media engagement framework, when applied to social media, will properly categorize each of these elements in order to determine the appropriate interim metrics and then finally how to value them in terms of incremental value to the brand.

CASE STUDY

SOCIAL MEDIA AND CUSTOMER SUPPORT

Using social media for customer support is a natural extension of social media technology—it allows companies to listen for customers speaking in their own voice about the things they care most relative to the company, the brand, their products and processes. Marketers have long been involved in retention strategies by investing in customer support, and social media has begun to be used in this area with really great success.

Customer support can be a key brand attribute that can sway many consumers to purchase the brand or remain loyal to the brand. Providing great social media-based customer support can significantly increase the brand image to those individuals who are active in social media.

Comcast

Frank Eliason, Senior Director in the National Customer Operations Center is the face behind the Twitter ID @comcastcares. The use of social media to enhance the customer service function within Comcast started humbly and somewhat under the radar. Working out of the Philadelphia customer support office, Frank began to monitor social media traffic and watched for posts that mentioned Comcast. When time permitted, he would call bloggers who wrote about their experiences with Comcast and interact with them over the phone one-on-one. He found that this kind of outreach was incredibly well received.

Frank explained, "If we were able to decipher who the blogger was and get a phone number, we would pick up the phone and call. Most bloggers don't think that anyone reads their blogs so they are shocked when they do get a call. They're just happy that you called. They love the fact that you helped them." Frank remembers when the marketing department took notice of what they were doing. "At one point, our PR department started to notice what we were doing because what was happening was we would reach out to people, and all of a sudden 'Hey, Comcast called me,'" reports Frank. The PR department was hooked and requested more. Suddenly they said to Frank, "This is great. We'd like this to be your job."

The widening of effort allowed Comcast to have highly valuable, one-on-one conversations with consumers on Facebook, Twitter, blogs and forums wherever the customer was communicating about the company. Frank suggests that "We were meeting customers where they already were. Listening and learning from them—it is very basic; almost customer support 101." The Comcast Digital Care Team's goal is "to listen to their customers and help if they can." They are not expected to deliver marketing messages to consumers, but rather a positive brand impression and customer service.

The most remarkable aspect of social media for Frank is the personalization that occurs between a brand representative and the consumer. Two years ago, Eliason was the only person responding as @comcastcares. He worked seven days a week, responding to customer tweets and helping to resolve issues with whatever resources he could muster. One time, when he took a day off, he found that customers started responding to other customers and letting one another know that Frank was on a day off that day. He believes this is fully attributable to the personal approach that social media demands. It is a one-to-one medium and it is this level of personalization that provided unexpected benefits and helps to drive the Comcast customer service social media philosophy today, which Frank says is "for a brand to interact in social media, it needs to be personalized."

Comcast's response protocol will differ by the site or type of social media in which the post or comment was found:

Blogs – Blogs are responded to first through email, then either through a call or by leaving a comment.

(continued)

Forums – Response is done privately through a private message, especially where only Comcast could solve the problem.

Twitter – Comcast simply responds publicly and openly. Twitter provides an early warning system because things seem to be posted here before consumers begin to call the support desk. Listening and monitoring the Twitter message stream allows Comcast to quickly change their interactive voice response (IVR) system when needed in order to improve and speed up the response during a wider service incident.

Facebook – Initially Facebook was pretty locked down relative to being able to message member-to-member if they were not already a 'Facebook Friend' and it was difficult for Comcast to respond to posts: the outreach on Facebook could only reach a handful of people. Since then, Facebook has opened up a bit, but, because of the spam policies, it is still difficult to respond on the social network.

YouTube – Comcast customer service monitors and connects with customers via messages and comments.

In terms of customer retention and call center call mitigation, the Comcast story is a great one on how a brand can improve the post-sale brand experience, mitigate negative word of mouth and drive positive word of mouth.

Source: Interview with Frank Eliason, Senior Director in National Customer Operations, Comcast on February 1, 2010. Published with permission. All rights reserved.

ENGAGEMENT IS THE KEY

The most remarkable aspect of social media compared with traditional media is with the level of engagement provided through social media. A message sent through television may be seen by the viewer or may not be seen. It may make a connection with the consumer or not. A consumer may further engage with the brand by talking to friends or acquaintances about the brand. Finally, the consumer may engage directly with the brand through purchase of the brand. In the social media space, engagement with the brand can be immediate and incremental. Individuals can make comments about their impressions or experiences with the brand. These experiences may be real or virtual and they have a high value as they relate to the individuals' perception of the brand. It is this area that will be discussed in detail in the book and provides one of the true differentiators between the impacts of traditional versus social media on consumers.

What's important for us to understand is how social media differs from, and is similar to, traditional media. Many of the tools and techniques used to measure traditional media can be easily applied to social media, with adjustments made for social media's unique nature. However, some of the value delivered by social media is very different from traditional media and we will need to adjust the financial linkages in order to capture and account for these differences.

Traditional and social media differ in the following ways:

Traditional media	Social media
One-way, one-to-many communication	Many-to-one, multi-path dialog
Here is what marketers think the brand value is	Consumers express how they perceive the brand
Consumers segmented by their demographics and viewing behavior	Consumers segmented by their social behavior
Content developed and finely controlled by the marketer	Content generated by the audience, influencers and the marketer; the content is only partially controlled by the company
Buzz driven by what's cool	Buzz based on message content, WIIFM[12]
Expert recommendation (e.g. Michelin Guide, etc.)	Peer and influencer recommendation (i.e. Circuit City, Amazon, etc.)
Content publishers control all channels	Users opt-in for publishers' content
Top-down strategic approach	Bottom-up, "voice of the consumer" strategy
Information managed by hierarchy	Information provided on demand
Emphasis on cost and ROI – CPM[13] metric to broadcast	Relatively low cost to participate

The table above compares the predominant characteristics of traditional versus social media, but we recommend care in delineating between the two. In clarifying our definitions, we are including Internet marketing as a traditional media channel—as far as ad sales and public exposure to ads posted online, there is no real difference. It is still a one-way, one-to-many, type of advertisement. For this reason, we have chosen to include Internet media in our definition of traditional media.

Traditional media has a "fire and forget" model as it relates to the interaction of the brand with the media. Once the message has been sent, individuals can't respond to it directly using that one-way media channel. On the other hand, the emerging social media model requires more than just creating and posting a message that shows up on Facebook or MySpace and leaving it for consumers to somehow observe. It requires the ongoing monitoring and engagement in the conversation about the brand, much like the process that Bravo Networks has developed around their "Talk Bubble" discussed in the case studies. The media engagement framework will be used to highlight the differences in engagement between traditional and social media and how measuring the level of engagement for each of the dimensions of the framework can help support better social media strategies and measure their success.

MEASURING TRADITIONAL MEDIA

For many marketers, measuring the effectiveness of traditional media has become straightforward. Last-touch attribution, (see box: Last Touch Attribution) experimental design, marketing mix modeling, predictive modeling, consumer behavior analysis and other techniques have been developed and are widely in use.

LAST-TOUCH ATTRIBUTION

Although it is known by many names, last-touch attribution is probably the best known of methods to measure the effectiveness of marketing. It is used by many marketers and simply attributes the entire weight of a marketing activity to the last measured or stated touch. For example, a coupon with a redemption rate of 0.75 percent assumes that all incremental revenue generated by that coupon drop is derived from those consumers who redeem their coupons.

Last-touch attribution ignores all prior and concurrent impressions from all other media. If the redemption rate were slightly higher because TV was running while the coupon was being dropped, its effect would be ignored and the higher redemption rate would still be fully attributed to the coupon.

In this book, we will briefly describe a few of these techniques as they can be used to measure the effectiveness of social media. We will show how they can be applied and adjusted to fit the measurement of social marketing activities. For a more detailed description of the latest marketing ROI and effectiveness methods, please refer to *Marketing Calculator.*

CASE STUDY

MAKING SOCIAL MEDIA A PART OF YOUR COMPANY'S DNA

The merger of traditional and social media is creating new opportunities and challenges for media companies to determine what are the right strategies, the right platforms and the best tactics to reach their audience and create an engaging brand persona.

Bravo Networks

Bravo Networks has a number of popular TV shows including Real Housewives of New York City, of New Jersey, of Atlanta and of Orange County; and Top Chef. Bravo is a fun, high-end entertainment brand focused on five key categories: food, fashion, design, beauty and pop culture and their audience is an educated, tech savvy and "forward-leaning" demographic, so the overlap with social media is significant and very important to them.

Ellen Stone, SVP of Marketing, and her team develop all brand strategy and manage the marketing presence for all the Bravo products. They are always trying to develop innovative and influential content that fans can start talking about and allow them to engage the brand in a variety of ways. "For Bravo, it is about conversation and buzz and it is the engagement that is core to Bravo." Ellen says that "social media is a part of their DNA."

As one of the first media brands to embrace social media, Bravo shared content with MySpace beginning in 2005, and today they have an effective and well-managed presence on a dozen social media platforms. They use social marketing to start a conversation

(continued)

with their audience, drive the conversation between fans and Bravo celebrities (also know as Bravolebrities) and create buzz around the programs they present on their broadcast channel. Social media leverages conversations around show premieres to help maintain momentum around a program or series in ways that uncovers opportunities for fans to connect with the brand. Bravo has developed related products for their brands that include cookbooks, clothing, games, food, wine and other consumer products.

Guides by Bravo

Bravo continues to integrate further into social media with the development of social media applications and partnerships. "Guides by Bravo" is an iPhone app that gives users the ability to find out where Bravo celebrities (Bravolebrities) from shows such as Top Chef and Real Housewives dine, eat and shop. They developed a partnership with FourSquare, the location-based social game, to provide an even deeper brand association for our fans when finding out about their favorite Bravolebrity restaurants and shopping venues by earning special Bravo badges particular to their favorite Bravo series.

Bravolebrities and the Bravo Talk Bubble

Bravo invented a new way for viewers of the Real Housewives series to connect with Bravolebrities and one another: the "Bravo Talk Bubble." The Talk Bubble merges the message streams from Twitter and Facebook. Viewers in the Bravo Talk Bubble don't need to be in the same room, or even the same state, to participate in a viewing party around the episode on the television screen. As their viewers engage, Bravo observes various metrics including page views, tweets and a proprietary set of metrics that help them understand tone and sentiment.

Aside from the Talk Bubble initiative, the key metrics Ellen and her team follow as they manage their social marketing efforts include:

1. engagement with the audience
   - how many fans on Facebook
   - how many times Bravo becomes a trending topic
   - how many top talent tweets get tweeted and re-tweeted

- how engaged consumers are with the brand
- what people are talking about from the show

2. online and mobile traffic page views and video streams
   - clicks and eyeballs
3. qualitative
   - positive sentiment and tone
   - getting the message content right and in context
   - being where the consumer is
   - giving the consumer as much Bravo as they wish to consume.

Ellen cautions that the voice and message being conveyed is very important, as well as the message frequency: the voice needs to be less corporate and the message more personal. The effort is made in context of looking for what the fans are wanting: the marketers want to make sure the brand can break through the noise and clutter in a way that is relevant and distinguishes them from their competition.

An example of how they expand the brand connection to the consumer is how they act on the "sticky" topics that come up. If they notice that a conversation about an article of clothing that one of the Real Housewives is wearing and that conversation is picked up by others, they will move to offer that item of clothing for purchase in the online Bravo store. Ellen says, "It's how they try and give the fan as much Bravo as they want, wherever and whenever they want. Bravo is acting to wrap the consumer in Bravo wherever they go and wherever they want on the TV, computer, mobile and beyond."

The future of social media for Bravo

As they get more competition from other brands in the same social spaces—and they do expect it—Bravo looks to be able to quickly determine what apps and platforms are going to best support the brand and what entertainment content is right in that platform.

What Ellen sees right now is that people *want* to share messages with one another and the sharing that goes on in social media has become a part of peoples' daily lives and a part of everything they do—even when it is watching television in a room by themselves.

SOCIAL MARKETING STRATEGY

There are three actors to consider within the social media value chain when developing a proper social marketing strategy: influencers, individuals and consumers. It must also encompass the interaction between traditional media and social media, including synergy and cannibalization. For example, Dell claims that through Twitter it was able to sell $19M in revenue.[14] But was this truly incremental revenue, or would this have been sold anyway through other existing traditional media channels? Social marketing strategy and measurement needs to encompass all these dimensions, because of the inter-relationship between the different social marketing and traditional marketing channels, and within each channel there is interaction between influencers, individuals and consumers. In addition, social media affects a number of critical corporate functions, including social marketing, customer service, product development, market research and operations. Social marketing strategy is one component of the over-arching marketing strategy to drive revenue, at least cost and risk for the short and long term. In order to determine the success of a social marketing strategy, all of these components must be managed in order to determine the response from each of the marketing investments, whether they are made in traditional or in social media.

Social marketing drives response through consumption and conversation in the social media space and, with a lag, drives response in terms of revenue and purchase in the real world. In the absence of social marketing, there is still some level of background or baseline conversation. Baseline conversation is triggered by the value of the brand, the quality of customer service and the level of operational excellence delivered by the organization. It is up to marketing to drive incremental conversation, engagement and revenue in the short and long term. Regardless of whether marketing is active or passive in driving conversation and engagement, all companies can take advantage of the activity in the social media space by monitoring it and responding to it. Radian6, Alterian and others have developed great enterprise-level applications that can be incorporated into a social media monitoring and listening process in order to measure the level of conversation and its sentimentality and tonality. They can also be used to mitigate negative word of mouth, develop leads and respond to customer service and operational issues as they appear.

INFLUENCERS

Driving social media value for marketers requires segmentation. Not only do marketers want to reach and engage with their target audience, but they want to reach and engage with influencers who are positively inclined toward the brand. These influencers amplify messages to the target audience by reaching many individuals with a positive (or sometimes negative) message in a persuasive manner, leveraging their reputations.

Like Mark Jenner and the team at Guinness Anchor Berhad (GAB) in Malaysia, social marketers must build a strategy to reach these groups as effectively as possible. In the case of GAB, they identified influencers in various categories: each selected by their ability to promote a message around the music scene happening in the Heineken Green Room events. Once the influencers were identified, they listened to them, engaged with them and then seeded them with messages and premiums in which influencers found value in forwarding and lending their reputations to.

From a measurement perspective, influencers represent one important dimension for measuring the impact of marketing.

INDIVIDUALS

One of the key differences between traditional and social media is in the engagement between a brand and social media-active individuals. Traditional media delivers a one-way engagement. The marketer sends the message and the individual (hopefully) receives the message. Based on that message, the marketer works to elicit a response to build engagement with the brand.

The marketer now has a new, second dimension—the community—to engage with the individual, regardless of whether the individual is a consumer, influencer or none of the above. The marketer needs to drive both virtual engagement in various online communities and offline (or online for online brands) engagement through actual, physical purchase. In social media: individuals join a community; they consume content and receive value from the community; they actively participate in the community by conversing, making posts, adding content, voting, rating, reviewing, commenting on and forwarding content from other individuals; and, lastly, they invite others to participate in the community. Sometimes they gain so much value from the community that they may even be willing to put their reputations on the line and advocate to their friends and acquaintances that this community can also deliver value for them.

This new dimension can add high value, but also can add complexity in how marketers needs to plan their marketing strategies and tactics. However, with the right framework with which to understand this marketing structure, marketers will be able to improve their entire

---

FALSE MEASURES OF ROI

Return on engagement—the duration of time spent either in conversation or interacting with social objects, and in turn, what transpired that's worthy of measurement.

Return on participation—the metric tied to measuring and valuing the time spent participating in social media through conversations or the creation of social objects.

Return on involvement—similar to participation, marketers explored touchpoints for documenting states of interaction and tying metrics and potential return of each.

Return on attention—In the attention economy, we assess the means to seize attention, hold it, and as such, measure the responses to activities that we engender.

Return on trust—A variant on measuring customer loyalty and the likelihood for referrals, a trust barometer establishes the state of trust earned in social media engagement and the prospect of generating advocacy and how it impacts future business.

Source: Brian Solis (http://socialmediatoday.com/SMC/176801?utm_source=smt_newsletter&utm_medium=email&utm_campaign=newsletter)

---

go-to-market approach. To assist the social marketer, we have developed the concept of a community engagement funnel, which we believe encapsulates these core concepts in order for the brand to successfully add this new dimension to their marketing mix.

CONSUMERS

Consumers make up a subset of the individuals who are social media-active. A marketer's activity in social and traditional channels drives brand value in terms of the consumer purchase funnel and the brand image. Consumer purchase-funnel effects are measured based on how consumers move down the consumer purchase funnel from awareness to consideration and then purchase, loyalty and advocacy. In the social media model, the marketer has the option to now generate so much enthusiasm for the brand that the consumer becomes an advocate for the brand. It is this new layer in the consumer purchase funnel that provides a critical new dimension to a brand's marketing goals. Brand enthusiasm can then be used by the marketer to increase advocacy, deliver valuable product insights, write valuable product reviews and improve customer support through advocate submitted comments on discussion forums.

Social media and social marketing can also have an impact on the brand image in terms of the value consumers place on the emotional attributes of a brand. For example, social media-active consumers may consider the customer service of Intuit extremely good because of the online discussion forum delivering immediate answers to searched and posed questions. Non-social media-active consumers may not rate the brand so highly, because they may not access this valuable resource.

CASE STUDY

METRICS FOR SOCIAL MEDIA RESEMBLE THOSE FOR TRADITIONAL MEDIA

The question on how best to measure and manage ROI is one that traditional media marketers have been struggling with for a long time. Processes, analytics and data gathering have been developed and the calculation of ROI is finally becoming *de rigueur* for many traditional marketers. Although there are a lot of metrics surrounding social marketing—making it apparently more measurable—what's missing is the connection between these metrics and incremental revenue. Many of the same concepts used in traditional media can be applied—controlling for the differences—to social media.

Edelman Digital

Steven Rubel likes to work with companies that have marketing initiatives that have a capital "M" as in Marketing Program versus marketing program. Steve is SVP, Director of Insights at Edelman Digital and according to him, there is "a nexus of digital and social media coming together to connect social marketing and PR that can enhance an agency's ability to more effectively drive the agenda of the client into the mind of the consumer."

An example he shared with us was about Ben and Jerry's premium brand of ice cream and a new product they introduced in 2009 called "Flip." Awareness around the product launch beat the

(continued)

client's expectations when the Edelman team launched a Facebook fan page that would take a short message and convert or "flip it" to be read upside down as a Wall post on either Facebook or as a message in a Twitter post. "The audience conversation and 'buzz' around that short bit of programming far surpassed the numbers and value of the messages that they could buy for the same price in traditional media channels," says Steve.

The measurements to assess the success of a social marketing campaign closely reflect the metrics they us in other media efforts. They include elements, such as:

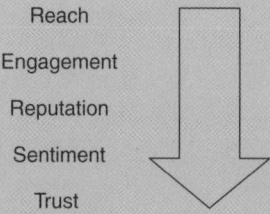

Reach

Engagement

Reputation

Sentiment

Trust

Each represents a level of message value that brands seek to express in creating a conversation with a consumer. The message value is a key element of the design of an engagement with any of their clients.

Crisis of attention

With digital and social media having opened a floodgate of content that a consumer can access, the growing challenge for marketers will be the ability to get the consumer's attention and develop top-level brand awareness. Steve says that "already there is a crisis of attention that marketers must face. With all that a consumer has the ability to access online—in an increasingly mobile format—the ability to get their attention of a particular brand is only going to get harder and harder." The other big challenge lurking beneath the surface for 2010, says Steve, "is the consumer privacy issue and what will happen when consumers realize how much information is being gathered and used about them."

Source: Interview with Steven Rubel, Senior Vice President, Edelman Digital and Director of Insights, Edelman on January 18, 2010. Published with permission. All rights reserved.

Measuring social marketing

Marketing is one of the elementary facets that drives successful businesses. Peter Drucker in 1954 said "the business enterprise has two and only two basic functions: marketing and innovation."[15] As marketing is such a critical function of the enterprise, the addition of both social marketing and the measurement of the overall effort is essential and worthwhile investment by management.

Social media measurement tools

In addition to the basic social media tools that make up a presence in social media, we have the technology or tools that are used to measure them. Some of these tools are designed to scour the entire web, looking for mentions in blog posts, micro-blog posts, social networks and more. They include Alterian SM2, Radian6, Scoutlabs, Brandtology and Nielsen BuzzMetrics. Others measure conversations on specific social media channels, and based on various criteria, grade them for their popularity, influence and other measures.

The tools and techniques referenced here are discussed throughout the book. More information can be found via our Facebook fan page at Facebook.com/ROIofSocialMedia.

Each of these tools provides metrics for measuring the success of social marketing and, using the media engagement framework applied to social marketing, will help to deliver valuable metrics that can lead to a robust and accurate calculation of ROI.

A process to social marketing ROI

We hope that by the end of this book, you will have captured the essence and concepts presented so you will be able to apply them to your business. To support you in this process, we are providing an eight-step process to first, implement the concepts in this book as part of the strategic definition process, second, to develop successful measures and last, apply to financial data to estimate and calculate their ROI. More information can be found at via our Facebook fan page at Facebook.com/ROIofSocialMedia.

The future of social media and ROI

A common comment about social media is how overwhelming it is. The stream of messages flowing into the organization or individual can be difficult to sift through and react to. As user, friend and follower counts increase, social media creates a stream of messages that can become meaningless—there is just too much content to examine, much less to absorb or find relevance in. Many of the messages are inane. Others are simply spam. Unrelated comments are blended in with the real, meaningful, useful information. It becomes a fire hose of blather negating the true value of social networks; it becomes a process of eliminating the noise from the signal, and the wheat from the chaff.

The potential failure of social media in a business context is not in the creation and delivery of a two-way dialog, but in the filtering of the massive amount of messages to deliver useful information. Where we see the market heading is toward a tool suite that uses intelligence to better manage this massive number of received messages combined to present that information when and where needed to the individual or parts of the organization that will be empowered to act on them.

New functions within the organization are evolving as well, with titles such as "social media switchboard," "social media listening post," "social media traffic cop," or "social media triage." They refer to that part of the organization that monitors and manages the message-sorting function. This same message flow can be used to measure the conversation regardless of where it is initiated. Today, we're seeing employees assigned to a bank of monitors with messages, posts and comments streaming by, clicking on icons to forward the comment to one person or another. In the next few years, we're likely to see improvements in the intelligence of the systems so that this process will require fewer employees with better results achieved over time. In this way, marketers will be able to better realize their results from their campaigns.

Using the response to Internet advertising as our guide, we expect that the future for social media marketing will also begin to diminish. As more brands participate in social media, consumers will also be overwhelmed by the fire hose of blathering messages. They will need to refine their activities to fewer messages in a category or to fewer categories—or both. Response to social media campaigns will decline and it will be more difficult to achieve the extraordinary returns that brands now enjoy. But, because of the unique value of social media, marketers will not now, nor in the future, be able to ignore this channel. It is a highly productive one, delivering great revenue, profit, brand and share in comparison with other traditional marketing channels—at least until the next channel comes along.

LET'S GET STARTED. . .

ROI is a business financial concept that helps executives make better resource allocation decisions, typically as to the level of investment to be made in various activities with varying levels of risk and return. It provides the executive a choice between investing, and by how much, or not investing, in a given course of action. The purpose of ROI as it relates to marketing is two-fold:

- to make better strategic and tactical decisions to drive more revenue, profit, brand and share
- to communicate the effectiveness of a given marketing action in terms the C-suite and the rest of the company will understand.

Establishing the ROI of marketing in the social media space will allow marketers to develop better social media budgets, defend those budgets and then grow them. Companies will be able to increase earnings and, more importantly, marketing will become a strategic component of corporate success. Because they measure their marketing and social media investments better, all else being equal, companies will be able to grow faster and be more profitable than their competitors.

Social media is changing the way businesses can, and must, engage with their consumers. The customer discovery process is becoming more immediate, but also more complicated. The ability to make a more informed decision based on predictable ROI and sound measurement is upon us. Welcome to the ROI of social media and social marketing.

ENDNOTES

1. http://www.brainyquote.com/quotes/authors/j/john_wanamaker .html

2. Rex Briggs and Greg Stuart, *What Sticks: Why Most Advertising Fails and How to Guarantee Yours Succeeds* (Chicago: Kaplan Business, 2006).

3. We add a further element to the 3C, 4P framework called the 1E, which represents the exogenous factors that can influence the model.

4. Valpak, a coupon direct mail service, is owned by Cox Target Media, Inc.; more info at http://www.valpak.com

5. Richard Jalichandra—October 2009 from State of The Blogosphere, BlogWorld conference.

6. http://www.slideshare.net/Olivier.mermet/universal-mc-cann-wave4

7. Sharon Gaudin, *ComputerWorld,* January 26, 2010, http://www .computerworld.com/s/article/9148878/Twitter_now_has_75M_ users_most_asleep_at_the_mouse eMarketer - http://www.emarketer .com/Article.aspx?R=1007271

8. See interview with Michael Buck, Dell at SocialMarketingConversatio ns.com

9. Facebook; http://www.facebook.com/press/info.php?statistics; collected May 27, 2010

10. Because this is a social media book, we would love to get your input on these and other obstacles. Please provide us your feedback at Facebook.com/ROIofSocialMedia.com.

11. Lon Safko and David Brake, *The Social Media Bible: Tactics, Tools, and Strategies for Business Success* (New Jersey: John Wiley & Sons, 2009), 6.

12. WIIFM: What's in it for me.

13. CPM: Cost per thousand

14. Dell Corporation; Michael Buck podcast, and transcript published at SocialMarketingConversations.com

15. Peter Drucker, *The Practice of Management* (New York: Harper-Collins, 2006).

2

SOCIAL MEDIA MOTIVATIONS AND BEHAVIORS

For marketers to be successful, they need to have the consumer squarely at the center of their thinking. Understanding the motivations and behaviors of individuals in social media will help to explain how the media engagement framework applies to social media. Social marketing analytics must also begin in the same way. This chapter will talk about the motivations and behaviors people have in participating in social media so that we can:

- understand how the three key players in social media—influencers, individuals and consumers—derive benefit and utility from social media
- provide insights on how marketers can use this understanding to help them improve their social marketing communications plans.

Once we understand these motivations and behaviors, we can define strategies and tactics to take advantage of them in order to make social marketing actions more successful. With these strategies, we can then develop metrics following the media engagement framework described in Section 2.

ROI is not just about measuring the past but also, more importantly for the marketer, providing insights *to improve marketing actions in the future.* Measuring the past within the media engagement framework can provide good insights for improvement, but these must also be understood in context of why individuals participate in social media. Understanding these motivations will then allow marketers to make significantly better decisions for the future given the highly dynamic nature of social media. Combining analysis of the past with a deep understanding of an individual's motivations to participate in social media will allow us to develop strategies that are significantly more successful than shooting from the hip.

MOTIVATIONS FOR PARTICIPATING IN SOCIAL MEDIA

Canadian research from a March 2009 study commissioned by members of the Canadian Marketing Association's Integrated Marketing and Customer Experience Council showed the following motivations for those who participate (79 percent participate, 21 percent do not participate) in social networks.[1] The percentages indicate the number of participants responding to each type of activity:

- researching (44 percent)
- reading (36 percent)
- engaging in conversation, commenting, posting feedback (29 percent)
- creating blogs, writing articles (5 percent).

There are a couple of interesting results from these statistics. Those individuals who actively submit content in the form of blogs or articles are relatively small—only 1 in 20—supporting roughly the ratios in the 90-9-1 rule often seen in the press. Those who occasionally provide feedback and engage in some form of conversation are a larger percentage, about 1 in 3.

INDIVIDUALS—SOCIAL MEDIA PARTICIPANT HIERARCHY

Individuals participating in social media fall into a number of different groups. These groups are defined based on their personas. As shown in Figure 2.1, individuals can be:

- influencers
- consumers
  - current
  - past
  - prospective
- individuals in general.

90-9-1 RULE

A popular rule of thumb in social media discussions is the "90-9-1 ratio," referring to the engagement you can expect from the social media aware audience. It breaks down as follows:

- **90** percent of the visitors to your social presence will only consume the content you or other users post. It's not that they dislike the site; it is more likely that they are not confident in sharing their voice, participating in the content creation or they may be apathetic to the site, the message or the brand.
- **9** percent will engage periodically, but only if or when the conversation strikes them as important or relevant
- **1** percent is the engaged audience driving the conversation in your social media community. They are the ones supporting and providing value for the community to read, hear or view.

Although the authors are not fond of rules of thumb, anecdotal evidence or comparisons with public benchmarks, this rule does provide some indicator for marketers as they plan, create and monitor their social media presence and campaigns.

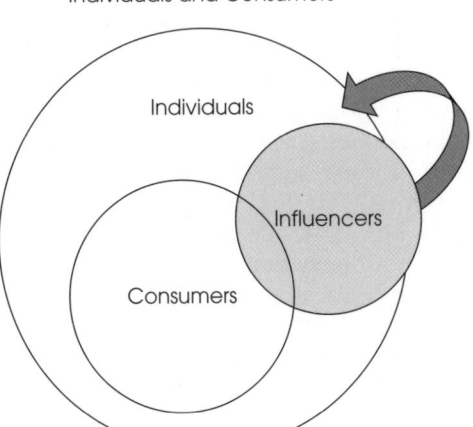

Relationship between Influencers, Individuals and Consumers

Individuals

Influencers

Consumers

Figure 2.1   Who connects to whom?

Each of these classes of individuals can change their behavior so that, in some instances, they may be influencers, while in others they may be prospective, past or current consumers (or they could be none of the above). For each of these classes of individuals, marketers must develop different strategies in order to move them to engage with, and advocate for, the brand. For example, a Mommy Blogger may be a consumer and advocate of the Pampers brand whereas another Mommy Blogger writing posts about other categories may be a past user of the Huggies brand, but may not be an influencer in the diapers category. It is important for marketers to identify the desires and motivations of the influencers, individuals and consumers in order to make certain they will either respond to, or promote, the brand in the desired fashion.

CONVERSATION HIERARCHY[2]

Concerning the dimensions affecting the sales volume of a brand, these individuals take part in conversations in social media in six ways:

1. at the consumer level
2. at the category level
3. at the brand level for your brand
4. at the brand level for competitive brands
5. at the distribution channel level
6. at the exogenous or external factor and trend level (for factors and trends affecting the category or brand).

In order to fully understand the conversations taking place in a category, marketers must monitor conversations along each of these dimensions in order to understand what influencers, individuals and consumers are saying about topics important to their categories and then how they should best participate and engage in conversations with each of these topics and segments. In social media, marketers should then build an appropriate strategy for each of these segments so that these conversations are most beneficial to their brands. Because the conversations are is no longer under the complete control of the marketers, marketers must build strategies at each of these six levels when promoting their brands using social media. For example, WalMart's Elevenmoms blog program talks primarily about saving money, thereby promoting the low price retail category within which WalMart is a dominant player. On the other hand, Greenpeace's posts about the use of palm oil from the rainforests of Malaysia and Indonesia affect all of the brands in the personal care category that include palm oil as an ingredient in their products.

THE THREE TIERS OF SOCIAL MEDIA STRATEGY

As we have seen in the media engagement framework, in order to build a successful social media strategy, marketers must develop strategies and tactics at three levels:

1. influencers
2. individuals
3. consumers.

INFLUENCERS

At the influencer level, a brand must provide value to target influencers in exchange for their desire to forward and promote your message to their followers. In this case, the marketer isn't primarily striving for the influencer to purchase their products: the objective is to have the influencer forward their message to their followers in a positive way as soon, and often, as possible.

Secondly, and more importantly, the brand is now in competition with a new set of competitors. For example, many marketers from many categories target Mommy Bloggers to have them write positive posts and forward coupons or promotion codes to their followers. Unfortunately, this plethora of marketers and categories targeting these same mommy bloggers for their time and influence leads to competition for the influencer's time and *endorsement share*. As more competitors develop more social marketing campaigns targeting these influencers, the cost to gain their endorsement will increase. Although the endorsement doesn't necessarily mean there is a paid, formal link between the marketer and the influencer, it will take more effort (which translates into money) for the marketer to build a strong relationship with key influencers as more and more brands target this same, limited number of influencers.

Influencers will want to avoid influencer burn-out. They will want to limit the number of posts they make endorsing various brands, as opposed to posts that are brand neutral. Marketers must now develop a clear strategy to reach these influencers, in concert with their traditional marketing strategies and other social marketing tactics, yet with a focused objective and different competitive set.

CONSUMERS

The primary goal of a marketer is to drive and deliver messages (at least cost and risk) to individuals to persuade them to purchase their

CYWORLD: CREATING SOCIAL NETWORK ENGAGEMENT

Cyworld was started in 1999 by a group of MBA students from the Korean Institute of Science and Technology. Initially called People Square, it was quickly renamed Cyworld. "Cy" in Korean means relationship, which defined the goal of the company. By mid-2007, Cyworld had 21 million registered users in a country of about 50 million people.

Users create their mini-home pages (called minihompy in Cyworld), which they use to display pictures or play their favorite music. These mini-home pages also contain bulletin boards on which users can record their thoughts and feelings. Users take great pleasure in decorating their own home pages by purchasing virtual items such as furniture, household items and wallpaper, as well as music.

A mini-home page is seen by users as a means for self-expression, and virtual items enable users to achieve this goal. In 2007, Cyworld generated $65 million or almost 70 percent of its revenue from selling these items. The remaining revenue was generated from advertising and mobile services. In addition to purchasing virtual items, members also engage in non-purchase-related activities. Members regularly update the content (pictures, diaries, music, etc.) of their own mini-home pages and visit the home pages of their friends to keep abreast of their updated content. If a user finds some content on a friend's mini-home page interesting, they can "scrape" it from their friend's page onto their own mini-home page.

The scraping function has the effect of replicating what members find interesting, thus generating a viral effect and increasing the value of the network for all members. Each minihompy also provides popularity stats, which can also support this viral effect.

Excerpt from: Raghuram Iyengar, Sangman Han, and Sunil Gupta[3]

brands over other competing brands. In the past, marketers used traditional media to deliver these messages. They operated in a relatively clearly defined category, so that the competitive set was defined as those competitors having products in the same category, each providing varying levels of functional and emotional value for the consumer. In exchange, the consumer was willing to pay a certain price for that value received. In social media, the marketer must still have messages delivered highlighting the value of the brand compared with other brands to move consumers down the consumer purchase funnel.

INDIVIDUALS

Individuals participating in social media may or may not be part of the marketer's target audience. These individuals participate in social media for a variety of reasons. Their participation and engagement is measured by the time they spend on various websites and the behaviors they exhibit there. The goal of the marketer is to develop a relationship with these individuals in such a way that they engage with the brand and become consumers, or that they engage with the brand and lead others to become consumers. This second type of engagement can simply be a series of brand-related posts, reviews or other conversations that consumers may read or that may get picked up in the search engines. In the social media space, the objective is then two dimensional in terms of driving the largest amount of high-quality engagement time possible with their brand and then using that engagement to win consumers over as customers or win others over as customers.

As in the individual level, the competitive set is also no longer the same as the traditional competitive set of consumers. It is made up of anything that competes for *time* with their target audience. Any second spent on another site unrelated to the brand is a second that could have been spent engaging with the brand. Marketers now compete against games, videos, news and many other Internet-based activities that could be undertaken by the individual. Marketers must now develop a second social marketing tactic to increase an individual's high-quality engagement time with their brands, rather than spending time doing other competing activities.

In that light, marketers must understand the motivators of individuals and influencers in order to increase the likelihood of success of their overall strategy to sell more products at least cost and risk. As we'll see below, these motivators are very different for individuals compared with influencers. The media engagement framework highlights that marketers must develop social marketing strategies and tactics that tackle the challenges at two new levels.

MOTIVATORS

Individuals participate in social media based on a number of motivations. They may use social media for their own purposes or sometimes they may be advocating (in a positive or negative way) a particular brand, thus acting as an influencer. By understanding these motivations, marketers can develop the right messages to impart at the right time in the right media channel to convert the individual to become an influencer or a consumer or both. The motivations for participating in a social community are:

For individuals
- communicate with friends and family; share (text, pictures, audio, video)
- meet and win new friends
- expand their business network
- fulfill sense of belonging
- learn from others; education
- self expression
- gaming
- entertainment
- participate in a cause (see discussion under influencer motivators)
- make better purchases
- get monetary rewards
- get more value out of current and planned purchases

For influencers
- be considered an expert
- become an influencer
- help others
- lead a cause
- develop and maintain business relationships; find a job

Not all of these motivators apply to all individuals at all times. Some individuals won't write a blog. Others don't want to develop business relationships. But, overall, these motivators provide a clear sense of why individuals and influencers participate in social communities.

MOTIVATORS FOR INDIVIDUALS

COMMUNICATE WITH FRIENDS AND FAMILY; SHARE
(TEXT, PICTURES, AUDIO, VIDEO)

Communication between contacts in the social community takes many forms. Discussions can be about the news or politics, what happened at school, or an infinite number of other topics. In the midst of all of these conversations, brands may be mentioned. They can be simple brand mentions, they can be outright endorsements or they can be praise or complaints based on a recent purchase, use or service incident.

Brand conversations can begin in numerous ways. The conversation can be instigated by someone considering purchasing a specific brand or asking a general category question, looking for a recommendation or store to purchase at the lowest price. It can be a full-blown recanting of a post-purchase experience reciting their impressions, both positive and negative, or it can be an opinion expressed by someone who has only seen branded advertising or heard of the brand experiences of others. By understanding these conversations, marketers can potentially leverage the pre- and post-purchase messaging to deliver either more messages, or more messages with a certain type of content. Considerations for marketers' communications include:

- what does it take to make their brand conversation-worthy?
- is their brand cool enough or valuable enough for a friend to endorse it positively (or at least not discourage its purchase)?
- is the category heavily or lightly talked about (as we'll see from our case studies, the beer, cooking and entertainment categories are highly talked about, whereas others are less so)?

An analysis of South Korea's Cyworld[3] (Cyworld is similar to Facebook and MySpace. See box on page 46) shows that certain segments are influenced by friends in a social network. The study defined social influence based on the level of activity in visiting other sites and their level of connectedness to determine a member's social influence on purchase behavior. This study found that the effect due to social influence was:

- neutral for 48 percent of the users
- positive for 40 percent of the users
- negative for 12 percent of the users

There is even a 'keeping up with the Joneses' effect where the social influence for moderately connected users can translate into a 5 percent increase in revenues of virtual purchases from Cyworld. On the other hand, highly connected users tend to reduce purchases of a brand if they see their friends using them, reducing revenue by up to 14 percent. "This finding is consistent with the typical fashion cycle wherein opinion leaders or the elite in the fashion industry tend to abandon one type of fashion and adopt the next in order to differentiate themselves from the masses." In this case, the communications was that of observation; that is, the viewing of a friend's purchases by visiting the "mini-hompy" (mini-home pages) and purchasing or not purchasing what they found there. The study found three clear groups of participants:

1. **Low status**—The least connected and engaged group, representing 48 percent of the studied members. Members belonging to this group do not imitate others because they feel that it will not help them gain more status. Purchases by this group were *not influenced* by social influence.
2. **Middle status**—Members of this group, representing 40 percent of the studied members, have an intermediate level of social activity, visiting other members' minihompy. They feel social pressure and fear falling in the social ranks. This group purchased 5 percent *more* due to social influence.
3. **High status**—Members of this group have a high level of social activity, representing 12 percent of the studied members. They do not imitate others very much because they feel quite confident in their own judgment and the legitimacy of their actions. This group purchased 14 percent *less* due to social influence.

This study also confirms that the highly active social members of a community are most likely to influence many of the other members, especially those of moderate activity levels. Interestingly, they are not necessarily large purchasers in the network.

In the midst of typical communications between friends and family, influencers arise that can drive purchases of the moderately connected. Regardless of where social media conversations take place, marketers can still gain by targeting influencers. For marketers, the implication is clear in terms of making their products and services and messages more readily available to the highly active members of a community, rather than to other members. Because social influence is a key driver of purchases, marketers can seed these influencers and/or target traditional media to them to drive purchases among the moderately connected. In addition, marketers can hone their messages to be more persuasive for the needs of this group of individuals. In this way, they can get an amplifier or multiplier effect to their advertising investment through the social influence of the high-status members in their target audiences.

Social media infrastructure providers (such as, Facebook, MySpace and Cyworld) can increase their revenue through advertising by making statistics available of the connectedness or social graph of their members. With these statistics, marketers can then hone influencer-oriented messages toward influencers and provide other messages to the moderately connected. Cyworld analysts could analyze the dynamic behaviors of individuals to determine which individuals are more likely to fall into the low-, medium- or high-status segments, thereby improving their ability to target the right individuals with the right messages at the right time to garner the most revenue from the sale of Cyworld services.

MEET AND WIN NEW FRIENDS

Individuals have many friends and acquaintances for many reasons and from many sources. They have college friends, high school friends and business friends. Individuals want to keep in touch with many of these friends, and social networks provide an easy way to do that. No longer do individuals have to maintain complex address books that are always out of date when Christmas or the holidays roll around. In addition, they can now track birthdays and anniversaries all in one place. Better yet, the individual to whom the data pertains is responsible for keeping everything up to date. With LinkedIn, when an individual changes jobs, all they need do is update their profile information and every one of their contacts has immediate access to the latest personal information for that individual. Communicating to LinkedIn connections is simple. With a few clicks and keystrokes, messages can go out to any number or group of friends in an individual's network.

Friends are classified into groups: the virtual world is just like the real world. "College buddy" or "golfing buddy" are terms seen in the real world. In the virtual world, terms include "BFF," "Facebook friend," "Farmville friend" or "a connection on LinkedIn." Based on the type of friendship and level of connection with that friend, the friend will have a lot, some or no influence over potential brand purchases. When received from friends, their messages will be weighted based on their reputations with their friends.

As illustrated in the Cyworld example, marketers will improve their success if they target influencers. Marketers can improve the response to their activities in two ways:

1. They can help and encourage influencers to build more and better connections. In this way, the marketer's influence can affect more of the moderately connected.
2. They can build and enhance the brand's connection with the highly connected, highly influential individuals. In this way, marketers can more easily leverage the social influence of the influencers.

FULFILL SENSE OF BELONGING

Social networks offer an emotional value for individuals through the fulfillment of a sense of belonging (e.g. Maslow's hierarchy of needs). In 2007 in England, the Social Issues Research Centre (SIRC)[4] "identified six key social identities in which people most frequently anchor their sense of belonging today (See "Belonging" box):"
- family
- friendship
- lifestyle choices (brand identities: how we spend our money and leisure activities; how we spend our time)
- nationality
- professional identity
- team spirit and shared interests

BELONGING

1. **Family.** Despite public debate about the decline of the family in modern society, family remains the most important focus of belonging. Of respondents in the national poll, 88 percent chose family as the key marker of belonging. The ways in which families are structured has certainly changed in recent decades, but family remains the most important category of human social organization.

2. **Friendship.** While the close proximity of a large extended family would have provided a structure for social support in the past, this function is now filled, at least in part, by an increasingly diverse and multilayered network of friendships. Increased geographic mobility and interconnectedness through new digital technologies allow us to connect with people in new ways. In the poll, 65 percent of respondents saw friendships as being an essential part of their sense of belonging.

3. **Lifestyle choices.** In developing friendships and social networks, we are also defining the kinds of lifestyle that we want to lead and the types of social capital—the social status, shared values and cultural practices—that go with it. We make choices about the kinds of activities that we are interested in, the kinds

of products that we buy and the associations that these involve. Importantly, we also make lifestyle choices by choosing not to consume certain products or engage in certain types of activity. What we do not do is as important to our sense of belonging as that in which we actively choose to engage. For many participants in the project, thinking about lifestyle choices revealed a far more entrenched sense of brand and group loyalty than they had initially expected or were prepared to admit.

4. **Nationality.** Advocates of cultural globalization point to the fact that national identity is on the decline. As the world becomes more connected, it is increasingly common for people to pass through the borders of individual countries, both physically and virtually. While there is certainly a greater awareness of the flexibility of national identities, and the possibility of shedding one in exchange for another, there still remains a strong tie between individuals and the nationalities with which they are born. People may question what exactly it means to be "British" or "English" in the 21st century, but this is by no means the same as rejecting the idea of being British altogether. Over a third of all people claim their national identity as a major factor in defining belonging.

5. **Professional identity.** In a society where our social status is to a great extent measured by the work we do and, perhaps more importantly, the money we earn, it is little surprise that professional identity is an important locus of belonging for both men and women. It is, after all, often the first characteristic that people offer up when introducing themselves to others. While occupational mobility has certainly increased for many people, and "re-skilling" is a normal part of modern-day professional life, we remain tied to the social significance of what we do for a living. Our sense of belonging in this context is greater than the affinity we feel with members of our extended families.

6. **Team spirit and shared interests.** For men, the football or other sporting team that they support provides a stronger sense of belonging than religion, social class, ethnic background or political affiliations. The clubs they belong to are also important

(continued)

> sources of social identity. Both men and women view the hob-
> bies and interests that they share with others as an important
> source of identity. For women, this sense of belonging is as
> strong as that associated with their nationality.
>
> *Source:* Research by SIRC commissioned by The Automobile Association

The fulfillment of the sense of belonging is a key driver of activities in a social network. Marketers can take advantage of this through
proper messaging and targeting. As profile information becomes more
available to marketers, they will be able to more highly focus their messages on these key emotional motivations based on the fulfillment of
the sense of belonging.

LEARN FROM OTHERS; EDUCATION

Whether individuals learn formally or informally, they are always
learning. Whether they learn to improve their standing in their social
community or simply to converse more knowledgably about the
football scores, there is always something that someone wants to
know. Individuals also gain valuable information based on the opinions and information provided by influencers. Social networks make
the process of information dissemination more valuable by presenting
valuable information in an important new way: its value can be rated
by the community. Instead of having to read everything about a topic,
the reader can use the crowd to help filter out the less valuable from the
more valuable.

Marketers can take advantage of this new presentation method by
providing the kinds of information relevant to the social network in a
format that they would want to consume them and comment on them.
This can be especially valuable for their brands by helping influencers
improve their category and brand knowledge by providing them potentially exclusive access to information that would support their standing
in their communities.

GAMING

Social gaming has become a new area for individuals to meet and interact with others. There are many games that are built around Facebook,
including Farmville and Mafia Wars. YouTube has made it easy for
marketers to offer contests. Marketers are already interacting with
individuals in the gaming space through display advertisements and
other placements. Gaming on social platforms has also exploded: witness
the 23,000,000 users of Zynga's "FarmVille" on Facebook and they've

ZYNGA'S FARMVILLE

Farmville notes, "The irony is that Facebook games typically share four characteristics that really do promise great things for both gamers and designers:

- True friends list: Gaming can now happen exclusively within the context of one's actual friends. Multiplayer games no longer suffer from the catch-22 of requiring friends to be fun while new players always start the game without friends.
- Free-to-play business model: New players need not shell out $60 to join the crowd. Consumers don't like buying multiplayer games unless they know that their friends are all going to buy the games as well. Free-to-play removes that friction.
- Persistent, asynchronous play: Finding time to play with one's real friends is difficult, especially for working, adult gamers. Asynchronous mechanics, however, let gamers play at their own pace and with their own friends, not strangers who happen to be online at the same time.
- Metrics-based iteration: Retail games are developed in a vacuum, with designers working by gut instinct. Further, games get only one launch: a single chance to succeed. Most developers would love, instead, to iterate quickly on genuine, live feedback.

These four pillars are the reasons why many game developers are flocking to Facebook. (Of course, many of these characteristics are not exclusive to Facebook, but combining them together with such a large audience makes Facebook the obvious choice right now.) However, Jesse Schell is right; a war is brewing over who will call the shots."

Source: http://worldsinmotion.biz/2010/03/opinion_fear_and_loathing_in_f.php

just agreed to present their games on Yahoo!. Farmville is just one of the suite of games Zynga has developed for Facebook, which includes Mafia Wars, Fishville and about a dozen others. Farmville provides players with a green patch of "farmland" on which they can create a farm that can include crops, livestock, buildings, landscaping, vehicles and more.

Participants can find other Facebook friends already playing Farmville or invite others to join them with their own farm and to place it next door. By planting crops, waiting for them to grow and then harvesting and selling them, players make gold coins. The coins can be redeemed for more seeds, livestock and whatever else in the marketplace. Some items don't require coins, but virtual bills, which come a bit slower. You can readily gift your friends with items for their farms as well and they, in turn, can gift you back, strengthening the social bond between players. A quick way to get your farm developed is to use a credit card and buy the credits, coins and bills needed for the items you want.

The impact of social platform gaming is that you can play the game with your friends asynchronously. When your friends are not around, you can visit their farms and help them by feeding their crops and livestock, which helps them in the game and also gains you coins and credits.

There is a sense of playing the game with real-life friends, and the obligation of real-life friendship between gamers extends the meaning of the game and will draw players back, even if they have lost interest. While not prevalent, branding opportunities in the gaming social platform are opening up. You might see the ability to get a can of your favorite soft drink in Farmville soon.

ENTERTAINMENT

Social media makes it easy to share videos, jokes and other content that is entertaining. Entertainment has countless themes. The YouTube video, the Flickr image sharing service and podcasting audio format are the most popular, allowing users to easily submit, view and hear content.

YouTube content can be in the form of entertainment or music or business related in the form of simple video recordings to support business-to-business marketing. Educational videos are also available.

Submitted videos can be commented on and ranked, and links can be shared or embedded in other websites. Videos can be sorted by popularity in terms of the number of views or their rank, most discussed and other criteria.

Marketers are using a number of options from YouTube to promote their brands. This includes submission of video versions of the TV commercials, contests and channels. Many other brands have channels on YouTube allowing a customized, branded page sorted by a handful of categories:[5]

Autos	How-To	Science	Musicians	Shows
Comedy	Music	Sports	Non-Profit	Movies
Education	News	Travel	Partners	Trailers
Entertainment	Nonprofits	Comedians	Politicians	Contests
Film	People	Directors	Reporters	Events
Gaming	Pets	Gurus	Sponsors	

MAKE BETTER PURCHASES; GET MONETARY REWARDS;
GET MORE VALUE OUT OF THEIR PURCHASES

Discussion forums and ratings and reviews help consumers gather valuable information prior to their purchase. This is especially important for highly considered categories, such as, cars, software and electronics. For low consideration categories, many brands offer special coupons to their fans (Facebook) and provide other valuable activities for their members.

In China, there is a new trend where groups of buyers ready to purchase the same equipment meet up online to form a purchasing group, called a "swarm." They go together in groups of 50 to 200 to an electronics retailer and begin negotiating a group purchase of electronic equipment.

Marketers can use these tools to generate leads and drive short-term revenue. For new product launches, marketers can entice brand loyalists to try their new products. They can also be offered through the branded social community to potential influencers to provide exclusive, pre-launch knowledge of the features and benefits of the new products. This feedback can help improve the messaging and support the experts and influencers in their desire to be ahead of the crowd.

MOTIVATORS FOR INFLUENCERS

BE CONSIDERED AN EXPERT; BECOME AN INFLUENCER;
HELP OTHERS

In both business-to-business (B2B) and consumer marketing, being considered an expert or influencer can have personal and career benefits. In B2B markets, being an expert can deliver more leads and revenue and can accelerate your career. In a consumer market, experts can lend their endorsements to brands and earn money or other rewards for that endorsement. To become an expert/ influencer in a social network, there are a number of tactics that can be employed:[6]

- **Establish a social networking brand**—Determine the social networking brand that will help to establish your position relative to other influencers. Build an online profile to support the brand. Writing style is also a key component to the social networking brand and reinforces your online personality.
- **Choose the right networks to participate in**—Determine which networks have the target audience most relevant to your area of expertise.

- **Choose where and when to engage**—Engagement is the key to becoming known as an expert. Frequently providing content and commenting on published content can help to establish your credentials in your area of expertise quickly.
- **Provide valuable content**—You will not be considered an expert unless you provide real value to your constituents. Here are some examples of value:[7] listening, providing support, providing empathy, providing validation, teaching, providing tutorials, entertaining and providing knowledge.
- **Engage and partner with other social influencers**—To be considered an expert and influencer, other influencers must also consider you an expert or influencer. With this status, your content will be cited more frequently, providing valuable credibility in your target social network. It will benefit your reputation as an influencer.
- **Market your social networking profiles, tie social networks together**—If you are active in multiple networks or have multiple online profiles, make certain they are all linked together so that they can reinforce one another.
- **Market your social networking brand**—Continue to promote yourself as the expert. For example, CakeCentral.com ranks members based on their level of activity. Members can be ranked from forum superstar and forum addict to frequent member and newbie. Recommendations these members might make about baking products have a higher likelihood of being trusted than general friends found in other networks. For example, the Wilton brand ("the leading food crafting company in the industry, with the number one position in cake decorating, bake ware and tea kettles"[8]) was mentioned over 37,000 times across the forums[9] in CakeCentral.com.

Marketers can improve their brand's standing in social media by helping experts and influencers improve their standing in the social community. This can be as simple as asking their opinion but can also be to help them further their knowledge or increase their following.

Lastly, you don't have to be an expert to be an influencer. Many individuals just want to help others. Potential purchasers may prefer recommendations from these individuals because they have less perceived vested interest and are genuine users of the products and services in question. This willingness to help can develop a strong following and eventually develop the individuals into influencers. They can continue to provide help by being the people individuals consult with before making larger purchases. In this way, they can build their reputations and gain respect and admiration, acceptance and acknowledgement.

Tremor[10] and BzzAgent[11] have built unique service offerings providing marketers access to groups of individuals willing to talk to friends and family about promoted products. Each of these new media channels has hundreds of thousands of agents in their communities. Based on various filtering criteria, marketers can develop social marketing campaigns, enlisting the agents to speak favorably about their brands and products. In so doing, the marketer can gain quick delivery of targeted messages into the market from trusted individuals. In addition, the agents provide reports indicating responses received, delivering valuable consumer insights that might not be gained from other sources. Lastly, these services follow strict guidelines set forth by the Federal Trade Commission (FTC) in terms of education, monitoring and enforcement so that marketers can make certain their social media marketing campaigns are fully following the established FTC guidelines on product endorsements.

LEAD A CAUSE; PARTICIPATE IN A CAUSE

There are literally thousands of causes that individuals can support through their social networks. Instead of just sending money and contributions, individuals can now participate by recommending others to the causes and by contributing comments and input to the causes. It is widely believed that the recent 2008 presidential campaign was won through the use of social networks to support the Barrack Hussein Obama presidential bid. Since then, just about every other politician has built a social network following in the various social networking communities and is communicating with their constituents using these tools.[12]

Politics aside, marketers can support these causes in a new way through social media to enhance their image with their consumer base. In some cases, as with the Dove brand from Unilever and the Greenpeace onslaught against its use of palm oil being grown in deforested rainforests, marketers must carefully consider their method of response in both traditional and social media (see box on page 60). A similar outcome arose more recently with Nestlé and their Kit Kat brand. Greenpeace was able to exert consumer pressure on Nestlé using a combination of social media tools.

DEVELOP AND MAINTAIN BUSINESS RELATIONSHIPS; FIND A JOB

LinkedIn provides many capabilities, as previously described. Facebook is also now competing with LinkedIn to capture the B2B market. Linkedin provides profiles, groups, email (Inmail) and other capabilities to help businesses build their online brand and generate leads. Searching for a job is also supported through social networks. LinkedIn has developed a number of great capabilities to provide new venues in supporting job

---

UNILEVER, DOVE AND GREENPEACE

Thanks to the staggering public support for our international Dove campaign in April 2008, Unilever has now agreed to play their part in saving the Paradise Forests of South-East Asia. As the biggest single buyer of palm oil in the world, Unilever has a special responsibility to help clean up the industry that's behind so much forest destruction.

Greenpeace's forests campaigners were invited to meet with senior executives at Unilever headquarters on Friday, May 9, 2008. In just two weeks, the company had received tens of thousands of protest emails from around the world, seen Greenpeace activists bring hoards of news media to their buildings in the UK, the Netherlands and Italy, and watched our viral video "Dove Onslaught(er)" take off faster than anything we've ever done before. Public pressure moved them.

The meeting with Unilever was a positive first step by the company, but there is a long way to go to get the bulldozers out of the rainforest.

Firstly, Unilever agrees to support an immediate moratorium on deforestation for palm oil in Southeast Asia.

Secondly, the company also agrees to use its leadership role within the industry to "aggressively" build a coalition of companies to support the moratorium. This includes them lobbying all the major players within and outside the Round Table on Sustainable Palm Oil (RSPO), including the likes of Kraft, Nestle and Cadbury.

Thirdly, they agreed to put urgent and substantial pressure to save forests onto their palm oil suppliers on the ground in Indonesia too. Once the suppliers are on board with the moratorium, then we have a real chance of stopping rainforest destruction.

Finally, Unilever agreed that they would lobby the Indonesian government to support the immediate moratorium.

An excerpt from "Public pressure for Indonesia's forests works, Ask Unilever,"; http://www.greenpeace.org/international/campaigns/forests/asia-pacific/ dove-palmoil-action, December, 2009.

seekers through improving and speeding connections that might be valuable in finding a job.

Marketers can support their brands by building branded pages (Facebook), company profiles (LinkedIn) and developing vibrant groups (LinkedIn). These pages help marketers deliver key brand messages to places where consumers are spending their time. They also allow marketers to conduct research to hone their messages and receive feedback. Once these pages are established, marketers can help to differentiate their brands and their ability to understand the key issues in making decisions in highly considered categories.

Behaviors

Social networks offer new and exciting ways to target customers who have important implications for improving marketing success. With the right information, marketers can improve the likelihood of consumers purchasing and advocating their brands and products for maximum long-term revenue, profit, brand and share.

Being able to identify more accurately the right individuals to target can significantly reduce marketing costs and increase response. Segmentation is the key, but it is probabilistic in nature. In an ideal world, we want to identify specific individuals who will absolutely respond to our marketing. In reality, we can identify only those individuals who are more likely than others to respond to a particular marketing activity given various identity markers. In social media, these markers fall into three broad categories:

1. levels of connectedness
2. privacy and demographic markers
3. behavioral markers.

Through segmentation using these and other markers, marketers can achieve a number of important tactical objectives in social media:

1. entice new visitors and members to the community
2. drive increased and deeper engagement on the site by members and non-members
3. identify and target influencers.

By using the right segmentation and executing marketing tactics taking advantage of these segments, marketers can increase their success and drive value for their brands. As we'll see in Section 2, the media engagement framework provides a segmentation framework among influencers, individuals and consumers. Once segmentation schemes have been defined and implemented, marketers can better target each group with the right messages at the right time in order to build engagement and long-term value in the social media space. In each case, marketers will need to build a strategic framework to market appropriately to each group and build a competitive strategy to target these individuals with the right messages and marketing activities in order to garner more of their valuable *time*, *engagement* and *endorsement* away from the competition. As discussed above, each group has different requirements, objectives and values.

CASE STUDY

SEGMENTING MESSAGES BY SOCIAL COMMUNITY

Sessions College for Professional Design

Established in the late 90s, Sessions College is a fully online college with students from over 100 countries providing instruction in graphic, web design, game art, fine art and multimedia. Students interact asynchronously in an online campus, building a portfolio of design work and then interact with prospective employers to find work in their field of design. Sessions provides three semesters per year, although enrollment and classes can take place at any time.

According to Scott Chappell, Chief Marketing Officer of Sessions, they have begun using social media to increase the touch points and the total number of communication opportunities they have with their students, prospects and alumni. Sessions has been able to use Facebook, LinkedIn and Twitter to build the brand through specific types of messages to the various audiences and connect a lot more without losing them or overwhelming them.

According to Scott, Sessions was able to increase their message frequency from 12 messages per month to over 36 without an increase in unsubscribes. Sessions was able to use this increased frequency and targeted messaging to increase conversions of prospects and visitors into sign-up and students. The messaging content model was designed around three key themes and through specific social platforms that are particular to Sessions and their online audience:

Culture—These are messages that convey the type of culture found at Sessions; these messages are primarily posted on Facebook.

Industry—Sessions' "Notes on Design" blog and their Twitter presence convey content designed to help build the prospects' confidence in the design industry and include ideas on how to support them when a change of career is being contemplated.

Sell—Sessions must also deliver enrollment. Messages around this topic are typically delivered through email, traditional mailers and, to a lesser degree, via a combination of the social media sites. These messages are time sensitive, enrollment-deadline oriented and more promotional.

Sincerity in its messages and consistency in frequency continue to be important tactical components to their integrated social media presence. Even though the number of touches has increased dramatically, the quality of those messages is much more important than quantity.

In growing their fan and follower base, Sessions has opted for patience. Instead of trying to artificially grow the fan base, Scott stresses patience and letting the social presences grow organically. Alumni are encouraged to stay connected to the social presence and they continue to interact with the brand and, as graduates, often become ambassadors for Sessions when questions are posted in a public forum. Recent graduates will often post on Facebook about their experience with Sessions when a question from a prospective student is posted, and alumni are invited to become part of a special LinkedIn group. In this way, Sessions can remain engaged and continues to support the university through contributions and pre-enrollment communications with prospective students.

Source: Interview with Scott Chappell, Chief Marketing Officer, Publisher, Notes On Design on February 3, 2010. Published with permission. All rights reserved.

SOCIAL MEDIA SEGMENTATION MODEL

Segmenting a market into target segments can help marketers invest their limited resources with groups of individuals who are more likely to respond over those who aren't. In addition, they can target specific messages to each of these groups at specific times to further improve the probability and value of their response. Historically, segmentation was one of the first concepts applying to all media, categories and brands that helped marketers improve their effectiveness. If a marketer can identify a certain set of motivations and behaviors specific to a certain group that is more likely to respond, the brand can exhibit faster growth and stay ahead of the competition. For social media segmentation, a combination of new and existing markers can be used. They fall into three broad categories: level of connectedness, privacy and demographic markers and behavioral markers.

1. **Level of connectedness**—Connectedness can be determined by the number of connections a particular individual has. This definition can be enhanced based on the number of invitations and forwards done by the individual. Although these tend to be less accurate, connectedness can also be enhanced further through self-reporting. In a branded community, and some public communities, the level of connectedness can be easily determined. In others, this data has yet to be made available to marketers.

2. **Privacy and demographic markers**—Members can provide personal profile and demographic information at varying levels of specificity. The level of information provided in the personal profile is often voluntarily given, so those members who provide a deep amount of information have high trust in the community and are willing to share their personal information with others. Often sites have specific privacy options concerning personal information and so all profile information may not be fully available to the marketer. It's not that the marketer needs to see the actual individual information: the marketer just wants to be able to target specific marketing activities to certain sets of individuals based on "selects" and "filters" garnered from these markers. For example, a marketer may wish to select the following three filters: all individuals over the age of 25, all individuals making their profiles public and all individuals who have a Bachelor's degree or higher.

3. **Behavioral markers**—Influencers and highly engaged individuals have certain behavioral markers. These markers may differ between communities, but they can help marketers identify those individuals with a higher propensity to engage in conversation about the brand or the community. Given that a large proportion of influencer conversation still takes place offline (where measurements are typically unavailable) identifying which members have a higher probability to engage in conversation about a brand can help marketers drive further word of mouth for their brands and marketing activities regardless of whether they take place online or off. Some of these markers are listed under "Influencer

segmentation" in Chapter 4. In addition, behavioral markers specific to the community can be very helpful to the marketers in identifying prospective influencers for their brands. These markers can include, for example, those individuals who have logged in to the network more than five times per week, made more than one comment per login and have sent out two invitations per week to join the community. With this segmentation scheme in hand, we can now identify individuals who have a higher propensity to engage in certain valuable activity. Marketers can now develop marketing campaigns to persuade the right individuals to talk about their brands, influence others about their brands and purchase their products.

BEHAVIORAL TARGETING

Behavioral targeting and behavioral marketing are often used synonymously. They are defined as analyzing past behavior (in this case on the web) to help marketers increase the likelihood that a particular offer or message will be more likely to be clicked on and converted by the targeted individual. Combining behavioral information with demographic information can lead to further insights and more highly targeted advertisements, leading to higher marketing success rates and ROI. Behavioral targeting is about reaching the right people at the right time with the right message. Behavioral targeting can be used to increase the acquisition of new customers, cross-sell different categories of products, up-sell to higher value purchases and retain and increase the frequency of purchase. As we'll see below, behavioral targeting can be used in similar ways by marketers to maintain and enhance engagement with the community.

At the moment, there is a lot of concern surrounding behavioral marketing. Individuals are concerned that companies are connecting their behavior on the web with their identities. Generally, behavioral targeting doesn't connect the individual with behavior. Instead, it seeks to connect an *anonymous* browser with a behavior.

LOOK-ALIKE MODELING

Behavioral targeting has been used by marketers in online and offline marketing activities for quite some time. One of the most well-known web behavioral targeting marketers is Amazon. Amazon makes two strategic offers to users based on their behaviors:

1. During the checkout process, the website at Amazon.com suggests other books with the phrase "customers who bought this also bought ..."

2. The Amazon.com website also suggests appealing combination offers at higher prices to entice a higher checkout value.

Each of these offers is based on past behavior and what's called look-alike models. A look-alike model analyzes all past behavior of previous customers and their purchases and then compares that behavior with your behavior to determine a most likely fit between the two to make a recommendation that is most likely to lead to conversion.

Advertising networks combine the behaviors of anonymous browsers across multiple sites to track how the users using these browsers clicked on display advertisements in the past. With this knowledge, the ad network can target more appropriate advertisements that have a higher likelihood of being clicked through. In this way, they can charge advertisers a higher premium for behaviorally targeted advertisements with a higher click-through rate, as opposed to a non-targeted ad, which will most likely have a lower click-through rate.

Because there can be so much information built into a web-targeting application, very specific offers and messages based on very detailed targeting algorithms can be presented to the browser. These can include messages and display advertisements, but can also include specific web pages that are presented or not presented.

THE SOCIAL GRAPH

A social graph is the social structure made of individuals or organizations that can be connected by one or more interdependency. Membership in a social network is one type of connection.

SINGLE SIGN-ON

A technology called "single sign-on" offers high value to both consumers and marketers alike. Consumers now only need to remember a single sign-on regardless of the website they are visiting. Single sign-on via a variety of providers is now available on many sites and bases its sign-on username and password on the consumers' accounts with the key players in this area such as Facebook Connect, Twitter OAuth or Microsoft LiveID. Single sign-on is popular for two reasons: simplicity and access. Consumers can participate in multiple sites with a single sign-on and for marketers, use of a preauthorized single sign-on presents the opportunity to also connect to the pre-established social network, the "social graph", of the consumer, a complete identity and their stream of posts without subsequent permission. This allows a much wider and faster opportunity for marketers to profile and attract users.

With single sign-on, marketers will now be able to gather statistics about users as they visit sites across each of these single sign-on based websites. Through this authenticated presence, marketers can be provided highly detailed information about the individual and his or her past behavior.

Through the single sign-on function, marketers can access statistics about the Facebook member and their profiles. Social media isn't just about richer media content or social networking or more applications. It is also about marketers finally having information available to tie consumer demographics and profile information to desired behavior. With single sign-on through online communities, it has become easier for individuals to navigate the web and more easily reap the value they're looking for from various applications. For marketers, single sign-ons can offer more valuable messages that can be more appealing to the individual. Just as sports programming has advertising more targeted to their male viewer demographic, web advertising can now be micro-targeted to deliver the best value for the browser and the best response for the marketer.

Segmentation allows marketers to improve the specification and purchase of the right list, the purchase of the right media at the right time to align these with the right marketing message and offering. With key demographic, connectedness and behavioral data available for each web visitor product, recommendations or specific messages can be further tailored in real time. Amazon's "customers who bought this also bought ..." is a great example of how to make the best offers to visitors whose past behavior matches other behaviors to drive the highest likelihood of incremental purchases.

THE NEW SUBSCRIPTION PARADIGM

The ability to simply and easily subscribe to a feed, or flow of messages and posts from a source such as a blog or social network, was greatly simplified with the development of RSS. "RSS" stands for really simple syndication and permits individuals to quickly and easily provide notice to a website that they want to updated and notified when new content is available.

(continued)

In a social network environment, the requirement to subscribe, provide an identity to or somehow otherwise identify yourself in order to access the site, has gone from users expecting to create an anonymous name or title to site users now expecting to provide an accurate identity that can be readily associated with the offline identity. The standard in social media is now the avatar that represents the person so that @AplusK is known to represent Ashton Krutcher, @TheRealShaq is really Shaquille O'Neil, @StevenGroves is really Steven Groves, @GuyPowell is Guy Powell and @JDimos is honestly Jerry Dimos.

This authentication is getting much easier: elsewhere we discuss the evolution of the Facebook Connect and, in April 2010, Facebook announced the next step of the Facebook Connect model, called Open Graph. The enhancements to the product are numerous and varied and will contribute to the development of what is being called the semantic web, but in the short term, they provide a ready technique to access some of the data behind the Facebook site. As users access a new site that has the new login capability, they can also be presented with their friends from Facebook who are already registered on the non-Facebook site. This will drive user adoption of new or complementary sites because they will not have to re-supply their credentials everytime they access another site.

Subscribing or logging into a site to access the content is a trend that we see diminishing, particularly with the advent of systems such as the new enhanced Facebook Connect and XAuth—a competitive credentialing system developed by Meebo and backed by big names in the industry such as Google, Microsoft, Yahoo, MySpace and Disqus. The exception to the user pushback of requiring extensive logon information seems to be online gaming sites where anonymity and an alter-ego persona are *de rigueur*. This makes the gaming environment one that may end up being the last bastion of social connectedness for the online because it will be much harder to connect the avatar ID with the offline, real person.

With this new paradigm, social network platform providers will now be able to glean more information about their members through their Facebook or Twitter profiles. This can be highly beneficial to the platform because they can now combine any information available on Facebook with what they may collect on their own sites in order to segment and target their users in a more detailed way.

BEHAVIORAL TARGETING IN SOCIAL NETWORKS

Behavioral targeting also applies to social networks. With accurate demographic profile information and good past behavioral information aligned based on the community engagement funnel (see Chapter 6), marketers can deliver more appealing messages to community members in order to maintain or deepen the visitors' engagement. The social networks can become more valuable to their members and visitors.

The goal of behavioral targeting in social networks is to increase the breadth of engagement across the community and the depth of engagement down the engagement funnel. Many behavioral targeting actions taken by marketing in e-commerce sites[13] can be applied to social communities. The table below shows some of these comparisons:

Comparing behavioral targeting for e-commerce and social media

Marketing action	E-commerce action	Social network action
Browsing history	This can include past sites visited, or on a particular e-commerce site what has been looked at but not purchased.	For social communities, marketers can review past engagement history to make suggestions to members about how to improve their engagement with the community.
Past email click-through	Understanding what might have been a convertible offer can help marketers make similar offers in the past.	For communities, this could include how members and non-members responded to any community communications to potentially deliver new and more targeted communications.
Any past purchase abandonment	Understanding what was almost purchased may help the marketer to make other similar offers that might be slightly lower in price or available in slightly different variants to finalize that conversion.	Abandonment in a social network could include the abandoned comment submission or invitation submission.

(continued)

(continued)

Marketing action	E-commerce action	Social network action
Actual past conversions	Understanding past purchases and when those past purchases took place can help marketers suggest other products that might be interesting for that individual.	Social communities may be able to target more specific information to members based on past discussions read, comments submitted or invitations sent. Display advertising may be able to be enhanced, but also sort options and other information presentment may be able to be improved and made more relevant.
Frequency and recency of visits	If a regular returning visitor starts to decrease his/her return frequency, it may be necessary for the marketer to understand why the individual has reduced his/her engagement with the site.	For social networks, a reduction in post frequency, visit frequency or invitation frequency can signal a loss of interest in the community. Monitoring this change in behavior can help marketers to make specific messages to these individuals in order to re-energize waning members.
Exploratory offers	Behavioral targeting can be used by traditional e-commerce sites to explore new areas of interest for past purchasers.	Marketers can use behavioral targeting to help members explore new areas of engagement that other members with similar demographics may have found to be interesting.

Marketers can use similar techniques to those shown in the table to understand the behavior of both individuals and influencers. Marketers can then apply these techniques to entice influencers to increase their engagement with their brands and to entice influencers to recommend the brands to their followers.

DYNAMIC SEGMENTATION AND BEHAVIORAL TARGETING

Individuals don't just repeat the same behavior over and over. They grow and mature in their actions. Their behavior is dynamic and changes over time. Understanding how behavior changes over time and the pathways of desired behavior can, for example, help marketers increase and accelerate the depth of engagement of individuals and lead to the identification of more influencers. Adding this dynamic component to the behavioral analysis can lend new insights for marketers to make certain they are delivering value to the community and whether specific actions with specific individuals can be taken to increase the value they receive from the community and, in so doing, provide value back to the community and the brand.

As shown in Figure 2.2, the non-member subscribes and becomes a member and after a certain period of time shows a certain level of engagement. After engaging at an initial level, the individual may show signs of being an influencer. If the community provides good value to the individual, engagement will continue and he/she may move to becoming an influencer or advocate. If the community fails to meet initial expectations or does something perceived by the individual as wrong, the individual may show little to no engagement and simply cancel membership and be gone from the community. By monitoring and analyzing behavior over time and comparing to other more ideal behaviors, marketers can determine whether an individual has the likelihood of being on the pathway to becoming an influencer, remaining simply engaged or canceling his or her membership. In each of these cases,

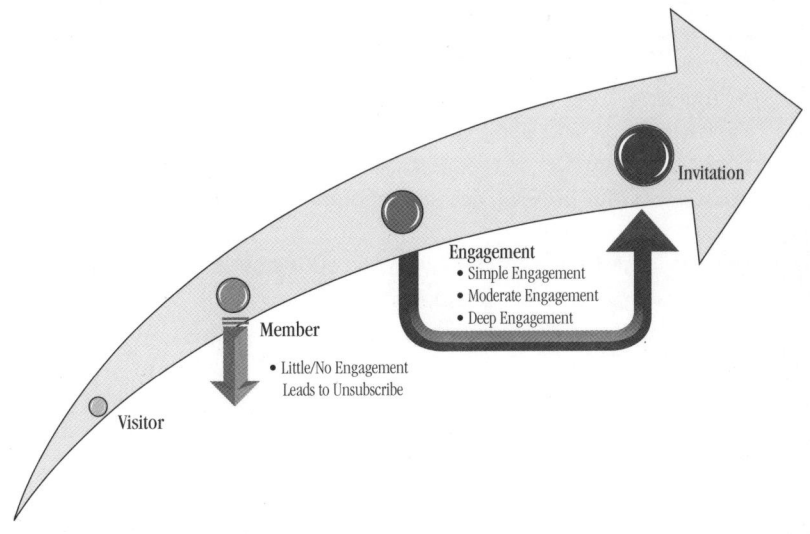

Figure 2.2 Dynamic behavior

marketers can then devise marketing actions to either drive more and deeper engagement and thereby increase member value and engagement and mitigate membership loss.

Klout.com uses this concept by monitoring a member's Klout score and, if it begins to drop off, it sends out an email with a few specific suggestions as to how the score can be improved.

KLOUT.COM ANALYSIS

"Our analysis shows that your influence on Twitter has dropped from 30 to 10. There are a lot of reasons this could have happened but don't worry, we are going to help you become more influential! The first thing we recommend is tweeting who your influencers are. This often sparks conversation which is the key to your Klout influence.

Tweet my influencers.

These are the things that you have improved:

- Activity – Wow, you've got influential people @ messaging and re-tweeting you. Your great content is being rewarded.

These are the things that we recommend you improve:

- Engagement – You should work on building relationships through conversation.
- Demand – Your network has either decreased in size or you've deliberately followed a lot of people to reach your current size. Follow anyone you think is interesting but try to engage with your network and don't just follow to be followed in return.
- Velocity – Offer original, creative and interesting content that adds value for your followers.
- Reach – The best way to build your audience is by listening and participating. There is no shortcut.

View your account.

We look forward to helping you grow even more influential. Please do not hesitate to contact us if you have any questions, comments or feedback.

Thanks!

The Klout Team"[14]

SOCIAL WEB–REPUTATION MANAGEMENT CYCLES

For example, Laurel Papworth[15] describes the dynamism as it relates to brand reputation (see Figure 2.3). She includes the reputation dimension as a key component in the dynamism.

"We create a Profile on a site, we make friends and add applications and groups and events to define Identity. We interact over time, offering content and comments and ratings which gains [sic] us a Reputation. That Reputation is then turned into a Trust factor—we decide how trustworthy a social network member is by the way they fill out their profile, by the connections they make and by the content they submit, all of which is over time, which is why Social Media is a long term engagement."

This dynamic can be modeled and marketers can use this dynamism to enhance engagement within the community, minimize churn and identify potential future influencers.

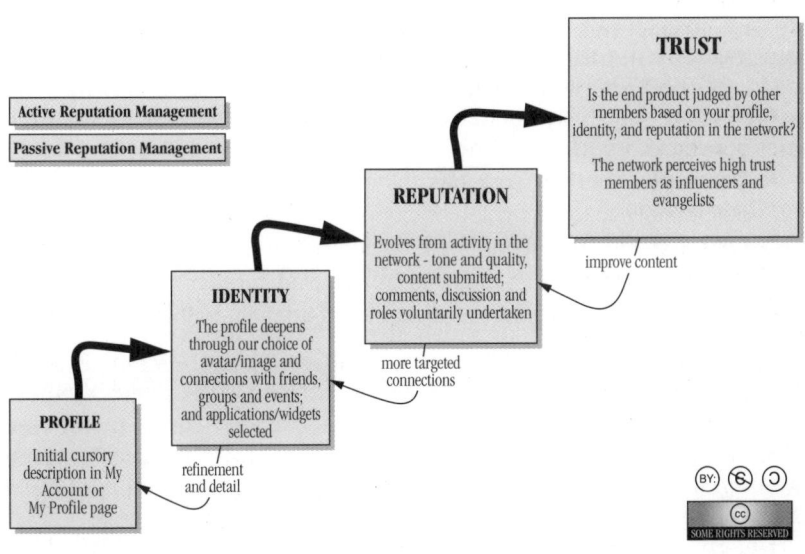

Figure 2.3 Social web: reputation management cycles
Source: http://laurelpapworth.com/ripple-social-network-influencers/, January, 2010.

CONCLUSION

There are many motivations for individuals to participate in social communities. These motivations differ for individuals, as opposed to influencers. In social media, marketers must now develop strategies and tactics to identify and differentiate individuals from experts and influencers. Understanding the motivations of individuals, as opposed to experts and influencers, will help marketers improve their social media marketing campaigns. Building models around these motivations will help marketers develop more successful social media campaigns at lower cost and risk.

Social media campaigns are designed to deliver three results:

1. those that take place in the physical world in terms of purchase and consumption
2. those that take place in the virtual world and deliver positive and persuasive conversation about the brand among individuals
3. those that take place with influencers to forward positive messages about the brand quickly and frequently.

Traditional and social media campaigns affect the quality and quantity of conversations individuals have in these three dimensions. These conversations, in turn, affect how others converse and then eventually act in the physical world. Through the understanding of motivations, marketers will be able to better coordinate their traditional media strategies and tactics with their social media activities to deliver and accelerate more positive and persuasive conversations about the category and their brands.

As we will see in later chapters, marketers can build metrics to evaluate individuals' social media actions and conversations in order to measure their impact at each level in the media engagement framework with each type of individuals. Just as important as the richness of the information they access is its immediacy. In fact, recent research shows that chatter in social media circles can be used as a very accurate predictor of new product success. Social media can help marketers see into the future.[16] For example, the level of new movie proceeds, which can then inform that marketers as to the level of post-launch marketing and promotion that will be required to hit their revenue targets.

Understanding consumer motivations and behaviors can help marketers understand how they can offer more value to their target audience and reap value in return. Behavioral analysis as it relates to social media can help marketers to significantly improve their social marketing tactics. Combining connectedness, profile information and demographics with the analysis of an individual's social media behavior can lead to valuable insights and more-focused marketing programs. Many of these motivations and behaviors apply to both traditional and social media. The design of the media engagement framework is based on this combination of motivations and behaviors as they relate to the social and traditional media channels.

ENDNOTES

1. *Are Consumers Really Shaping Marketing through Social Media?* By Stephanie Bullock, Director, Segment Management, Direct Marketing, Canada Post Corporation. Ivana Mazon, Vice President, Client Services, FUSE Marketing Group. July 23, 2009.

2. See White Paper on "Dimensions in listening in social media."

3. Raghuram Iyengar, Sangman Han, and Sunil Gupta, "*Do friends influence purchases in a social network?*" *Harvard Business Review*, working papers. May 21, 2009.

4. Portions quoted and excerpted from Research commissioned by The Automobile Association July 2007. The Social Issues Research Center (SIRC). http://www.sirc.org/publik/belonging.pdf, December, 2009. Dr Peter Marsh, Simon Bradley, Carole Love, Patrick Alexander, and Roger Norham.

5. www.youtube.com/channels, February, 2010.

6. Modified from RealEstateMarketingBlog.org. Become A Social Networking Influencer. Submitted by John on Wednesday, December 17, 2008.

7. Elliott TS. Social Networking and Group Psychology, October 23, 2009 01:05. http://www.ts-elliott.com/social-networking-and-group-psychology, December, 2009.

8. www.wilton.com, December, 2009.

9. Search of CakeCentral.com using the term "Wilton", December 2009.

10. http://www.Tremor.com, December, 2009.

11. http://www.BzzAgent.com, December, 2009.

12. http://www.greenpeace.org/international/en/news/features/Sweet-success-for-Kit-Kat-campaign/

13. Modified from http://behavioraltargeting.wordpress.com/, Anil Batra's Behavioral Targeting Blog, December, 2009.

14. Email received by Steven Groves from Klout.com: 3/26/2010.

15. http://laurelpapworth.com/reputation-management-in-social/, January, 2010.

16. Sitaram Asur and Bernardo A. Huberman, "Predicting the Future with Social Media," http://bit.ly/dBOrur

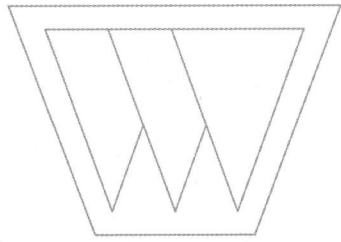

SECTION 2
THE MEDIA ENGAGEMENT FRAMEWORK

3

INTRODUCTION TO THE MEDIA ENGAGEMENT FRAMEWORK

Many books on social media and social media metrics look at social media in a partial or complete vacuum. They consider social media as a stand-alone media, but ignore how social media absorbs synergistic affects from traditional media and how social media can enhance the response to traditional media campaigns. This book takes an entirely different approach, realizing that social media and traditional media are inextricably linked. All media channels have nuances—and social media is no different—but they all work together to drive value for the brand. Because TV and most traditional media channels have existed longer, they have been studied in much more detail and are much more understood by the marketers using them.

With each of these traditional channels, marketers have learned how to purchase, improve and manage them optimally. These channels are simply better understood. Just as television has many different channel types—such as syndicated, network, cable and local—so too does social media have more than one type of channel. With sophisticated tools, media buyers carefully plan a TV media buy, reviewing each program and network to optimize their purchase. They plan integrated marketing campaigns to provide the highest reach, frequency and quality to reach their target audience optimally with the right message at the right time and place using a surround sound set of marketing impressions. With social media, each channel also needs to be treated separately and distinctly. Micro-blogs work differently from blogs, which work differently from ratings reviews and so on. Yet, although these channels differ, they also need to be planned in the context of one another. Smart marketers build integrated social marketing campaigns and they build integrated marketing campaigns including both traditional and social media. The case studies concerning the social marketing campaigns for the Guinness and Heineken brands in Malaysia show how these can work most effectively together (see pages 120 and 121).

TV advertising is planned based on the currency of reach, frequency and quality of impressions. Social media is planned in a similar fashion, although reach, frequency and quality must now be interpreted with an added dimension of influencer, individual and consumer. The planning of social marketing now needs to consider how to best reach influencers, how they can be persuaded to advocate a brand, and how individuals will receive those advocacy messages and turn into consumers. Instead of impressions, social marketers work with the additional currency of engagement.

With this in mind, we have developed a new concept: the *media engagement framework*. Although most of the discussion in this book will focus on how the media engagement framework (MEF) pertains to social media and social marketing ROI, it can apply equally well to traditional media.

CASE STUDY

STRATIFICATION OF ENGAGEMENT

Establishing a type of engagement for a particular level of consumer communication allows a fuller experience for the consumer. At one level, the best engagement for the consumer is via another consumer. At other levels, a direct-to-consumer tactic might be better. Developing metrics for each of these levels can provide great insights in determining the success of the engagement with customers and prospects.

PitneyBowes

PitneyBowes was founded in 1920 by Arthur Pitney and Walter Bowes to provide large and small businesses alike with customer engagement solutions, business insights, workflow management and mail solutions. They now serve over two million customers with one goal: to help their customers meet *their* goals with collaboration, integrity and accountability. While the company began by providing mail and document management services to help companies become more productive managing their mail, they now provide a wealth of services including predictive analytics, location intelligence and relationship marketing.

For the organization to tell their story to their audience, the company has developed a number of key tactics as part of their strategy: a functional listening post, technology training and an internal social media council. They have also developed a "loose governance" policy and structure that provides a framework for employees that supports the desired persona of the PitneyBowes brand.

Aneta Hall is the Emerging Media Manager in charge of all that is social at PitneyBowes and similar to the model advocated by Chris Brogan and Julian Smith in their book *Trust Agents* — she positions herself as a true trust agent in her work building a social media road map for the company. Already her work has developed to the point where everything about social media is measured so that valuable insights from experiments can be gained and the process can be continuously improved. For PitneyBowes, social media is well along the way to becoming the fourth leg of the marketing communications infrastructure alongside advertising for driving one-way messages, PR for writing press releases and investor relations for issuing earnings reports.

Although the company sells primarily to businesses, social media can provide great value in developing one-to-one relationships with all their customers, prospects and stakeholders. In a B2B environment, where sales cycles are typically longer than they are in B2C, using social media is an ideal way to engage with customers and deliver real value before, during and after the sales process.

(continued)

Three-tier measurement model

PitneyBowes has implemented a three-tier measurement model to assess the effectiveness of their social presence:

1. Attention metric—At the top level, the number of mentions needs to be counted, representing eyeballs and raw traffic attributed to the social presence.
2. Participation and engagement metric—Social media interactions need to make lasting connections so that customers and prospects pay attention to the message. At PitneyBowes, this is measured primarily through time-on-site because they see that time is one of the truest indicators of engagement. Other metrics are online word-of-mouth spread based on re-tweets and comment counts.
3. Influence—For PitneyBowes, influence is tied directly to their business goals. It is then measured through the level of sales generated, which, as Aneta Hall says, represents "the holy grail" for the company's social marketing efforts.

This three-tier model initially received a mixed response from much of the PitneyBowes marketing team, where most marketers gravitated to the attention metric. This is slowly changing as marketers begin to see the value delivered through deeper and deeper engagement by customers and prospects as they participate in the PitneyBowes social media community.

Holiday Mail for Heroes

PitneyBowes has been very successful in increasing engagement with their brand through affiliations with philanthropic efforts. They were able to increase their response on Facebook by double digits and significantly accelerate growth on their Twitter channel through the "'Mail for Heroes" campaign. The campaign is run in conjunction with the American Red Cross to give consumers the opportunity to send a postcard to US servicemen and -women who are serving around the world.

The campaign has been running for three years and Aneta says that "the Red Cross is a very social brand, and leads to a lot of engagement for PitneyBowes" in the joint campaign. The site included a video of celebrity sponsor Amy Grant and video montages of participants, and generated over two million cards in 2007 and 2008.

Customer support forums

For post-sales customer support and retention, Aneta talks about how PitneyBowes "invested a lot in a community-driven customer support because, if at the end of the day you don't clean up your own backyard, as far as the community is concerned in social media you won't get permission to talk about your product or marketing initiatives."

PitneyBowes developed a user forum which is a customer-focused, customer-driven site linked from the main site at PB.com. "PB reps moderate the forum, but they have a policy that they can only engage with a complaint after 24 hours." The lag time for engagement is such that other customers can get involved and often it occurs that a customer provides an answer to *another customer*. A major goal for the development of the forum was to deflect calls from the PitneyBowes call center.

Using the cost estimate statistics gleaned from Groundswell that for every five visits to an answer posting, or 25 visits to a general posting, one customer service call will be averted. Aneta shares that they "analyzed the number of views to a rate change post and were able to realize that at the end of the day in a period of three months, we were able to avert over 30,000 calls to our call center." At an estimated cost of $10 per inbound call, this translates into over $300,000 in call deflection in one quarter.

Looking to the future, Aneta explains "it's time to be patient, to adjust the metrics and to continue exploring."

Source: Interview with Aneta Hall, Manager, Emerging Media, PitneyBowes on February 4, 2010. Published with permission. All rights reserved.

Applying the Media Engagement Framework

In order for the concept of the MEF to be successful, it must be media channel agnostic. It can't work for just one channel and not for another. It must work across all channels and be flexible enough to handle the nuances of each of these channels. It must be parsimonious. The media engagement framework integrates many of the concepts from traditional and social media in order to comprehensively describe the key elements of building a social marketing strategy and measurement framework. Although this book is primarily about social marketing ROI, it has its foundation in building the elements of social marketing strategy. The two are inextricably linked.

MEDIA CHANNEL AGNOSTIC

As we'll see in the ensuing chapters, the media engagement framework can work with all media channels, both social and traditional. In this book, however, we will only talk about how it applies to social media. For example, it will apply perfectly to targeted and integrated campaigns using any combination of Twitter, Facebook or YouTube.

Based on this framework, we will present many other related concepts to show how to build successful social marketing strategies and tactics and then to measure their success and determine their ROI. As mentioned earlier, for those marketers unfamiliar with the concepts of marketing ROI, it is highly recommended you first read *Marketing Calculator*.

THE PERSONAS OF THE MEDIA ENGAGEMENT FRAMEWORK

The media engagement framework is made up of three segments or personas:

1. influencers
2. individuals
3. consumers.

Each represents the types of persona or target audience marketers must engage with in order to drive value for their brands in social media (Figure 3.1). Each target persona interacts and overlaps with the others. Influencers write posts to their followers, who are made up of individuals. Individuals can either be consumers or prospective consumers or may never be consumers. Consumers are the target market for selling products and services.

INFLUENCERS

Just as these three personas are important for social marketing, so too are they important for traditional media. PR targets editors to write articles to influence and inform their readers. PR would manage endorsement

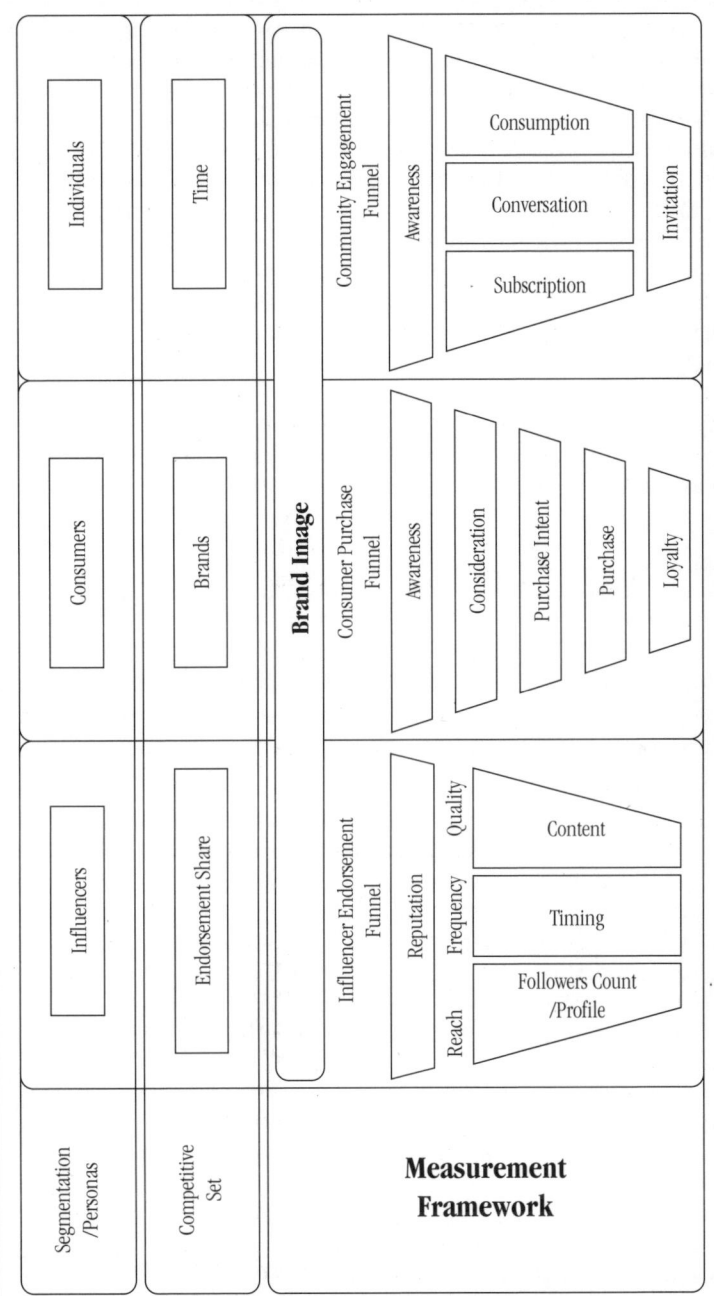

Figure 3.1 Media engagement framework

campaigns where celebrities would endorse a brand in the hopes that celebrity fans would then purchase the endorsed products. NASCAR is the shining example of utilizing the endorsement of drivers to promote their sponsored brands. In a similar vein, before the advent of social marketing, email was often employed as a component of a marketing technique to promote a particular brand in the hopes it would go viral. Other media channels such as TV communicate directly and simultaneously to all three target audiences simply because a broadcast media can't narrow-cast its message to only influencers or only consumers.

It wasn't until the advent of social marketing that it was imperative to develop a framework that would address the special needs of social marketing, with the added benefit of being also applicable to traditional media. Social marketers implicitly developed programs for each of these personas. They reach out to influencers by first identifying key influencers, commenting on their blogs and then engaging with them directly using both social media and/or traditional media (such as email).

ENDORSEMENT

The top-level objective for social marketers with influencers is to gain their endorsement. They gain this endorsement through the engagement process described above. Social marketers target influencers based on their ability to reach the marketer's target audience; to reach out to them with a frequent posting cycle and with content that will be positively persuasive toward the brand.

INFLUENCER SEGMENTATION

Similar to consumers, influencers fall into segments. In order to fully develop an influencer program, social marketers must develop communication and engagement strategies to reach out to each of the influencers in each of the segments. In one dimension, influencers can be targeted based on the reason for their influence. For example, celebrities can be determined to be influencers in a category. So, too can "normal" social media-active individuals have influence over other individuals in a particular category.

Influencers can also influence different aspects of the category. They can be influencers for specific brands—yours or the competitors—for specific distribution channels and for certain external factors important to the category. For each of these classes of influencer, marketers must develop an influencer campaign that can drive the most share of endorsement that will help either grow the category or grow the brand's share within the category.

CASE STUDY

CO-CREATING A BRAND WITH THE CUSTOMER

One of the most powerful aspects of leveraging social media as a corporate tactic is that a brand can be defined together with the consumer. What the customer wants to see in a product or service can now become an integral part of what the company provides. In that way, the product or service is more closely aligned with the consumer's wants and there can be a premium that the customer is willing to pay for getting precisely what they want.

Delta Airlines

Delta Airlines is one of the world's largest airlines, serving more than 160 million customers each year. Based out of Atlanta, Georgia, Delta has a strong website and a fully integrated frequent flyer program: Delta SkyMiles. We spoke with Jennifer Miller, Manager for Marketing and Content for Delta.com, about the Delta social media experience launched in 2007. What started out as an effort to try and speak directly to customers about the state of travel evolved into a moderated blog designed to connect them with their customers.

Early efforts included a contest of videos developed by fans and posted on YouTube. Since then, social media for Delta has evolved from a marketing effort to become a way to listen and engage the consumer about the travel experience. Obstacles to growth in their social presence have to do with the industry and the economy; the industry has shrunk significantly and the marketing and social media teams are just now entering a growth phase. Social media for Jennifer and her team is about managing the resources to support the engagement with the consumer around the travel experience.

The key metrics for Delta aren't yet centered on a hard ROI. They are centered on creating a program where first they increase the reach of the brand and learn how to measure the consistency and quality of the conversation. To be able to monitor the conversations around the brand, Delta is using Visible Technologies to establish the key topics for monitoring and to get the data processed into meaningful information. So far, Delta has set up a listening post, established a social media policy, created a crisis communications plan and examined

(continued)

how to create advocates across the company to represent the brand in marketing, corporate communications and customer service.

One of the key insights that came out of the social media development process was that they have learned that it's no longer about what a brand wants to say: it's about co-creating the brand in a conversation and an engagement with the customer. Delta is now looking to grow the conversation and make it a valuable and dynamic part of the way Delta goes to market.

Source: Interview with Jennifer Miller, Manager, Delta.com Marketing, Content, & Social Media, Delta Airlines on March 12, 2010. Published with permission. All rights reserved.

INFLUENCER ENDORSEMENT FUNNEL

In Chapter 4, we will define in more detail each of the elements of the influencer dimension of the media engagement framework. A new concept called the influencer endorsement funnel will be more fully defined, describing how social marketers can define their influencer outreach strategies in order to develop highly successful social marketing campaigns. The influencer endorsement funnel draws upon metrics already known and understood by marketers—reach, frequency and quality—and applies them to the development of influencer marketing programs. In this way, successful influencer marketing strategies can be defined, executed and measured in such a way to drive the most value for the brand at least cost.

CONSUMERS

The use of social media to target consumers will continue to grow and provide benefit for the brands supported by these new tools. Social media will become a strong new media channel as an equal peer alongside other existing traditional media channels. Traditional media channels are measured in many ways, but primarily based on two key dimensions: the consumer purchase funnel and the brand image.

CONSUMER PURCHASE FUNNEL

Just as the brand image of social media-active consumers may differ from social media-inactive consumers, so too, will the consumer purchase funnel status differ for social media-active consumers compared with social media-inactive consumers. Awareness, consideration and purchase intent will build differently for social media-active consumers.

Awareness may take place more quickly, but consideration or purchase intent may lag (or some other combination may occur). In any case, the traversal of the consumer purchase funnel will differ for social media-active consumers compared with social media-inactive consumers. Social media-active consumers represent a new sub-segment that needs to be measured using similar consumer purchase funnel and brand imagery measurement techniques, with the expectation that they may have different perceptions from those consumers receiving primarily only traditional media. The MEF addresses this by simply applying these familiar concepts to this new social media-active persona.

Whereas the other two dimensions of the MEF discussed influencers and individuals, this dimension will discuss how it can apply social marketing to consumers. Many of the familiar topics of brand imagery, the consumer purchase funnel and segmentation will need to be applied to both social media-active consumers and social media-inactive consumers, yet these tools will support important metrics in determining the relative success of social media versus traditional media.

Segment by social media activity

A new segmentation criterion for consumers will need to be added to the mix when considering social media. As discussed above, the social media-active consumer will develop different brand impressions from those that aren't social media-active. Social media-active consumers will need to be tracked in a similar way to social media-inactive consumers, but the results of these tracking studies may deliver new insights for marketers. Social marketers may need to develop new strategies for their social media-active target audience to influence consumer perceptions in some new way to the advantage of the brand. Opportunities for social marketers may be uncovered where a brand can reap quick rewards against the competition based on the newly determined insights. Traditional marketers may also gather valuable insights for their social media-inactive consumers as they start to listen to the voice of the consumer in social media. This is already taking place because promotional materials often include verbatim quotes from consumers found in the brand's social media properties.

INDIVIDUALS

Social marketing campaigns reach many individuals: those who are consumers, those who might become consumers and, unfortunately, those who may never become consumers. Because of the nature of social media, social marketing is more of a broadcast media. Thus messages posted by an influencer will reach their followers who are made up of many individuals. Their followers may not necessarily be target consumers. The hope is that a significant portion of their followers are in the brand's target market. Just as TV advertising reaches a broadcast market measured in gross rating points (GRPs), so too, does social marketing reach a large market measured in follower counts and fan counts.

COMMUNITY ENGAGEMENT

Social marketers wish to develop social marketing campaigns that develop increasing engagement with these individuals. This engagement increases as the individual progresses down the engagement funnel—the community engagement funnel—as individuals consume information about the brand, converse about the brand and invite others to also engage with the brand. The top-level objective for marketers is to drive an individual's engagement. With increased engagement, the individual is more likely than not to write posts about a brand or, if they are in the brand's target segment, to become a consumer.

Because of the opt-in nature of social media, social marketers compete not only against other brands but also against the amount of time an individual has to spend conversing about or engaging with their brands versus having those individuals engaging with other entertainment opportunities on the web. Their social marketing tactics concerning the brand must be highly engaging and entertaining so that the individual will spend more time engaging with these activities or reading posts from pertinent influencers, as opposed to doing anything else.

Chapter 5 describes the individual segment marketing process more fully. We introduce a new concept called the community engagement funnel, where marketers can measure the level of engagement individuals have with the brand so that specific marketing tactics can be developed to drive increasing engagement. Social marketers can use the community engagement funnel in two ways. Marketers can increase the number of individuals engaging with the brand at each level in the community engagement funnel, and they can move individuals deeper and deeper into the funnel. In this way, the marketer can develop short- and long-term value for the brand.

As communities and the statistics surrounding communities become more mature, we see these concepts of community engagement being implemented in sophisticated social customer relationship management (CRM) applications.

BRAND IMAGERY

Social media is heavily used by many brands to provide improved customer support. The brand image, as it is perceived in the minds of the influencers, individuals and consumers, plays a decisive role in how each of these three personas will respond to marketing actions. Brands with low brand equity are less likely to evoke a response from these three personas than brands with high brand equity. Influencers are more likely to endorse brands that have a high brand value, than those that have a low brand value. Similarly, individuals are more likely to engage with brands with a high brand value than brands with low brand value. Unfortunately, this works in both a positive and negative way. Less prominent brands are more than likely to elicit negative word of mouth than more prominent brands upon a customer dissatisfaction event. More prominent brands, on the other hand, are more likely to be "preyed upon" by issues-oriented activists because they are more likely to evoke change in behavior of the brand manufacturer and they are more likely to elicit a response in the press when taking on "big corporations." Greenpeace's social media attacks on Unilever's Dove brand (Onslaught(er)) and on Nestlé's Kit Kat brand are great examples of how a big brand can suffer disproportionately in social media because of its size (see page 60).

Intuit, for example, has a very sophisticated and advanced discussion forum that Intuit users can visit to search quickly for answers or potentially pose questions to other knowledgeable users in the community to answer. In this way, customer support calls have been deflected and, for those actively participating in the community, the perception of Intuit's customer service has increased. If however, there were social media-inactive Intuit users, they wouldn't log in to the community and they wouldn't utilize the shared knowledge of the Intuit support community. They would use the traditional telephone support channel to gain support and, in so doing, may have a totally different perception of the quality of customer support offered by Intuit. Therefore social media delivers a different brand image to social media-active consumers compared with the brand image perceived by social media-inactive consumers.

Social media also offers other challenges to social marketers. Messages received by consumers are no longer directly transmitted by the marketer. Influencers, individuals and other consumers are talking about the brand using their own voice, and the marketer may not have any control over this voice. If the messages sent by these individuals are negative or are slanted in one direction versus another, they will have a tendency to affect the brand image for social media-active consumers. They are receiving very different messages than social media-inactive consumers and therefore will most likely develop different brand perceptions and a different brand image. Marketers in general, and social marketers specifically, must now measure the brand image of each of these social media-active segments in order to understand what's happening to their brands in social media and potentially take corrective actions to improve their image among social media-active consumers.

COMPETITIVE SET

As individuals participate in social media, they choose to engage in one activity versus another based on the value it offers versus other potential activities that could be undertaken. These competing activities differ for each persona type and must be considered by the marketer when developing a successful marketing campaign. They are described below for each persona.

INFLUENCER: ENDORSEMENT SHARE

Influencers can only endorse so many brands. In many industries, marketers compete at the influencer level against other marketers for the endorsement of influencers. There is a limited set of brands that an influencer can endorse.

CONSUMER: BRANDS

Marketers compete against one another in the consumer persona as they migrate through the consumer purchase funnel. For example, once consumers become aware of a particular brand, now the battle is set for their mind share as they create a consideration set of products to purchase.

INDIVIDUAL: TIME

The most essential element in terms of competition at the individual level is the irreplaceable dimension of time. Once expended, time cannot be regained, so obtaining the individual's attention for even a moment is increasingly becoming the task of marketing. The elements that compete for that time are becoming more varied, and easier to access, in the individual's world.

MEASUREMENT SET

To manage the effort in traditional and social media, a measure of the activity, and results of that activity, is essential. Each of the personas has a measurement set that applies and is particular to the effort around that persona. The measurement set is covered in subsequent chapters: a short overview of each is presented here.

INFLUENCER ENDORSEMENT FUNNEL

The influencer endorsement funnel has components that help the marketer to understand the potential reach, frequency and quality of an influencer's messages. The model has elements that will help identify the best influencer for the brand image and track their relative activity.

CONSUMER PURCHASE FUNNEL

The concept of the consumer purchase funnel was developed showing the relative level of engagement a consumer has with a physical brand. Marketers have been using the construct of the consumer purchase funnel to measure and determine the relative effectiveness of their efforts to drive purchase and loyalty. Measurement and metrics in the consumer purchase funnel are only reviewed here, but a more in-depth exploration can be found in *Marketing Calculator*.

COMMUNITY ENGAGEMENT FUNNEL

The community engagement funnel (CEF) describes the increasing levels of engagement an individual has as they engage with a social community. The deeper they go into the funnel, the higher the level of engagement. The CEF contains elements that the marketer can monitor and measure so that tactics can be developed to drive increased engagement of the individual with their brands in a social community.

CONCLUSION

As we more fully define the media engagement framework in the ensuing chapters, marketers will gain new insights into how they should build their marketing strategies, develop their tactics and gather valuable metrics. With the right metrics in place, ROI can be estimated or calculated to improve the results of marketing investments. With these improvements, the brands will grow faster and develop a strategic advantage over the competition, leading to higher profits, growth and valuation.

Employment and adoption of the MEF will provide a construct that a marketer can more easily apply to the development and execution of a marketing plan. With it, the marketer can develop a series of appropriate measurements and key performance indicators (KPIs) that can be shared with the executive team to report on effectiveness and allow for a tighter level of control and manageability in the social marketing effort.

4

INFLUENCER PERSONA IN THE MEDIA ENGAGEMENT FRAMEWORK

Influencers in social media are an important group because they can amplify your message for your benefit, regardless of whether the message is online or off. This amplifier effect is critical to reap the most benefit from social media. However, influencers not only send out positive messages, they can also send out negative messages to your target market. The utmost level of care should be undertaken to develop this class of market participants.

THE INFLUENCER AND THE MEDIA ENGAGEMENT FRAMEWORK

The influencer component of the model describes how marketers can approach influencers in their category, set internal targets and measure their effectiveness with the goal to gain their endorsement for issues and brands that will have a positive impact on the category or the brand. There are other dimensions to define an influencer strategy, and they may be important for some categories, but, overall, we have found these three dimensions to be the most important with regard to the MEF.

These three dimensions relate to the influencer in the following ways:

- *audience segmentation:* influencer celebrity, category strata and audience target profile
- *competitive set:* endorsement share
- *influencer endorsement funnel:* reputation, reach, frequency and quality.

In social media, influencers represent potentially the most important group of individuals for marketers. Influencers in social media have followers. These followers are made up of individuals, some of whom are other influencers who you want your message to reach, and many of these individuals are the consumers you want your message to reach: those who belong to your preferred target segments and who are most valuable to the brand.

CASE STUDY

THE THREE PILLARS OF MARKETING

Microsoft is one of the best known technology brands on the planet. They vie with Google and Apple for the top slot for the best known technology brand. Because they have grown from their beginnings in software to become a major services and media company, they see social media with a different slant.

Microsoft, Southeast Asia

We interviewed Andrew Pickup, Chief Marketing Officer of Microsoft Asia Pacific, to understand how Microsoft sees social media in general, and specifically in Southeast Asia. Having just launched Windows 7 with a major social media component, it was interesting to hear how they employed their cadre of millions of beta testers around the world and hundreds of thousands in Asia Pacific to drive awareness and acceptance of this new operating system.

With 93 percent of PCs having Windows, and because many of the millions of PCs sold are used to connect to the Internet, Microsoft has a unique advantage over other non-technology brands, such as BMW or Starbucks when it comes to social media. With this direct connection to social media, they employ three pillars in their communications strategies generally and with the Windows 7 launch campaign specifically:

1. paid media
2. earned media, (where earned media encompasses the category of social media)
3. owned and operated media.

Paid media are those media assets that Microsoft can make an investment in to promote their products and services to improve visibility or awareness. Paid media, however, is just the start of the engagement cycle. The media assets Microsoft puts into those venues is often subject to consumer interpretation or re-interpretation. Microsoft has realized that the comments and conversations that occur in the social ecosphere are part of earned media and they too help promote the Microsoft brand. The goal of all these efforts, interactions and conversations is to get the consumer to Microsoft's owned and operated media network.

As it relates to owned and operated media, Microsoft is a "media player in its own right." With their online presence at Microsoft.com, Windows Live and Bing, they have three of the top 10 domains in the world.

For Asia Pacific, this means they have a reach of about 160 million consumers through Microsoft, MSN, Hotmail and Windows Live Messenger. But in earned media, "we're a blogger, we're an issuer of PR, we're a thought leader and we put that content, whether it is in written form, digital form or video form, out into the marketplace. And we ask people to comment on it, re-tweet on it, adapt it, take it and make it their own, *etcetera*."

Because of its large presence in social media, Microsoft splits individuals making comments—"hundreds of millions of people" every year—into a number of segments. At the top level is the Tier 1 segment, which includes bloggers in any geography. These may be engaged one-to-one, depending on the requirements of the day.

(continued)

Other tiers and segments are defined as well to support the messaging requirements as necessary.

Measurement

With the level of volume Microsoft has, they have many tools in place to measure, monitor and take advantage of what's being said about them and their categories. From a measurement perspective, they see three components:

- volume of coverage
- the level of influence of the commentary
- tonality—positive, negative or neutral.

Their approach to social media has led them to be the most talked about brand—"The most tweeted, the most referred to, the most social media engaged of all the brands in the world. Eight percent of those were positive and 17 percent were negative or neutral"—based on a study by Advertising Age in America in 2009. Compared with Google and Apple, which had "lower levels of commentary and were also on a lower level of positive nature" Microsoft enjoys over 650 million unique visitors to their web properties every month.

A segmented approach

Looking at different markets in Asia Pacific, they range from Australia and South Korea, which mimic the infrastructure in Europe or America, to Southeast Asia, which still has connectivity issues, and yet is very strong in its level of mobile Internet connectivity. This requires a very segmented geographic approach to be successful in social media. "Indonesia was the fastest-growing country, in terms of percentage, on Facebook anywhere in the world, followed very quickly by the Philippines and Thailand." Southeast Asia is a great emerging market for social media and "has a strong appetite for consuming [digital] media in this way."

"I think our role's what is changing generally. How the [power and influence of the] brand is diminishing over time and the power of the community is increasing and what's happened is that consumers as well as business people are now connected, they're aggregated, they're unionized if you like, they have a voice and they want to engage in something that we call collaborative marketing."

With Microsoft's three-pillared approach, they see their best ROI coming from their investments in owned and operated media, followed by their social media investments. By making this media very sticky, they can use their own media to engage with their audiences and then to motivate them through earned media to comment on their experiences with Microsoft. It's a powerful statement about how the value of content drives value for the company, which can then be leveraged to drive earned (social) media through conversations within the community.

The future of social media and the Internet

Looking forward, Andrew brings up two key trends shaping the future:
- Single sign-on, where Microsoft is leading the charge with their LiveID functionality.
- Mobile connectivity. Mobile will replace the PC as the most popular device to access the Internet by about 2013. Mobile access, especially of Twitter and search, will drive the mobile Internet.

Source: Interview with Andrew Pickup, General Manager, Marketing & Business Operations, Microsoft Asia Pacific on May 31, 2010. Published with permission. All rights reserved.

EVALUATING INFLUENCE

In building a successful influencer strategy, marketers should first "listen" to the influencers by analyzing their messages and postings in the social ecosphere to understand where they spend most of their time, what their interests are and what their role is in the unofficial hierarchy of the community. The marketer needs to understand the types of topics the influencers write about, the style they use to write with and where the content they focus on overlaps with the content pertinent to the brand.

Targeted influencers can be evaluated further to determine the frequency of posting and the reach of their efforts relative to the size of their audience and the second-level reach of that audience. If the targeted influencer is a blogger, the traffic to their site and how many subscribers they have and how those subscribers have opted into the influencer's posts (e.g. RSS or email) are important in evaluating the worth of the influencer to the brand. At the next level, marketers need to evaluate the influencer's subscribed audience: how many subscribers they have and what their behavior is when it comes to commenting or reposting the influencer's content.

With this information in hand, the brand team may then opt to prioritize and approach the influencer. There are a number of tactics that can be employed to engage with the influencer in order to get them to write in a persuasive and influential manner about the marketer's brand.

INFLUENCER SEGMENTATION

Because influencers are so critical to marketing success, let's dig deeper into segmentation schemes that are generally most important when classifying and targeting influencers.

Influencers can be segmented not only based on their follower profile but also based on their motivation and impact on sales volume in the category. The follower target profile will be discussed under the consumer model in Chapter 5. Here are two influencer segmentation dimensions that are critical to developing a brand's influencer engagement strategy and metrics: influencer celebrity and category stratification. Metrics surrounding the audience target profile are described below under the reach dimension of the influencer endorsement funnel.

GENERAL INFLUENCERS

There have been a number of studies that have determined a set of generic markers that help to identify individuals who will more than likely be influencers. Individuals with these characteristics may be online influencers, offline influencers, both of these or neither. Influencers will have a particular profile and set of behaviors that marketers can search for. Marketers can design their social community sites in order to identify these individuals more easily. Through *ad hoc* surveys, member profile questions and other means marketers can gather information concerning influencer markers in order to market specifically to individuals who have a high likelihood of being influencers. This model can be improved by comparing the following markers with those that have self-identified themselves in your community already. In this way, based on these markers, marketers can:

1. Target specific types of non-member individuals who have a high likelihood of being influencers to join the community, or
2. Target current members who have a high likelihood of being influencers.

John Berry and Ed Keller describe influencers as follows:

"They generally have an activist approach to life that extends from the community to the workplace to leisure time; a network of contacts broader not only than the norm for the society but also broader than the networks of people often labeled as demographically desirable, for example, the affluent; a tendency to be looked to by others for advice or opinion; restless minds that seem to be constantly engaged in and fascinated by problem solving; and a pattern of trendsetting in areas that have made a substantial difference to the mainstream society."[1]

Influencers[2,3] differentiate themselves from other individuals in the following ways:

1. They are willing to pay more for a product if they believe it is of higher quality.
2. They are willing to try the latest thing.
3. They want to tell others about the new products they like.
4. Friends and family often ask them for advice about using different products and services.
5. They are less trusting of information and seek out many more information sources.
6. They have a large social network. They are:
   a. highly likely to belong to five or more organizations
   b. speaking to many people across many walks of life, socially active and participatory in the community
   c. meeting new people, volunteering and traveling.
7. They love to talk. They:
   a. love to talk about products and services
   b. are very likely to recommend a brand they like
   c. gain personal value when sharing information
   d. have a strong desire to continue to learn.
8. They are highly persuasive. They:
   a. are viewed as "experts" by others
   b. are self-aware of their expertise and want recognition for their expertise
   c. spend time researching brands
   d. actively seek advice from others.

According to Berry and Keller, they span just about all demographic, political, geographic, gender and income segments. They are generally "college educated, mid-life, in the child-rearing years and upper-middle income."

PEER INFLUENCERS

Peer influencers are those persons who are influencers in their own right because they have certain characteristics and have developed a following of friends and family. They regularly influence small groups of individuals both online and offline. The Cyworld example found in Chapter 2 discussed peer influencers. For many marketers, peer influencers represent an untapped opportunity to build their brands.

Influencers exist in just about every market and category. They have knowledge that can help others to lead better lives and they enjoy helping others with that knowledge. They belong to a number of communities and organizations. With the right tools and marketing strategies, marketers can enlist them to help successfully promote their brands, both online and off.

Successfully marketing to influencers can improve the success of marketing campaigns. Unfortunately, influencers don't always self-identify themselves and say "here I am." Instead, they simply act the way they've always acted, and through those actions, they influence others. They can influence others in many ways in terms of the products and brands they purchase, causes they support and communities they participate in. In order to identify influencers, we need to understand what makes influencers special. We need to track those behaviors and develop and reach out to them with specific messages so that they will, in turn, influence their followers in the brand's favor. Based on their behaviors and markers, we can determine which individuals in our communities are more than likely to be influencers. By scoring individuals against these markers, the highest-scoring individuals can then be targeted with specific messages and offerings at the right time and place.

PEER INFLUENCERS

SweetSugar never thought of herself as a bakery expert. However, as her interests in baking became more pronounced, she started to spend more time online exploring what other bakers were saying and realized that there was a wealth of information that could be gained from many of the baking communities. SweetSugar joined a few of them, but really felt at home at CakeCentral.com. She joined about five years ago in 2005 and has since moved up the ranks to now be a "forum superstar." She has posted over 5,900 times and continues to post at the rate of well over 100 per month. Each one of her posts elicits 10 to 15 comments within the first seven days from many members she doesn't even recognize.

She just loves helping others, posting pictures of her creations and even participating in a number of baking contests. They're not really cakes: they are works of art and the 80 or so pictures attest to her artistry. Whether it's dogs, alligators, guitars or pumpkins, SweetSugar has built it, baked it, served it and ate it.

Although she hasn't yet won any contests, she has come close a few times. Every once in a while, she thinks she has gone overboard because she turned the laundry room into a cake supplies storage room. (The washer and dryer were moved down the hall.) But, on the other hand, she is having a great time and finds it an easy way to be involved with her passion while her kids were sleeping or now while the oldest is away at school. Two years ago, she sold her first cake and now provides cakes to a lot of her friends and acquaintances for birthdays and special events. She has even made special wedding cakes, which were her biggest challenge because she knew they had to be just perfect.

SweetSugar has been juggling a number of activities including the PTA, the swim team mom and volunteering at church, but still finds time to help out others at CakeCentral. Since joining, she has been invited to participate in a number of events with some of the big names in baking supplies and has realized she has a real following in the community. One of her goals is to travel to meet some of her peers who she has gotten to know through the community. She would love to finally meet up with a handful of them and has actually done so with a few people on their last vacation down to Orlando and DisneyWorld in Florida.

SweetSugar isn't different from many other influencers who aren't celebrities. They just happen to have the behaviors that end up influencing others. They belong to a special group of influencers called peer influencers.

The individual as influencer

Influencers are generally always influencers, but the question often arises as to whether an individual can, in some circumstances, be an occasional influencer. The answer is "yes": an individual can emerge at times and perform actions that influence other individuals. This occurs when the individual is so moved by the brand, cause or issue that the individual will actively forward messages to friends and acquaintances. Just as influencers need to be motivated and find value in forwarding and advocating for a brand, so do occasional influencers. For example, kids were found to influence their parents to purchase a BlendTec blender after having viewed the WillItBlend series of YouTube videos.

Self-identified influencers

On the one hand, some influencers can be identified through their known behaviors and profiles. Individuals who have large followings and send out invitations and advocate for a brand in the community have self-identified themselves through their actions. They actively seek tactics that increase follower or friend counts and they recognize the value of regularly posting fresh content for their audience.

They will likely have self-selected their topic or topics, developed a knowledge base or expertise around a category, products set or service and established themselves in numerous social sites. These two markers—the number of followers, the number of invitations or the number of brands they advocate—represent the first level of classification of peer influencer.

Latent influencers

The next class of influencers can be identified by profiling the self-identified influencers. Matching their profiles to others in the community with the same profile can help to identify latent influencers who may be influencers elsewhere but haven't yet exhibited influential behavior within the community. These individuals may be influencers, but not for your brands, or they may simply have the right profile but just aren't influential. Using look-alike modeling based on the right behavioral and profile markers, individuals who have a high likelihood of being influencers can be found. Conversely, individuals who are highly unlikely to be influencers can be removed from the target list.

Near-celebrity influencers

Near-celebrities aren't quite celebrities to the general population, but are well-known in a very small targeted, specific group. They have become influential only because of what they have been able to achieve for the specific group or groups through their online presence. Near-celebrities build their follower base with the express purpose to have large audiences, sometimes reaching follower counts in the tens of thousands. They may not be celebrities in the general population, but have built a reputation as experts in their own domains of expertise. They may have grown from being peer influencers and evolved into near-celebrities.

Near-celebrity influencers belong to a different class from peer influencers. Near-celebrity influencers have extremely large followings and are well known for their knowledge and reputation.

A great example of using near-celebrity influencers is a recent Audi promotion done to promote the new Audi R8. Guy Kawasaki has written a handful of books including *The Macintosh Way*, *Selling the Dream* and *Rules for Revolutionaries*. Through these books, he has developed an enormous following and, in some circles, may even be considered a celebrity. He isn't known for his automotive acumen because his "other" car is a Toyota Sienna—not that there's anything wrong with that. He is, however, a rock star in the technology and innovation space. So, the marketers for the new Audi R8 decided to approach a new "Audi-enc"' in a new way by offering a test drive with an influencer in the tech sector.

In February 2009, Guy Kawasaki was given an Audi R8 for a week.[4] Because of his influencer status and many connections, it was quite certain that he was going to blog about it upon completion of the test drive—and he did just that in a post titled "'Audi—like my belly button?' Life with four kids and an Audi R8." The post itself included numerous pictures and short mentions of others introduced to the car, including his kids (his daughter is the source of the quote). Once posted, the article generated 321 comments as of January 2009, some of which were very interesting and supportive of the Audi brand experience. Some, however, acted to leverage Kawasaki's blog popularity including discussion and a link to http://www.theofficialbellybuttonforum.com.

CELEBRITY INFLUENCERS

Celebrity influencers are those who are generally widely known by the public at large and are widely known both online and offline. Celebrities have a large following because they became famous based on their profession. Oprah Winfrey and Ashton Kutcher are prime examples of celebrities who have enormous social media followings.

INFLUENCE MEASUREMENT TOOLS

Tools and technologies are being developed to help marketers to determine the relative influence of influencers. Klout.com analyzes a Twitter presence to determine the level of connectedness and influence a particular Twitter account may have.[5] For each submitted

Twitter ID, they develop a "Klout score" and a four-dimensional bubble map of key connections. These four dimensions—connector, persona, casual and climber—provide valuable insights into how well a marketer's Twitter account may be scoring or whether a particular influencer may be worth targeting.

From their website:

> "Klout is the standard for influence. We believe that every individual who creates content has influence. Our goal is to accurately measure that influence and provide context around who a person influences and the specific topics he or she is most influential on.
>
> Klout tracks the impact of your opinions, links and recommendations across your social graph. We collect data about the content you create, how people interact with that content and the size and composition of your network. From there, we analyze the data to find indicators of influence and then provide you with innovative tools to interact with and interpret the data.
>
> The Klout Score is the influence metric. It measures overall influence through 25 variables broken into three categories; True Reach, Amplification Score and Network Score."

The use of these kinds of technologies will increase as brands seek out the influencers who can help propel their brand messages into the target audience.

COMPENSATING INFLUENCERS

Although influencers are generally not paid, there can be successful paid influencer programs at each level. Compensation can be in terms of free demonstration products or actual cash payment. In all cases, when engaging bloggers and influencers in social media in the US, payment relationships with the associated conditions surrounding that payment should be fully disclosed per FTC guidelines.[6] As influencers achieve higher and higher celebrity status, it is more likely than not that you may expect to pay them for the endorsements they deliver regarding products or brands. Marketers are also now experimenting with paid and in-kind, influencer programs (e.g., the use of free products, travel to influencer group meetings and the like) for influencers at all levels.

INFLUENCER COMMUNITIES

To drive influencer behavior, many brands have come up with privately branded online communities to support the effort. Intel, WalMart and Microsoft have developed formal influencer relations programs with varying levels of recognition and rewards. The influencer channel has even become a new media channel through agencies such as BzzAgent and Tremor. A few examples are described below.

INTEL INSIDERS

Intel Insiders[7] are made up of a handful of social media experts to help Intel "connect with online audiences interested in technology and innovation."

> "We seed Insiders with products and whenever we do, we explicitly require them to publically acknowledge Intel's support, whether a gift from Intel is involved or if sponsorship or travel was provided by Intel. We follow rules set forth by WOMMA and our legal team guides us to adhere to rules set forth by FTC. Our aim since the first blog post kicking off the Intel Insider program in June 2008 is to build relationships, learn ways to improve our own communication and openly share our intentions and experiences."

In December 2009, the Intel Insider influencer relations program was voted the best by the Society for New Communications Research.[8]

WALMART ELEVENMOMS

The WalMart Elevenmoms program began with 11 moms but has now expanded to 21, with the primary focus of saving money. In December 2008, the program was expanded to their Hispanic site. Their clearly stated engagement policy is as follows:

> "Participation in the WalMart Elevenmoms program is voluntary. Participants in the program are required to clearly disclose their relationship with WalMart as well as any compensation received, including travel opportunities, expenses or products. In the event that products are received for review, participants may keep or dispose of product at their discretion."[9]

The WalMart Elevenmoms program is defined around its key message and brand position of saving money.

MICROSOFT MOST VALUABLE PROFESSIONAL

Begun in the 1990s, the Microsoft Most Valuable Professional (MVP) recognizes individuals with strong records of contributions to the community for any of a number of specific Microsoft technologies.

To become an MVP, the program is described as follows:

> "Potential MVPs are nominated by other technical community members, current and former MVPs, and Microsoft personnel who have

noted their leadership and their willingness and ability to help others make the most of their Microsoft technology.

"To receive the Microsoft MVP Award, MVP nominees undergo a rigorous review process. A panel that includes members of the MVP team and Microsoft product groups evaluates each nominee's technical expertise and voluntary community contributions for the past 12 months. The panel considers the quality, quantity and level of impact of the MVP nominee's contributions. Active MVPs receive the same level of scrutiny as other new candidates each year.

"MVPs are independent of Microsoft, with separate opinions and perspectives, and are able to represent the views of the community members with whom they engage every day."[10]

The Microsoft MVP program is designed around those influencers who can support each of the company's key technologies and products. There are over 88 communities, which are broken down by technology or product line subdivided into 15 main categories.[11]

INFLUENCER MARKETING AGENCIES

As mentioned earlier, BzzAgent and Tremor have developed unpaid influencer programs primarily for individual influencers to engage their friends in promoted campaigns. With each agency, there are hundreds of thousands of individuals who have signed up to be part of this specialized media channel.

INFLUENCER STRATIFICATION

Influencers can be classified into five distinct strata based on the conversation hierarchy as they relate to the category of the brand and the different dimensions against which they may directly or indirectly influence the volume of sales of a brand in a category. Some influencers may only write in one dimension, whereas others may span multiple dimensions. These are:

Consumer-related influencers—Writing about consumers themselves in a particular category can have influence over a particular segment in the category or the overall category. It can influence their purchasing behaviors or their participation in a particular category.

Category-related influencers—Category-related influencers are those who may affect the size of the entire category. For example, posts on potential changes in the long-term interest rate may have an effect on mortgage rates in the real estate market. Most posts in a category don't reference a specific brand. In the beer category, for example, four out of five of the posts mention beer, ale, stout or other generic terms, whereas only one in five mentions a brand. If any of these generic influencers can be engaged with to mention your brand, they can have a large effect for you.

Some category-related influencers have a degree of power over trends driving the size of the category. For example, if a brand sponsors a particular athlete, influencers writing about this athlete can also affect the value of the brand.

Category-related influencers must also consider the relevance of master brands and the categories they operate in. The Unilever Dove Brand can be found in the hand and body lotion category as well as in shampoo and is therefore a "master brand" spanning multiple categories.

Brand-related influencers—Brand-related influencers write posts directly about your brand. They are so enamored with your brand that they are willing to lend their credibility to your brand. They become advocates for your brand. These influencers are typically the easiest for marketers to engage with. Because these influencers are already writing for you, marketers must endeavor to:

- increase the number of posts
- help them increase their follower count
- help them to provide more value to their follower counts
- help them to write more persuasively.

Competitive brand-related influencers—Similar to the brand-related influencers, these are the influencers who are advocates for competitive brands. Although generally more difficult, if these influencers can be engaged with to also write positively about your brand, then this can become an important component of your influencer strategy.

Distribution channel-related influencers—Because the sales in a particular category can also be affected by the distribution channel, if there are posts written negatively or positively about a category-related distribution channel partner, they can have an impact on the category as a whole, or on your brand or your competitor's brand.

External factor influencers—External factors can affect a brand or a category. If there are influencers writing very persuasively about a particular topic related to a brand, then social marketers must monitor these posts and build a relationship with them in order to potentially mitigate any posts that may have a deleterious or negative effect on the category, the brand, the distribution channel or a competitor. An example of this could be the alleged influence Bill O'Reilly had when, in March 2003, he announced the boycott of French wines during the second Iraq war. Although no mention was made of a particular brand, these posts clearly helped the American wine business.[12] This particular influencer announced the boycott in traditional media, illustrating how the MEF can apply to both traditional and social media.

OTHER INFLUENCER SEGMENTATION DIMENSIONS

There are many other segmentation schemes important to marketers as they develop their influencer strategy. Some important components include the social media channel; that is, which type of channel the influencer is influential in. Some influencers may have large Twitter followings, others may have large Facebook followings and yet others may have a powerful blog or a LinkedIn group they manage. Depending on the specific marketing action, target audience and message, marketers may want to only approach those influencers who are influential in a selected channel. If the target audience is primarily on Facebook, then an influencer in Twitter may not be as valuable as an influencer in Facebook. In a similar way, influencers could also be segmented based on the primary target device used by their audiences. These could include the standard laptops, but could also include smartphones or the iPad in Asia.

Getting the influencer segmentation schema right is critical in developing a successful social media strategy and can lead to great success for marketers. By targeting specific influencer profiles, marketers can target their messages, prioritize their efforts and minimize potential burn-out of the influencers. Segmenting influencers along these three dimensions can lead to lower costs, improved results and lowered risk of influencer burnout.

THE INFLUENCER ENDORSEMENT FUNNEL

In an ideal world, a brand would like to reach out to all influencers and have them deliver a credible message, repeating the brand's position to all of their followers as fast as possible and as often as possible.

REPUTATION

At the upper level of the influencer endorsement funnel is influencer reputation (Figure 4.1). Those influencers in a specific category or segment must be viewed by their audience as experts in order for their messages to be highly credible. Expertise can be derived in many ways. As we saw in Chapter 3, influencers have many different motivations. Experts can be knowledgeable and know more than their audience, or they can relay messages about a brand simply based on their experiences. Influencers seen as experts carry a different weight and can write in an authoritative way about how a particular brand or product can be evaluated. On the other hand, personal experiences with a product or brand can also be written about, but they have a different weight and sentiment than those written by an expert.

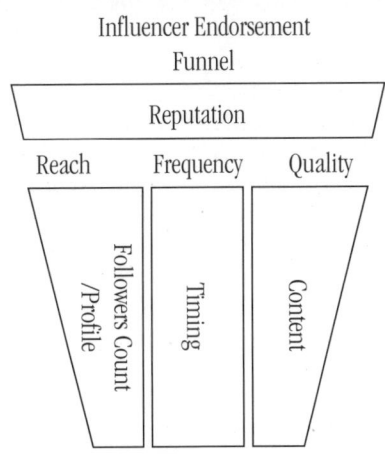

Figure 4.1   Influencer funnel

Great messages valuable to the brand can be sent by anyone, but if the source isn't credible and doesn't have a good reputation, the value of the message will be diminished. For example, a technology message sent by a non-technology influencer won't lend the same level of credence as a technology message sent by an influencer with strong technology credentials.

REACH, FREQUENCY AND QUALITY

At the lower level, the influencer endorsement funnel is made up of three metrics familiar to all marketers: reach, frequency and quality. They are similar to those found with traditional media and represent an output metric at this stage of the MEF. That is, a social marketer can use influencer reach, frequency and quality as interim success metrics for their efforts with each influencer. As with any advertising, the brand needs to deliver valuable, high-quality messages to a target audience with a certain frequency and timeframe. These three dimensions are defined as: reach of influencer audience, frequency and timing of content and content quality.

REACH OF INFLUENCER AUDIENCE

Reach has two components: audience quality and follower count. The audience quality is made up of individuals who fall into the influencer's audience. From the perspective of the brand, marketers want the influencer's audience to have a large overlap with the marketer's target audience. With many influencers, and with many social media channels, the exact reach can't be exactly determined, but several external services can rank them and group them by relative size (e.g., Alterian SM2 and Radian6).

Audience quality can also be subdivided further if marketers want to reach certain target segments that may only be reached through certain influencers. For example, Burger King may wish to reach the young demographic. They may then engage with top rock stars who have large youth followings. On the other hand, if Burger King was trying to promote its salad offerings, marketers may want to reach out to Mommy Bloggers to entice them to write posts to their followers—other moms—to bring their kids to Burger King so the kids can have a hamburger while their moms have salads.

FREQUENCY AND TIMING OF CONTENT

Post frequency and timing measure when and how often a particular influencer writes posts. Some influencers may only post once per week, others once per month, but the appropriate metric is the timing and frequency of posts about issues important to your category (see the discussion on influencer stratification).

This dimension becomes more and more important as the social marketing effort reaches a real-time, global effort. If the influencer makes posts on a schedule or if they follow a more *ad hoc* schedule, say in a blog only, the post may lack the impact to successfully support creating a buzz or getting a viral response to a campaign.

If the influencer makes posts in a micro-blog, those posts are generally much more frequent and the timing of posts is less of an issue, but the regularity of posts is relevant. A social media influencer cannot connect or disconnect at will with his or her audience—periodic and persistent content is how they got to where they are in the rankings, and that requires regular attention and activity.

CONTENT QUALITY

Post or message quality is a good metric for how persuasive the message is about your brand or category. Metrics for the success and quality of an influencer's post can include the number of re-tweets for Twitter, the number of comments for a blog post and the number of fan page visits or "Likes" for Facebook.

Post content is relatively easy to assess. Scrutiny of the message stream and posts made will reveal whether or not they talk about products and brands often enough for his or her audience not to be caught off-guard by the introduction of brand-oriented content—if the posts are deemed to be overt or disingenuous, the influencer may lose his or her audience, or he or she may find that his or her messages are adopted by another audience, who are perhaps more valuable to the brand.

Post quality, however, is somewhat subjective. The language used in social media is relevant to the audience to whom the influencer is connected. The *Elements of Style* by Strunk and White or *The Chicago Manual of Style* means little to the legions of Millennials who have opted into social media—contractions are what they use in texting (ur = you are, LOL = laugh out loud, etc.), and jargon and slang are expected by their audience—not using it may indicate that they don't know their audience and they are not connected. It is this lack of consistency and standards that present a huge challenge for the automated determination of tone, sentiment and meaning to the listening-tool manufacturers. The language may be appropriate for the audience the influencer is writing for, however, and must be assessed in that context.

Social media marketers, however, can't just purchase the reach and frequency of influencers as they can with traditional media when they submit their advertising content. Similar to PR professionals approaching editors, social media marketers need to build a relationship with influencers in such a way that they will be highly likely to write or forward many messages about the brand in a positive light. They need to engage with them in the right way, to elicit the right output from them and also not violate FTC guidelines on endorsements. Social media marketers want to identify the right influencers who have the right target audience and will reach that audience at some period of time and potentially more than once. They want to spend the most effort and time identifying those influencers with the largest audiences falling into their target audiences who can deliver a credible and persuasive message about the brand.

To measure the results of these activities, marketers must measure:

- the audience profile and the number of followers
- the frequency and timing of messages sent by the influencers
- the sentiment, persuasiveness and content of the message.

BUILDING A SUCCESSFUL INFLUENCER PROGRAM

Executing a successful influencer strategy with the appropriate success metrics can be done with a simple six-step process:

1. Determine the objectives desired for each segment in terms of message quality, content and frequency.
2. Identify your target influencers based on the segmentation schemes outlined above, or other segmentation scheme relevant to your brand. Prioritize each of the segments based on these criteria. Once the segmentation scheme has been defined, identify credible influencers and their estimated influence based on reach, frequency and quality in each of these categories.

3. Begin listening to each influencer and determine the types of message content they deliver to their audiences. Develop a profile on each of the target influencers based online and offline activities. For example, offline activities might include attendance or speaking at specific trade shows or conferences. Gather other profile information as available through a detailed web search.

4. Develop an outreach strategy based on an analysis of the influencer's content, audience and other profile information. Determine if there are specific individuals in the organization who may be more aligned with certain types of influencers. Determine if these individuals already have a relationship with the targeted influencers.

5. Determine the type of reciprocal value you can offer the influencer. This can include exclusive access or early product demos, but generally shouldn't restrict the influencer to writing only positive posts about the brand. It can also include public recognition and badging so that he or she can deliver an even higher level of perceived value to his or her audience. Lastly, if more than one influencer is engaged, it may be valuable to them to develop an exclusive community specifically for them to converse among themselves. All details of the arrangement should be disclosed, especially in the US, and especially if there is a paid relationship as in the Intel, WalMart and Microsoft programs mentioned above. Make sure you have a clear disclosure policy in place and publicize it. Always allow influencers to say whatever they wish, even if it appears detrimental to the brand, without reprisals or other limitations.

6. Develop and monitor metrics based on the framework outlined in the influencer endorsement funnel. Help influencers to increase their followings and entice them where possible to increase the frequency with which they write about your brand. Providing them exclusive content can also help to improve the quality and persuasive value of their posts to your target audience.

Conclusion

Influencer segmentation and behavioral targeting will become key marketing tools to help marketers provide more value to their target audiences found in social media communities. Already, many large firms employ these tactics with phenomenal results. Once audience target segments and influencer target segments have been identified, marketers can start to determine strategies to identify and market to influencers. Influencer marketing tactics provide an amplifier effect and can accelerate and enhance many marketing campaigns.

Reputation and reputation management applications are on the rise. A characteristic of the next iteration of the social web is one that is "vetted" or evaluated by reputable sources. The reputation of the source will be relevant. Choosing the right influencers with the right reputations will be critical in improving the value of the brand in the minds of the influencer and target audience.

Lastly, influencers must be chosen and engaged with based on their reach, frequency and quality. These last three metrics are familiar to all marketers and represent the number, timing and quality of messages reaching a marketer's target audience.

ENDNOTES

1. Jon Berry and Ed Keller. *The Influentials: One American in Ten Tells the Other Nine How to Vote, Where to Eat, and What to Buy*. 1st ed., (Free Press, January 2003).

2. From SPI(Social Persuaders & Influencers)-Report, December 2006.

3. Source: WOMMA Conference, December 2006 USC Annenberg.

4. http://blog.guykawasaki.com/2009/02/audi–like-my-b.html, January, 2010.

5. Klout.com CEO, Joe Fernandez if interviewed in the tool developer case study in Section 3.

6. FTC 16 CFR Part 255 - http://www.ftc.gov/os/2009/10/091005endorse mentguidesfnnotice.pdf; collected May 28, 2010.

7. Intel Insiders Community Page - http://scoop.intel.com/insiders

8. http://scoop.intel.com/2009/12/intel-insiders-voted-best-influencer-relations-program.php, April, 2010.

9. http://instoresnow.walmart.com/Community.aspx, April, 2010.

10. http://mvp.support.microsoft.com/gp/mvpbecoming, April, 2010.

11. https://mvp.support.microsoft.com/communities/mvp.aspx, April, 2010.

12. Bill O'Reilly declares end to his France boycott in wake of Sarkozy victory, Media Matters for America, May 2007, http://mediamatters. org/research/200705090008, April, 2010.

5

CONSUMER PERSONA IN THE MEDIA ENGAGEMENT FRAMEWORK

Social media has quickly become a new arrow in the marketing communications quiver. Because of this, marketers are beginning to scrutinize their knowledge of the consumer decision-making process against how those decisions are influenced by the messages consumers receive. Regardless of the source, messages have many components to them, which are primarily centered on five attributes: authority, persuasiveness, reach, frequency and recall (if they are memorable). Messages are received by the consumer or prospect and the consumer responds to them in specific ways. There has been, and will continue to be, a good deal of research in this area. The following represents the state-of-the-art research about how consumers respond to received messages in the marketplace and then eventually make purchase decisions at the "first moment of truth"[1]—the store shelf. The consumer purchase funnel and brand image—a model that has been in use for many years—represent how authority and persuasiveness translate into metrics that can be measured. They are the defining component of the MEF and represent the endpoint—the purchase—for traditional and social media marketing.

We have talked about how, in many ways, social media is similar to traditional media. Messages are received by individuals who process those messages and then act. Upon receipt of a message with traditional media, the individual could:

- do nothing
- act by telling a friend or
- act by purchasing a product.

With traditional media, as the authors of Groundswell point out,[2] it is difficult to tell others through traditional, non-social means. Those non-social means could include:

- writing a letter
- writing a comment or letter to a printed or video media outlet (e.g., a newspaper, a TV or radio station)
- sending an email
- calling a friend over the phone
- talking personally with friends and family.

The individual could also purchase the advertised product or service, or a competitive product or service.

Upon receipt of a message from a social network, the individual has all these options plus many others. They might:

- instantaneously forward the message to friends and acquaintances by writing on a Facebook wall
- send a Tweet
- write a blog post.

Messages received from any source, whether traditional or social means, cause the recipient to act in various ways, many of which can be directly measured. Some can only be measured through survey techniques, such as a brand tracking study or a choice-based conjoint study. Messages deliver:

- a level of engagement as described partially above
- an emotional impact on an individual of lending their reputation and forwarding a message to a friend
- the emotional value a message has when received from a friend as opposed to other media.

Messages received from different sources determine how much impact they have in driving a consumer down the purchase funnel.

Those media channels that are highly engaging and destination oriented, such as a YouTube video, will have a much higher probability of making the consumer aware (probably near 100 percent) and of driving significantly higher levels of consideration and purchase intent than those media channels that are less engaging and more interruptive, such as TV.

With this framework in place, each media and message can be measured and classified as to the level of incremental awareness, consideration, purchase intent and brand association scores it delivers. Knowing the reach and frequency of each message can then determine the overall level of impact it will have on each of these scores.

INTERRUPTIVE VERSUS DESTINATION MEDIA CHANNELS

Each media channel can be classified by its level of incremental impact on the levels in the consumer purchase funnel and brand-association scores. However, it has become clear to the authors through several case studies and other anecdotal evidence that media that is more destination oriented will have a significantly stronger impact on the viewer than interruptive media channels.

Unfortunately, with destination media channels, it is difficult to determine whether the viewer belongs to the target segment or not. So, in this case, there can be a lot of wastage in its overall impact. This is not to say that traditional mass media doesn't also have a lot of wastage, it's just that traditional mass media has a significantly higher reach than social media. Where TV mass media can reach tens of millions of viewers, social media may only reach tens of thousands of viewers.

This was made evident in Lisa Wellington's comment at the MeasureUp 2010 conference about the millions of followers in the Coca-Cola Twitter or Facebook presence and how they compared with the billions of servings of the Coca Cola product every day.

Source: Lisa Wellington at the MeasureUp Conference, 2010. Chicago.

CASE STUDY

AMPLIFYING THE EFFECT OF OFFLINE WITH ONLINE SOCIAL MEDIA

comScore reported last year that a social presence could affect the click though rate in search engine marketing by more than two-fold. How well does it work when you leverage online for offline though? In Malaysia, a country with over 28 million citizens, one company is learning how best to use online social media to drive attendance at branded, offline events.

Guinness Anchor Berhad

Guinness Anchor Berhad (GAB) is the corporation charged with brewing and marketing the Heineken and Guinness brands of beer, as well as several Asian regional brands, in Malaysia. GAB—under the direction of Mark Jenner, Director of Marketing—is learning to use social media as part of an integrated campaign development process, leveraging both online and digital properties and traditional media elements.

The act of consuming beer is a social one, making the addition of a social marketing component a natural extension. Mark recognized this early on, and social media has become a new platform for them to communicate with their audience as an essential part of an integrated campaign between various media channels—online or offline, in magazines, music events or in cinemas—GAB uses the same look, feel and tone in each channel.

Heineken and social media in Malaysia

For the Heineken brand, they leverage with another highly social activity—music—and they use the global Heineken "Green Room" campaign as a foundation to promote a series of exclusive music events for Heineken beer drinkers. They began by identifying influencers (bloggers, Tweeters, etc.) in the community. They then used the Green Room event to drive engagement with the influencers and to get visitors to their Heineken Malaysia Facebook fan page and a 'mini-site' (http://www.GreenRoom.com.my) developed to support the event.

They targeted influencers through an analysis of the bloggers' content, their writing style, the topics they wrote on (focusing on content creators who wrote mainly about music, fashion or hip culture) and anything else they could glean about the bloggers and their lifestyles. They checked the size of their respective audiences and then invited them to smaller events to get to know them, sharing things about the GAB product and the brand, and intentionally avoiding a hard sell. They then helped these bloggers increase and improve their reach by giving them packs of tickets that could be used to invite their followers to upcoming physical Green Room events.

GAB crafted the campaign so that as one Green Room event wraps up, they leverage the pictures and comments posted by consumers on social media sites to promote the *next* Green Room event. The effect is that one event builds on the success of the previous event, amplifying the offline activity with the online buzz. Each event grows larger and becomes more talked about than the previous event.

For GAB, content is key in growing the fan base and being able to engage. They've realized that if they post fresh and interesting content, consumers will share it with their friends. Over the last three months, the fan page grew from just over 43,000 fans to now over 75,000: a much larger following than most other brands in Malaysia.

Guinness and social media in Malaysia

In 2009, another GAB brand, Guinness, celebrated its 250th anniversary and GAB leveraged the power of social media again. As part of the global celebration, GAB hosted a large regional party and presented a concert in Malaysia that featured an internationally popular music group, the Black Eyed Peas. To create awareness for the event and the Guinness brand, they took to the street by sending out an actor in the likeness of Arthur Guinness (the founder of Guinness) to outlets and pubs throughout Kuala Lumpur. As the character moved from one location to the next, he posted messages about his location and encouraged people to meet him at the pub. If they offered a toast to Guinness, the toaster would receive a pair of tickets to the upcoming concert. Individuals tweeted and made their own posts with photos of the action. This

(continued)

generated an enormous amount of conversation and buzz about sightings of Arthur, where he was going to be next and how to get in on the event. It's almost a perfect use of social media by the brand. Start the conversation and get out of the way: the brand provides the spark and the conversation takes off. When Guinness drinkers got to talking to one another, it met an objective of the team to get consumers socializing and discussing the Guinness brand and product.

Although the quantity of visitors, messages and interactions are considered to be still small in their social presence, GAB is trying to more closely evaluate the quality of the responses and the level of engagement. They are looking closely at the tone of comments, the percentage of the fan base clicking "Like" on the fan page and the number of posts made. In the future, they want to connect the investment in social media to the level of incremental sales of products in the various outlets.

As GAB have learned how to leverage social media, there have been efforts that did not pay off. The short story is that just dumping content isn't the way to go in social media. This perspective came from the attempt to simply post a television ad for a regional brand on a fan page and then try to prompt engagement around the ad. The tactic showed that consumers were not interested in simple re-tasking of content that they were already familiar with. Conversely, when a fan posted a Heineken TV ad from another region, it did end up driving more traffic.

According to Mark, two of the biggest obstacles to being able to invest more in social marketing are:

1. finding effective ways to measure the social marketing ROI
2. convincing management that there is an ROI in the endeavor.

Whether the ROI is generated through additional product sales or if the brand's health in the market is improved, these show management that there is a payoff for the effort. Mark says that social media ". . . feels like the right thing to do and people are saying the right things, but we've not been able to isolate the effect of social media on the brand health or brand equity and measure it properly."

Mark shares that "we see that this kind of attention leads to a personal recommendation and the personal recommendation from another consumer to another is the best kind a brand can get. Ten years ago, we'd say that a friend recommended us. Social media allows that (same action) to happen much quicker and broader."

Source: Interview with Mark Jenner, Director of Marketing, Guinness Anchor Berhad on May 20, 2010. Published with permission. All rights reserved.

THE CONSUMER AND THE MEF

Consumers represent a subset of individuals in social media. Just as with traditional media, when marketers embark on a marketing campaign, their messages reach many individuals: not just consumers, but also prospective consumers and non-consumers, and influencers. Consumer and prospective consumer behavior in response to a message can be described through a consumer purchase funnel as originally developed by McKinsey[3] and a brand image. Marketers can influence this brand image and the level in the purchase funnel a consumer resides through marketing and delivery of their products and services. This chapter will first describe the consumer purchase funnel and then apply it to all media, and specifically social media. In Chapter 8, we will talk specifically about the brand image and how the three persona's perceptions of the image can affect their actions in social media.

The impact from social media on the brand image and consumer purchase funnel is different from that derived from traditional media because the marketer is no longer in full control of the message. Messages are received by consumers from other consumers, prospective consumers, individuals and influencers. These new sources of messages can have a totally different content, frequency and reach from that desired by the marketer. Nevertheless, using social media, marketers who can harness the power of these messages can go a long way in positively affecting their brand image and driving consumers further down the purchase funnel.

CONSUMERS AS A SUBSET OF INDIVIDUALS

Consumers represent a subset of individuals participating in social media. Individuals can potentially use products and services from a particular category, or they may not. Similarly, influencers may be users of products and services within the category or not. For example, as Tom Dickson with BlendTec mentions, kids who have seen the YouTube WillitBlend series can influence their parents to purchase a BlendTec blender, even though the kids aren't direct consumers in the blender category.

Consumers, of course, fall into segments and, with social media-active consumers, a new dimension of segmentation must overlay the marketer's original segmentation. Because the consumers' demographics may now be the same, the fact that they are social media-active may now change the perceptions that consumers have of the brand and the category. Because social media messages are now received from many sources and have a different tone and content from other traditional marketing controlled sources, these social media-active consumers are significantly more likely to have a different perception of the brand from those who are not social media-active.

Let's consider, for example, two different consumers of Comcast. Each is very similar in their demographics and lifestyles. They receive a similar number of messages through traditional media. The only difference is that one is social media-active and the other isn't. They have similar expectations of the service level provided by Comcast. The consumer who is social media-active perceives that Comcast offers extraordinary customer service because of the individualized and immediate response found on the plethora of social media resources employed by the company. On the other hand, the social media-inactive consumer with the same preference for good customer service may feel that Comcast customer service is unacceptable, because the hold times are too long when calling in for service. The level of social media activity provides a new segmentation criterion that marketers need to respond to in order to improve the value of their brand in the minds of their consumers.

CONSUMER PURCHASE FUNNEL

The consumer purchase funnel describes the emotional path a consumer takes from initial awareness to final purchase. There are many variations for the consumer purchase funnel, but the one we find most valuable is the one presented in Figure 5.1. There is a natural flow as a brand moves through the mind of the consumer, as described by the consumer purchase funnel. It is a key component of the MEF, representing how consumers make purchase decisions. It should be the end result of a marketer's actions in moving a consumer to choosing their brand, as opposed to the competitors' brands.

The consumer purchase funnel can be defined differently for different categories[4], but we can simplify it into five primary levels that represent the medium- to long-term effects of advertising as they pertain to individual consumers (see box below). These values for consumers overall in the category can be measured through brand imagery tracking studies.[5]

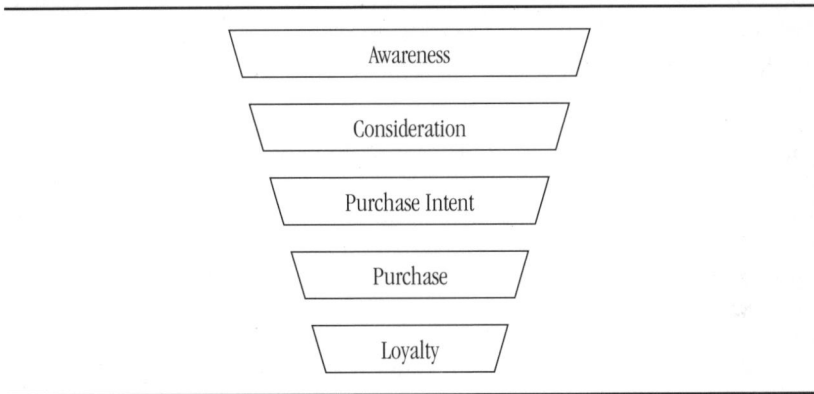

Figure 5.1 Consumer purchase funnel

SOURCES OF MESSAGES

There are five sources of brand messages:

1. From the brand through mass and direct media, such as TV, radio, print
2. From experts and endorsers, such as Oprah Winfrey, Kelly Ripa or Guy Kawasaki
3. From trade, such as, Kroger or Walmart
4. From the competition, such as the beer wars between Anheuser-Busch and SABMiller Brewing
5. From other consumers, such as you and me and our associations.

Each of these sources of messages has a related probability of being seen as embodying persuasiveness, authority and other characteristics. Interestingly, the most understood, yet probably least powerful, is mass media—yet the most powerful and least understood is social media.

Awareness

Awareness[6] for a brand typically has a medium- to long-term effect. Awareness decays over time, where a particular consumer is either aware of the brand or unaware of the brand. A consumer can't have partial awareness: he or she is either aware of the product or brand or not. The sum of all aware consumers is typically what is reported in a brand imagery tracking study.

There are primarily two types of awareness: spontaneous and aided awareness (see box below). In practice though, as messages are inserted into the market, consumers have some probability of seeing those messages based on the medium employed by the brand in a spontaneous way. They may be seen on TV or they may be heard on the radio or read in a magazine, billboard or newspaper. Whether they were seen and made a powerful enough impression on the consumer for the consumer to become aware of the brand, means that with every message inserted into a market, there is some discernable probability that a consumer will become spontaneously aware based on the number of messages and frequency with which those messages were placed into the market.

SPONTANEOUS AWARENESS

Spontaneous awareness (aka unaided awareness, unaided recall)

Spontaneous awareness is the mention of your brand name when a respondent is queried about brands that he or she knows of in the category without providing any earlier prompting of brands active in the category.

Spontaneous awareness is indicative of the brand's cut-through power in the category, which could have been driven by relevance and distinction (differentiation) of the brand proposition. In many consumer packaged goods (fast-moving consumer goods) categories, spontaneous awareness of the brand is a good predictor of presence in the consumer's consideration set. This means that the brand has already succeeded in establishing itself in the consumer's mind through messaging only, without necessarily having seen it in a retail store. The presence of the brand on the store shelf accentuates the brand's properties and pushes the brand closer to purchase in the mind of the consumer. As opposed to brands with only aided awareness, consumers with spontaneous awareness of a brand may still search for the brand even if the brand is not immediately found on the shelf.

Spontaneous awareness is not always a clear indicator of value for the brand, but not having spontaneous awareness is a clear negative indicator for a brand. Other issues concerning spontaneous awareness include:

- Spontaneous awareness could be due to a consumer's negative perception of the brand due to some previous negative experience with the brand or through negative mentions of a brand from other information sources.
- For all brands, it is important to differentiate spontaneous awareness among users versus non-users, regardless of whether the relative brand size is small or large, new or old.
- Spontaneous awareness is not necessarily a great indicator for heritage brands or brands that dominate a category. In these cases, top-of-mind awareness may be a better indicator of marketing success. Top-of-mind awareness is defined as the number of times a brand is measured first when asked about brands in the category.

Today, messages sent with traditional media typically have a very low probability of driving awareness. On the other hand, messages received through a social media contact typically have a high probability of driving awareness. The authority and reputation of the sender of the message in social media is usually high and pre-established. Therefore the consumer's needs or desires to read and engage with the message are also high.

In a social media context, such as the campaign around the A1 Steak Sauce YouTube Contest (see http://www.youtube.com/a1), consumers can engage with the brand by either creating a video and uploading it to YouTube and thereby participating in the contest, or by viewing the uploaded videos and ranking and rating the entries.

In either case, there is a very high probability—probably close to 100 percent—of becoming aware of the brand. From a metrics perspective, what would be important for a brand is to monitor the number of unique viewers in the YouTube account playing the entire video as opposed to only parts of it (measuring actual viewing is not possible).

AIDED AWARENESS

Aided awareness reflects the response, "Yes, I know this brand" upon prompting with the brand's name. Aided awareness is, of course, better than no awareness but, in terms of value for the brand, it is only slightly higher than no awareness.

Visibility in the shelf is in itself not enough because a strong message is required for the consumers to pause and reconsider the brand. Hence, in many categories, aided awareness is looked at, but not necessarily seen as a good indicator of success of marketing.

Other issues concerning aided awareness include:

1. Aided awareness is a good indicator of marketing success if the brand is in the early stages of being launched.
2. Aided awareness is a good indicator of success if the business question surrounds the awareness for a brand's variants.

Awareness for a brand is also dependent on the engagement a consumer has had with a brand. If a consumer has purchased a brand and consumed it, then that brand will have a 100 percent awareness with that consumer for a long time (generally longer than the decision timeframe of the brand manager). We can expect that the consumer may never forget having used that brand.

If a brand is new or has low category penetration, then it may be that many consumers have never tried the brand. They may become aware of the brand through messages received or they simply remain unaware of the brand.

Consumers who become aware of, but have never used, a brand can also lose awareness if, after receiving messages, the messages cease. The consumers may then end up not using or purchasing the brand. Certainly this can happen regardless of the media carrying the message, although for some types of messages—especially for messages in social media—the probability of becoming unaware after initial exposure can be very low.

For example, for social media, if a consumer views a YouTube video and engages with the brand in a virtual way, the interaction will establish a strong connection with the brand. It will have a relatively low probability of the consumer losing their awareness of that brand compared with the low level of engagement a consumer typically has with a TV ad. In this way, virtual engagement in social media with a brand can have very long-lasting effects for the brand.

Messages that necessitate high virtual engagement and are delivered from authoritative sources have a very high value for the brand. Because these messages are sent from friends to friends, they have a high probability of being seen. A typical TV message may have a 2 to 5 percent probability of making a consumer aware, whereas some social media messages, such as those videos in the A1 Steak Sauce example, may have a near 100 percent probability of making the consumer aware.

CONSIDERATION SET

Just having awareness of a brand doesn't mean that the brand is in the consumer's consideration set— that it will be considered when the consumer makes a purchase in the category. As the discussion showed though, spontaneous awareness strongly suggests that the brand is in the consumer's consideration set. For a purchase to take place, the advertised brand must be considered by the consumer as one of the choices in the category. For consumers who have never used the brand, or for new products in a category, advertising is the only way to insert and keep the brand in the consumer's consideration set. If advertising is discontinued, a brand may eventually fall out of the consumer's consideration set. For each consumer at any point in time, the brand has some probability of falling out of the consideration set. This is especially true for categories that are highly considered. This includes circumstances where the consumer is expecting that the value of their purchase will provide long-term benefits through functional attributes, such as a valid warranty, or through emotional attributes, such as the brand impact of a purchase among friends.

Consideration also decays over time, just as in the case of awareness: the consumer either holds the brand in the consideration set or not. As time progresses, if the consumer has never used the brand and no further messages from the brand are received, there is some probability that the brand will fall out of the consumer's consideration set.

Social media drives consideration for brands in both positive and negative ways. As consumers see messages for the brand, they will either enter it into their consideration set or not. Negative messages may lead the consumer to take the brand out of their consideration set. This is especially true for ratings and reviews, where a brand or product can receive both positive and negative messages. Because of the value consumers place on these, peer review/peer rating services, such as Yelp!,[7] are growing fast in popularity. If the messages are truly negative along the lines of the consumers' most important preferences, the consumer will remove the brand or product from the consideration set as they continue along the purchase decision-making process.

Similar to awareness, consideration is also determined by past engagement with the brand. Once the brand has been tried, it can only leave the consideration set if the consumer has a bad experience with the brand or the consumer has received negative messages about the brand. If the consumer has never used the brand, then the brand can fall out of the consideration set more rapidly. This happens if the consumer loses awareness or the consumer receives no further messages in order to maintain or promote the brand into the consumer's consideration set.

Consideration is not to be confused with preference. It may be that a consumer prefers the taste of Coca Cola over Pepsi, but Pepsi may be chosen if the price difference is large enough. In this case, both Coca Cola and Pepsi are in the consideration set, although Coca Cola is preferred over Pepsi. Preference will be discussed in Chapter 6 in much more detail.

PURCHASE INTENT

The incremental intent to purchase can be increased through repeated advertising exposures. The impact of a message can be very persuasive in social media. With a combination of more messages and advertising, the purchase intent can be increased. If advertising stops, intent can decay. Purchase intent isn't on or off, as is the case with brand awareness and inclusion in the consideration set. It is generally higher for those consumers who have purchased a brand in the past and had a positive experience with the brand than it is for consumers who have not previously tried the brand. In order to have purchase intent, the consumer must have awareness for the brand. If the consumer is no longer aware of a brand, purchase intent falls to zero and remains zero until the consumer becomes aware again. Similarly, the brand must also be in the consumer's consideration set before the consumer can have a positive intention to purchase.

Social media messages can have a high impact on purchase intent because they can come from individuals with a high authority and reputation and because the consumer will have opted-in to hear their views. If they are friends of the consumer or considered experts in the category, then their messages will have a higher weight than other messages that are delivered through other means, such as through traditional advertising where messages are simply broadcast from the brand.

Messages can come from many sources in the social media ecosphere—blogs, micro-blogs, social networks, photo sharing services,

CONVERSER AND INVITER VIRTUAL ENGAGEMENT

Those persons who positively (or negatively) comment and converse about a brand, as well as invite others to brand-related communities, typically increase (or decrease for negative comments) their purchase intent for the brand. For positive comments, the fact that they are willing to put their reputations on the line concerning a brand means that they have very high purchase intent. Each recommendation re-affirms that purchase intent, making it more difficult for that inviter or commenter not to purchase the brand at the next opportunity. It would be difficult for them to invite someone to a brand-related community and then go off and recommend a different brand. This, however, is not necessarily the case for activities that in and of them-selves have value. For example, if a brand is running a great game as part of a promotion, a member of the community may invite friends and others to participate in the game, and yet have no affinity with the brand.

They aren't inviting their friends to participate in the brand-related community as such: they are inviting their friends to participate in the game. This invitation is not seen as an endorsement for the brand, but simply for the game. In this case, the marketer needs to make certain that the value of the game can drive participants to a longer-term engagement; otherwise they will simply play the game and then end their engagement with the brand.

The San Diego Zoo case study exemplifies this as they advertise on Cartoon Network for the gaming aspect of their Polar Bear Plunge website (see pages 172 and 173).

video sharing and via virtual 3D communities, such as Second Life, Blue Mars, Kaneva or any number of emerging 3D social platforms.

Measuring the increased purchase intent delivered by each social media channel can be done by considering the level of virtual engagement a particular marketing activity delivers. For example, messages about the brand may more strongly or less strongly influence the consumer based on the time a visitor spends on a branded community and whether or not the messages might be part of an immersive experience.

The incremental value the Huggies brand receives from a consumer spending five minutes on Huggiesbabynetwork.com is significantly higher than the value received from a 30-second visit. Measuring the time-on-site for a branded community can yield a very predictive interim metric to gauge the persuasive value of the community in delivering purchase intent.

PURCHASE

The goal of marketing is to deliver messages at the right time and right place to the right customers to influence them to purchase more of the brand faster and faster. One of the most valuable steps in the consumer purchase funnel is to purchase the product. In the end, the goal for the marketer is to have the consumer select the brand in the store or on the web over others that may be available from other competitors.

LOYALTY

Once the brand has been purchased, marketers can continue to reach out to customers to influence them to purchase more products through up-selling and cross-selling as well as to continue to renew their purchases. This can be done through loyalty marketing.

Loyalty is similar to purchase in that it represents the ongoing decision to continue to purchase the brand. The messages received must be in line with the brand experience and show that remaining with the brand is going to provide more utility and value than switching to a competing brand. Many consumer purchase funnels don't include this level, but it is certainly a key component to marketing and operations to drive loyalty once the consumer has been won in the hard fought fight in the upper funnel levels.

B2B MARKETING

In a B2B market, the buying decision isn't made by an individual, but instead by a purchase committee. The committee may be informal—comprising a manager and subordinates—or it may be a formal group of managers and executives, each with a responsibility to represent the needs of their departments and workgroups. All of the dimensions of the message value framework apply, but now must be modified to fit *each* member of the purchase committee. Awareness and consideration are values related to individuals, but now each individual in the committee must be made aware and they must put the brand into the consideration set.

Each member of the purchase committee has differing preferences. Lower levels are trying to grow their careers, whereas senior executives or middle managers are trying not to make a mistake. The "you can't be fired for recommending IBM" in the past was an important component for many business decisions. Marketers can use social media to support each of the members of the purchase committee through the segmentation of their social marketing actions.

Joan Koerber-Walker, CorePurpose Chairman and CEO, has four separate Twitter accounts and three different blogs to target specific messages to specific types of audiences with little audience overlap between them:

1. @joankw
2. @JKWinnovation
3. @JKWleadership
4. @JKWgrowth

Source: Podcast and case study with Joan Koerber-Walker / CorePurpose in Chapter 8.

Social media and B2B marketing and selling

Although the sales team may not want it described this way, in B2B categories, the sales team has begun to act as an extension of the marketing message. Each sales person can deliver sales messages, social media messages, gain useful feedback and answer customers' and prospects' questions about the product, the company or the brand. They provide significant value in the selling of products, not least of which is the ability to take the final step moving from prospect to customer by asking for the order and "closing the deal." The following discussion needs to be seen in this light, with the goal to understand how social media can support the B2B sales team and make the marketing function more effective.

THE PURCHASE COMMITTEE

Larger ticket purchases in the B2B space are not made by one decision maker: they are made by a team of people—the purchase committee. The roles in the decision process include influencers, information gatherers, champions, naysayers and budget owners. Decisions are made by a team, taking into account the budget, many emotional factors, a brand's reputation, the total cost of ownership, the switching costs and many other factors. The decision is often more of a consensus determined through a formal or informal committee that takes into account internal politics and priorities that may have nothing to do with value propositions of the competing brands or otherwise. We call this the purchase committee. The committee can include any number of participants, from the nominal department head (and direct reports) who has final say on the budget to a formal team of participants including the line manager, a purchasing function, a financial function and other stakeholders in the proposed solution.

Michael Buck of Dell's SMB effort in Europe, the Middle East and Africa (EMEA) suggested that because of all the different people who have to approve a transaction in a B2B sale, Dell have to manage social media conversations differently for each of them: one for finance, one for IT and so on.[9]

In the informal case, the manager with the sign-off authority may want to make certain that his/her direct reports are full and equal participants in the decision-making process because they will also be responsible for the implementation and execution of the purchased solution. If the project fails, the manager will end up with a "ding" on his/her credibility and this may have far-reaching career implications. The manager must do what's necessary to make the project a success and therefore will provide a lot of leeway to direct reports to gain strong commitment, leading to a higher probability of project success once the decision is made and the project implementation begins.

Social media can support the decision-making process in a number of ways. Most importantly is making certain that relevant and pertinent information is easily and quickly available to each of the members of the purchase committee. Each purchase committee member has different decision preferences and desires. Social media can be a great method to provide very quick and targeted information to the sales team and purchase committee members because it is much more immediate than other media. Commissioning a white paper or case study can take months. Writing a blog post from a senior executive addressing a specific and current topic can be done almost immediately, if necessary, and, once written, can be easily forwarded to the right members of the purchase committee for their review. A blog

> # UNSUBSCRIBE, UN-LIKE, UN-FAN AND UNFOLLOW
>
> Generally neglected in any marketing effectiveness study is the impact of "unsubscribes," typically due to an email campaign. These are counted by email delivery services such as ConstantContact, but what aren't counted are the emails that land in the Junk/Bulk box of subscribers. Based on a recent survey by Return Path, July 2009, together these can account for up to 3.3 percent of mail sent (January through June 2009).
>
> In a similar way, unsubscribes from Twitter accounts or Facebook fan pages, although maybe not as permanent as an email unsubscribe, can also be an indicator of a marketer's effectiveness. These un-follows can be especially devastating if they are from your best prospect's VP.
>
> *Source:* Delivered email Metric May Not Be Accurate, Jack Loechner, the Center for Media research, August 3, 2009.

post's semi-formal nature can address issues that just aren't easily discussed in other media.

MESSAGES MOVING B2B CONSUMERS DOWN THE CONSUMER PURCHASE FUNNEL

Social communities also help the sales and marketing teams in identifying potential decision makers within the prospective company. LinkedIn and Plaxo allow the sales and marketing team to search out key decision makers and then to reach out to them directly. Twitter also allows followers to contact company Twitter account holders directly with questions. These social communities also provide critical background information that can be helpful in developing a good relationship with each of the purchase committee members. Each of these functions corresponds to similar levels in the consumer purchase funnel. A response to a well-directed and worded LinkedIn InMail or a connection invitation could be defined as an early indication of consideration.

Serena Software develops business application software to automate software development and improve productivity. The company used creative videos to help support the launch of a newly released software product called "Business Mashup Composer". The company developed an entertaining series of videos posted on YouTube[10] tied to a Facebook[11] contest referencing the "Just @#$% IT" SuperMasher campaign to drive awareness for a new piece of software. The campaign successfully drove 1.1 million views with a click-through rate of just under 0.8 percent, where many of these click-throughs also downloaded a product white paper. The click-throughs and white-paper downloads represent a good proxy for the number of potential business consumers entering this newly released software into their consideration set. Serena Software was able to use a B2C Facebook community to promote its new product release and garner high awareness and consideration for primarily a B2B product.[12]

Purchase intent can be enhanced as members of the purchase committee are reached through various touches, whether from the sales person, traditional media, brochures and downloads or social media. Although there are differences in the B2B decision-making process, the concepts of the consumer purchase funnel and brand image represent the process the purchase committee goes through individually and as a group.

CASE STUDY

MARKETING IS THE NEW FINANCE

The people who control the purse strings in a company have historically been the finance department. There just isn't enough money to do all the things you want to do in marketing, sales, manufacturing or any other department. When Dell implemented social media back in 1995, even Michael Dell was not sure where it might go, but since then they have discovered that the payoff for social media has been well worth the investment.

Dell Computers, Inc., EMEA

According to IDC, Dell is the number one supplier of computer systems in the United States and the number two worldwide.[1] In the social media space, they made headlines when they stated they were able to realize $19 million dollars in revenue directly attributable to their activity using Twitter. Initially, the Dell Twitter channel was designed to help quickly move certain types of expiring inventory, but it has become significantly more successful than was expected.

Michael Buck is the Director and General Manager for Global SMB and, according to him, Dell positions their online activity around the "four pillars of the online presence" that drive their social media interactions with consumers:

- Dell.com – the primary platform for e-commerce and the place to integrate customer interaction
- Dell-branded communities – IdeaStorm, Blogs and forums and communities
- External communities – Facebook, Twitter, Linkedin and others
- Employees – essentially 96,000 people who are Dell brand ambassadors.

By listening to customers and incorporating their feedback, the organization has made great strides in tangible operational improvement.

The power for Dell in social media comes from the top down. Michael Dell participates in the company blog and that company-wide philosophy flows down to almost all Dell employees. That kind of participation makes a difference in business-to-business (B2B) and consumer (B2C) marketing at Dell. What they have found is that B2C consumers are very proactive and readily provide feedback, reviews and comments about how Dell is doing, while in the B2B market, it is very different. Business customers appreciate the access to help-ful content and staff through corporate social media presences. Due to the complexities in selling B2B high tech products, customers seem to require a bit more hand-holding. There are many more touch-points in the purchase process within a business that they must address—finance, sales, management, IT and others. They all have different needs so the social media portfolio needs to be more diverse and robust. For a B2B social engagement, the buyer and user are not one person: they are often a committee of people. Even with the chal-lenges in managing this broad scope of social media objectives, the benefits far outweigh the investment.

Dell is very metrics driven, but they look first at the customer-value drivers. In social media, there are five:

1. A meaningful connection to Dell based on shared interests that allows them to express themselves

(continued)

2. Receipt of rewards and recognition for contributions provided, especially if they provide feedback and learning
3. Getting advice and validation
4. Receiving assurance about their decisions; learning from peers and the company
5. Solving their problem; avoid a call to support.

The metrics that correlate to the value drivers are:

1. Using customer insights to drive innovation—how many customers are changing or affecting Dell products?
2. Marketing spend efficiency—social media is not free, but it is much less expensive than traditional media online conversion rates—streamline the e-commerce offering
3. Customer lifecycle value—loyalty and recurring investments
4. Cost savings—eliminate friction in the system for customer support interactions.

On IdeaStorm.com,[13] a Dell-branded community that is over three years old, the statistics show that the community has:
• contributed 14,043 ideas
• promoted an idea 720,890 times (i.e., voted positively for the idea)
• posted 89,452 comments.

And, of those, Dell has implemented over 416 ideas submitted by customers.

Michael suggests that "Marketing is the new finance at Dell." Direct selling is not in the foreground—first they listen, they build the ecosystem and the supporting environment and as customers see the effect of their work, they vote with their dollars. The starting point is trust; something they have to earn from their customers—it is not a given that consumers will engage; Dell treats social media as a serious effort that has serious consequences. Dell is investing in promoting that perspective to their customers as well—the Dell Facebook fan page has several guides that can help business owners understand how to leverage social media to target their audience.

The future of social media at Dell

Dell is in social media for the long run, says Michael, "There is nothing worse in social media to start something and not taking it seriously. Or to fail to set up an end-to-end path for the consumer interaction. The consumers will notice and they will suspect those that treat a social media presence as nothing more than a gimmick and they will call them out publicly. Dell is very committed to social and offering the platforms because of the success we've seen and our customers are openly and readily accepting it."

The future they see is in using social media with a more geographically balanced presence, focusing more in BRIC[1] countries, which are developing very rapidly in social media. They expect an increase in activity and a re-balancing of social media assets so that they can approach a global audience. "Search" and influencers will play an expanding role in the social media model and they see search as a core element of social media. Search is particularly relevant for global companies, because search is where the customer is when they're in need of help and information.

Dell will also be looking for the key social influencers and brand lovers that multiply the effectiveness of the investment made in social media and they expect to target those who can improve and enhance the impact of the Dell message in social media. Michael sees that social marketing in the SMB space will become much more targeted to influencers and that mobile will play a larger and larger role in social marketing. For Dell, social media provides a strong foundation that is measurable and has the power to influence consumers with a positive experience with the brand regardless of the access device used.

Source: Interview with Michael Buck, EMEA Director and General Manager for Global SMB, Dell Computers, Inc. on March 5, 2010. Published with permission. All rights reserved.

Conclusion

The consumer is the individual who has become aware of the brand and is considered to be in a process that leads to the purchase of a product. Increased engagement with the consumer can lead to the best opportunity for the brand to establish a relationship with the consumer, such that he or she remain loyal and continue to purchase the brand.

An influencer who is also a consumer is one of the best possible outcomes for a brand. By virtue of their presence in social media, influencers will likely continue to promote and evangelize the brand well past the purchase. It is the place beyond the consumer purchase funnel that all brands want consumers to progress to: promoting and extolling the virtues of the brand to others in their circle of friends and followers.

ENDNOTES

1. *Wall Street Journal*, September 21, 2005 front page article "Procter & Gamble Co. believes shoppers make up their mind about a product in about the time it takes to read this [sentence]."

2. Charlene Li and Josh Bernoff, *Groundswell: Winning in a World Transformed by Social Technologies*, (Harvard Business Press, Boston, MA, 2008).

3. The customer decision journey, *McKinsey Quarterly*, https://www.mckinseyquarterly.com/Media_Entertainment/Publishing/The_consumer_decision_journey_2373, July, 2010.

4. Other forms include AIDA—awareness, intent, desire, action.

5. These are ongoing surveys of consumers brand perceptions, generally performed on a regular basis. They track consumer perceptions over time.

6. Thanks to Ramesh S., Chief Analyst for DemandROMI for the comparison between spontaneous and aided awareness.

7. http://www.yelp.com

8. Sorry, but I live in Atlanta.

9. Podcast and transcript posted at http://www.SocialMarketingConversations.com and in the case studies in this chapter.

10. Serena Software YouTube Posting; Mrmashup; http://www.youtube.com/watch?v=qLTs6jlbkjE; collected May 28, 2010.

11. Serena Software, SuperMasher Campaign Page on Facebook; http://apps.facebook.com/supermasher/campaign_memberships/home; collected May 28, 2010.

12. MarketingProfs—Facebook Success Stories.

13. http://www.ideastorm.com

6

INDIVIDUAL PERSONA IN THE MEDIA ENGAGEMENT FRAMEWORK

The media engagement framework (MEF) includes a segment under social media that addresses the role of the individual in the social media mix. Individuals participating in social media are an important part of the marketer's target audience. Individuals participate in social media for a variety of reasons. Their participation and engagement is measured by the time they spend on various websites, the engagement level and the behaviors they exhibit there. The goal of the marketer is to develop a relationship with these individuals in such a way that that some level of engagement translates into more engagement overall and into some individuals becoming consumers, making purchases or influencers writing positive messages about the brand, or by sheer volume of conversation increasing the rankings in search.

THE INDIVIDUAL AND THE MEF

Individuals make up all consumers, non-consumers, influencers and non-influencers. They are important to a marketer because they may be, or may become, a consumer or an influencer or their participation in a social community or social marketing activity may lead others to become aware of that social marketing activity or make it more enticing. The authors have often asked the question, "Is it better that only a subset of target consumers are aware of some social media activity or is it better that many individuals including a same sized subset of target consumers are aware of some social media activity?" We believe it is the latter. In the *Will it Blend?* series of videos, those individuals who aren't consumers for blenders may make target consumers aware of the *Will it Blend?* series of videos just because they engage with the series. Through engagement, the videos are downloaded more often, more highly rated, linked to and appear higher in the search engines. In this way, the brand gains value from non-consuming, non-influencing individuals being engaged with the social media property in ways that don't take place in a similar way with traditional media.

This behavior for any individual, whether he or she is a consumer or an influencer or not, is characterized and classified using the community engagement funnel (CEF). The following discussion describes how marketers can measure this engagement in order to determine the level of success they have in general in social media.

The connection point for individuals in a culture and in the social network varies. In North America, we watched as Facebook grew from beginnings in Ivy League schools, throughout universities and then into the cities and mainstream culture. If you became a member of LinkedIn or FastPitchNetworking.com, you quickly found that the community there revolved around businesses and various functions of a business-to-business relationship. Twitter grew not out of any particular type of relationship, other than the early geek crowd at South by Southwest (SXSW) and now it, along with Facebook, is more mainstream.

Around the world, we see a similar paradigm with social networks emerging around shared experiences such as the school that the individual might have attended, a province he or she may have come from or lived in or a corporation that embodies the country's culture.

CASE STUDY

DRIVING VALUE AND USERS IN THE COMMUNITY ENGAGEMENT FUNNEL— TWITTER VERSUS F150ONLINE

The following two examples illustrate how one company actively worked to drive their users deeper into the CEF and how the other—Twitter—hasn't.

Twitter

Since their launch in 2006, Twitter has been able to reach over 75 million users by January 2010. One of the issues they are dealing with is that Twitter has not yet found a way to increase the activity of most of its users—only 17 percent of those 75 million accounts have sent one or more posts. Douglas Quenqua of ClickZ wrote "about 25 percent of Twitter users have no followers, and about 40 percent have never sent a single Tweet," the study said. "Eighty percent of Twitter users have sent fewer than 10 tweets since signing up." Only 60 percent have engaged further than a few posts and created a follower base, with 83 percent not conversing in the last month prior to a survey in December 2009.

"On the upside," the ClickZ study found "tremendous loyalty and engagement from those Twitter users who stay on the system after their first week. "Although just 20 percent of users sent tweets in their second month with the service, those users tweeted so often it made up for the lack of activity from the inactive users." The lack of deep engagement across the community was made up for in traffic generated by those users actively using the service and engaging as part of the community.

Relating Twitter to the CEF would be done as follows:

Engagement level in the CEF	Twitter-based actions
Awareness	Awareness of the Twitter micro-blogging offering
Subscription	Signing up for an account
	Subscribing to other users posts ("following")
Consumption	Reading others' posts ("tweets")
Conversation	Creating and posting messages
	Repeating other users' posts ("re-tweeting tweets")
Invitation	Telling others and encouraging them to get an account

(continued)

The Twitter community has been pointed at as a very success-ful one, but often not for the introductory user, who may not fully comprehend the why and how-to of Twitter. Social media profes-sionals and marketers are using the tool, but new users have yet to grasp the tactics and reasoning to engage more deeply and con-tinuously with an audience. That engagement means logging in more often (via the website or a third-party tool such as Tweetdeck or Seesmic), posting messages ("tweets") to a community of "fol-lowers," and subscribing to other Twitter users' posts ("following"). Twitter, as the host of the service, has not undertaken a notice-able effort to increasing engagement down the funnel with its user base—it is the community and savvy marketers who are driving consumers to adopt the service and use it.

F150online,[1] the unofficial resource center for Ford Truck enthusiasts

On the other hand, F150online.com worked hard from the beginning to drive engagement with all their users. Begun in 1996, F150online.com was an early online community for owners and enthusiasts of pickup trucks: specifically the Ford Truck F150. It has grown to be one of the largest sites for late-model truck enthusiasts on the Internet, boasting over three million monthly page views and over 300,000 monthly unique visitors.

The parent company, Internet Brands,[1] also owns and operates a number of social communities and e-commerce websites in a variety of consumer categories: automotive, careers, health, home, money and business, shopping and travel and leisure. Over 95 per cent of the traffic to its websites derives from non-paid sources. Automotive sites managed by Internet Brands cover a number of makes and models of vehicles including Audi, Camaro, Chevrolet, Land Rover, Mazda, Mustang and Ford. With these sites, Internet Brands offers a wealth of highly targeted users to advertisers.

F150online.com started by allowing F150 truck owners and enthusiasts to post pictures and exchange messages in discus-sion forums and message boards. It all began with Steve Eppinger, founder of the site and serial entrepreneur, posting pictures of his recently purchased F150 truck on the web, and within a week, he saw that the pictures had more than 50 visitors. After looking around, Steve could not find any other resources online for F150 owners and that led him to start an email discussion list about the F150. Within four months, the list had over 400 members and it was this that led to the F150online website.

The issue for Steve was that F150online.com needed money to support the site; in April 1997, Dunlop Tires approached Steve to advertise on the site. However, the challenge was that Dunlop didn't have any money budgeted for this type of advertising channel. Through a give-and-take negotiation, Dunlop offered up a barter arrangement exchanging advertising on the new site for four new tires. Today, the site still maintains its preeminence in the truck category and remains such a hit that when "F150" is searched under Google, F150online still comes up number one or two in the results pages.

Initially, the site focused on the needs of their members by providing tools they needed to connect to other users. It has grown from photo galleries and technical articles to providing discussion forums, info on recall notices, product reviews, classified advertising, industry news and a national events calendar. As the site reached a certain critical mass, advertising revenues could now support it. Steve began to employ traditional online and offline media to further drive awareness and membership. These efforts brought people to the site, where now the effort turned to engagement tactics and keeping people involved and active on the site.

Steve explained how the metrics have evolved over time relating to social media: "Initially as the site grew, monetization of the community had to do primarily with the number of eyeballs and page views and CPM (cost per thousand) we could offer advertisers. What is now more important is the amount of time spent on the site and the amount of interaction between the members in the community and in the social network. If only 5 percent are participating and the rest are 'lurkers,' the numbers don't mean as much. Having 10,000s of lurkers aren't going to be very influential for the other members or the advertisers. The advertisers are [now] looking for members who promote and strengthen their brand to other members—how frequently are members participating, getting involved and making their voice heard."

Relating back to the CEF, this means measuring the volume, or amount, of conversation and using this as a way to monetize the

(continued)

community and build value for potential and current advertisers. This presents a unique dynamic for monetization—advertising on social communities can evolve into a two-tier price structure: one is a straight eyeball and click-through approach, and another significantly higher rate could be based on the level of conversation generated about the brand in the community.

With this in mind, Steve and his team quickly realized that new users needed to be encouraged to participate and make their first post. The community managers began encouraging member participation and made it easier and less intimidating to get involved. This tactic allowed F150online.com to increase their post-to-visit ratio to over 20 percent and their percentage of members posting to over 30 percent. To drive engagement on the site, Steve explains, "We created an environment where everyone was encouraged to participate." Incentives were developed to reward members as they submit posts.

The F150online.com engagement building model includes:
- access to the classified advertising section
- reduction in the level of advertising
- access to the private email system
- custom signature on your profile
- membership status designation ranging from "Junior Member," "Member" (30 posts) to "Senior Member" (100 posts), "Technical Article Contributor" or "Global Moderator."

These tactics, backed up by metrics, were instrumental in increasing the level of content consumption and driving conversation on the site. The activity drove incremental value for members and advertisers.

F150online is able to drive high levels of engagement for over 30 percent of their members, as opposed to roughly 17 percent for Twitter.

Source: Interview with Steve Eppinger, President & CEO, Ownersite Technologies LLC and former founder of F150Online.com on February 2, 2010. Published with permission. All rights reserved.

THE COMMUNITY ENGAGEMENT FUNNEL

The idea that individuals in a community can be driven to a higher level of engagement is exemplified in our case study with Steve Eppinger of F150online.com. As Steve worked to develop the community, he noticed that individuals varied widely on their levels of engagement. The relevance and frequency of posting and the interest in completing a profile were areas he saw needing support in the community. The tactic he utilized was one that provided levels of recognition for time spent on the site, completing a profile or posting and responding to others. Various levels were awarded as the tasks were accomplished and F150online.com used email to provide gentle reminders to new members to complete the profile, post a picture of their vehicle or to make their first post. The designations of "Junior Member" up to becoming a "Senior Member" or a "Global Moderator" became more and more meaningful and drove their behavior as members of the community.

At particular levels, as the user showed dedication to the subject and the willingness to connect and help others, special privileges were given to moderate a group or a forum of other members. Each level or title in the community contributed to driving the consumer to deeper and deeper levels of engagement in the CEF (Figure 6.1).

Engagement with a brand takes place either physically or virtually. Before the advent of social media, consumers engage physically with a brand when they go to the store, pick up the item from the shelf, examine it, read the label and either put it in the shopping cart or put it back on the shelf. When they get home or back into the car, they or their family members consume it. For an existing brand, advertisements were seen on TV, in a magazine and billboards or heard on the radio. Signage may have been seen in the stores. Before seeing a new brand on the shelf, the consumer may have seen messages or heard about it. Up until this point, the messages have been all one way and the delineation between the receipt of the message and the engagement with the brand has been quite clear.

The lines started to blur when someone either asked you about a brand or you asked them about a brand. It may have taken place in the

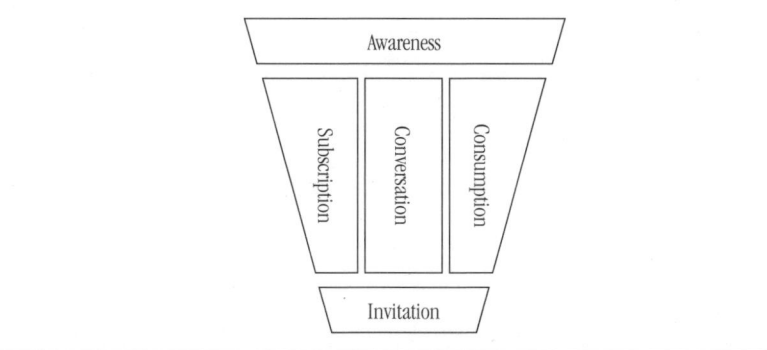

Figure 6.1   Community engagement funnel

living room between family members, at a restaurant with friends or at the water cooler with colleagues. If your experience with the brand was bad enough or good enough, you may have even called the company or wrote a letter. There was now a dialog taking place about the brand. The level of dialog, however, was low and only with a handful of brands and products did this engagement with a brand between consumers have any significant impact on the brand. With highly considered purchases, consumers may have consulted the *Consumer Reports* magazine or other expert sources. Still, these interactions were still one way. There was no significant level of dialog between consumers. Only a mere handful of products were able to go viral on any scale. Hula hoops were one of the first: going viral primarily through observation and conversation in schools. They were augmented by contests broadcast on radio stations to see who could hula hoop the longest. An early record holder for the longest duration of hula hooping according to recordholders.org[1] is 10 hours, 47 minutes by Mary Jane Freeze from the USA, which was established on August 19, 1976.

There were a few brands and categories that nevertheless were able to thrive based on their ability to create a social network surrounding their brands. The Palm Pilot was one of the first: initially seeding airline pilots with early units. Business persons and frequent flyers saw them and realized that the problem of handheld communications and information processing had just been solved. They could track their calendars, use a calculator and synchronize information with their PCs. In fact, this social marketing method was so successful the company was able to forestall the raising of capital to finance traditional media because this method of social network observation was so successful.

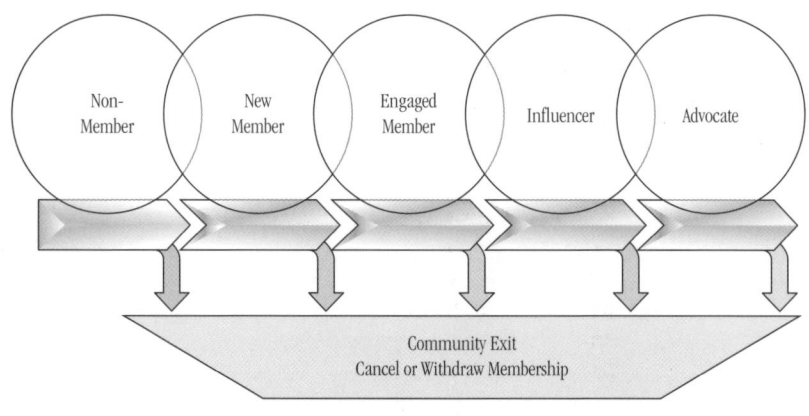

Dynamic segmentation: member pathways

Even now, some brands try to reinforce their conversation-worthiness through their traditional advertising. It used to be that when you saw a turquoise box, you knew someone was about to receive a Tiffany's gift. Now, Helzberg Diamonds is using a similar advertising approach mimicking the conversations they hope will take place about the brand when consumers see the burgundy box.

Until the Internet became widespread, social networks were severely limited in their ability to drive conversation about a brand. That changed in the 2000s as online social communities became mainstream. Now, individuals are talking about brands all the time. With all this talk comes a new level and high volume of engagement that can now influence the success of a brand. The CEF talks about these new types of virtual engagement in a way that makes it possible to classify different behaviors that consumers exhibit and then how marketers can use the tools in their arsenals to affect the level of engagement in a community in favor of their brands.

The CEF concept was designed to help the marketer understand how consumers reaped value from a community in ever-increasing ways as they participated in a social community. By classifying specific community activities to varying levels of value, these actions can now be measured and linked to measures of success for the marketer. These interim measures described by the CEF help marketers to make significantly better decisions in how they promote participation in their communities and how they design their communities. The CEF has become a key social media ROI concept: delineating key interim metrics that marketers can use to measure their success. KPIs can now be set and progress can be measured against these KPIs.

THE COMMUNITY ENGAGEMENT FUNNEL DEFINED

In order to better convey the marketing effectiveness of social media, we need to break down the impact of social media into component parts. Individuals participating in social media activities will engage with a brand in a number of ways as they participate in a community. Regardless of the type of community, if an individual is unaware of the brand's community, the individual cannot engage with the brand in that community. Once they are aware of the community, they can participate in the community either by becoming members, consuming materials (through reading, listening and viewing), adding value to those materials through conversation (through voting, commenting and forwarding) and finally invitation and advocacy (through inviting others to participate in the community). There are some differences between private and public communities but, in general, these five levels describe the level of engagement an individual can have with a community. With this in mind, we can now understand the level of virtual engagement a consumer might have with the brand regardless of whether it is through a branded or unbranded community or is in some other way related to the brand, its competitors or the category.

Awareness

Although individuals can engage with the community at different levels, the CEF represents the relative value the brand receives through that engagement. At the top end of the funnel is external awareness of the community. If the individual isn't aware of the community, engagement can't begin. At lower levels in the funnel, for example with a public community, engagement can begin by consuming the material in the community. They can view the Facebook wall or watch a video on YouTube. A blog may be read, but in order to comment on it, the blog must be joined, by submitting an email address and signing up to the blog. On the other hand, a private community may require an individual to join prior to consumption and conversation. At the bottom of the funnel is invitation and represents the highest value for the community. The three middle layers of the funnel differ in importance, depending on the design of the community. That the three middle stages could be experienced in different sequences indicates that:

- Social media participation is dependent on the design of the community.
- Any successful measurement framework needs to be flexible enough to encompass the potential variations.

The Dove Campaign for Real Beauty

As an example, the Unilever Dove "Campaign for Real Beauty" (CampaignForRealBeauty.com) was very successful at driving initial awareness and participation. The company used traditional channels (magazines, television, billboards, etc.) to drive awareness for the program. Young teen girls were invited to participate in the CampaignForRealBeauty.com website. They could download materials, participate in online workshops, take an online self-esteem quiz and become a member.

The site now links to a Facebook fan page with over 72,000 fans as of December 2009. It facilitates donations to a group of non-profit organizations providing self-esteem programs (called "self-esteem partners"). This is done by entering UPC codes from purchased products and encouraging community members to share their stories with others (by adding to the "real beauty wall"). The primary site for the brand and the campaign (dove.us) has on average over one-half million (See compete.com) unique visitors on a monthly basis.

Before individuals can engage with the brand in the social community, they need to first become aware that the community exists, what it provides and how it might support the individual according to their interests and needs. Building a brand's social media connection takes time—individuals need to understand what the community will do with the connection once they make it. Will the marketer spam them with unwanted messages or send them valuable discount coupon codes? Will they be provided the opportunity to attend unique events or will they simply receive re-purposed mass media invitations?

Awareness for a community can come from many sources. It often needs to be supported by many mechanisms, both off- and online. It could come from a message or invitation from a friend or it could come from an influencer. It could come through search. It could come from an advertisement, online or off, that lets the individual know that the brand is being represented in some form in the social media ecosphere. It might be a Facebook or Twitter "chicklet" at the bottom corner of a print ad, or in a television commercial. As the individual recognizes the logo on the chicklet, individuals can make the connection that this brand also has an account on Facebook. If the individual is so inclined, he or she can find the page, view the page and either "like" the page, become a fan or follow a link to a branded network and join up as a member.

Awareness isn't measured by just the number of unique visitors to the site. Nevertheless, the measure of the number of monthly unique visitors can be a good proxy for those individuals who are aware and have the impetus to visit the site to learn more. Using available web metrics tools, these can be relatively easily measured for both the brand's social presences and a competitor's social media presences. Using our example of the Campaign for Real Beauty, the task for Unilever and the Dove brand would be to convert their half million monthly unique visitors into subscribing members. Of course, Dove's primary goal isn't to build membership, but instead to use that membership as a stepping stone to further engagement with the brand so that, when the member purchases products in their related categories, the individual will be more inclined to purchase the Dove brand, as opposed to any competing brands.

Once an individual becomes aware of the brand's online presence, then the brand manager can start to understand how the experience in the community can be measured and managed and drive additional virtual engagement with the brand.

The next three dimensions of the CEF have varying degrees of value depending on the type of community. Reading a blog requires only awareness, but not subscription. On the other hand, in order to converse (that is, submit a comment), the individual may need to subscribe to the blog by providing an email address or use some other method of subscribing. Or the individual can simply subscribe to the blog using an RSS reader.

Or, as with Facebook, the individual must be a member of the community (community subscription). Then he/she must become aware of a specific fan page (awareness) and then that individual can consume the content of the fan page (assuming it is public). At that point, the user can "become a fan" and subscribe directly to the page. On Facebook without subscribing—that is, becoming a fan—content can be shared, comments submitted (conversation) and other actions can be taken.

CHICKLETS

Chicklets are small community logos that can be found on many websites and now also on mass media indicating the availability of a Facebook fan page or Twitter account.

Icons courtesy of Benjamin Reid / www.nouveller.com

CONSUMPTION

As visitors visit a social media site, they will initially be seeking to consume the content presented, regardless of whether the content is staged and provided by the marketer, is user generated, or is some mix of the two. Consumption plays a very large part in the social marketing model because most visitors will only ever consume content. We've outlined the 90-9-1 engagement model as 90 percent of the visitors to a social site will consume content, 9 percent will participate sometimes and the over-arching bulk of the user generated content will be produced by 1 percent of the community.

With consumption playing such a large role in the CEF, it is incumbent upon the marketing organization to produce content that sparks conversation and user-generated content. The content should be tailored to the audience, but quality content will continue to dominate the discussion. Quality content does not always imply a high production value in the content, but it does imply content that adds value and enhances the experience for the individual. Quality content should though be presented in context to the brand, the community and the media being used.

In the drive to consume content almost continuously, the individual will seek out many sources. Simple reading of articles (and comments) or viewing of pictures and videos (and comments) represents the primary value a visitor or member can receive from a community.

Community members can move to the next level of reading by clipping or tagging an article. Clipping can be done for various reasons: some of low value and others of high value. For example, it can help the individual find the article at a later date for future reference. At this point in the engagement funnel, the reader has yet to formally interact with others and is still receiving only "one-way" value from the site.

Marketers can use this consumption behavior to potentially target specific marketing campaigns to move low-volume consumers to mid-volume consumers and then potentially further to "conversers" or "inviters." Marketers can ask through surveys what other types of information they would like to see in the community. Or, by analyzing the pool of low-consumption members, marketers might try to understand what might be missing in the community offering to entice low-volume consumers to become mid-volume consumers.

A member's consumption activity can then be a proxy for the level of engagement an individual has with the brand. For communities that can measure the level of online purchases or paid advertising, the correlation between site consumption (and engagement) with purchase or ad click-through rates can be easily determined. With this correlation, the value of marketing that may drive incremental consumption can then be directly determined using a last-touch attribution measurement approach.

For brands purchased offline, marketers can then field specific research to determine if consumption and engagement correlate with the level of brand loyalty and purchase. In this way, marketers can determine whether higher social community engagement leads to more offline, in-store purchases. If the two are correlated, marketers can then devise creative social media strategies and tactics to drive more consumption, with the knowledge that it will lead to additional offline purchases at some point in the future.

In 2008, Adobe® Systems, Inc. launched a social media engagement initiative titled "Real or fake?" (Figure 6.2)[2] Aimed at college students, it ran for one month to promote the range of Adobe Creative Suite® products. During the month, the game delivered 14,000 plays with over 5,000 and 6,000 in the first two weeks, respectively. During this time, the Adobe Students' Facebook page received an additional 3,000 new fans and more than 53,000 page views compared with an average

Figure 6.2 Adobe real or fake?

of 5,000 views per week prior to the campaign. In the second week, 4 percent of the players shared the game with friends and 6 percent clicked the "buy now" button. In this instance, the Adobe marketing team and agency were able to significantly increase consumption on the Facebook page, which also delivered a high number of clicks to potential conversion. They were also able to deliver a good number of invitations to share in the excitement and fun of the game through the number of players sharing the game.

Conversation

Social media is by its nature conversational. There is an expectation by the individual that there is a conversation that is open to them with the company, the brand and the other members of the community. It is this discussion that individuals will expect to have with all brands in coming years.

A measurement of increased engagement with a brand can be determined by the level of conversation engaged in by an individual. If an individual is providing a comment or a new post, this is highly indicative of the increased engagement for that individual. Other conversational measures of engagement include Diggs, re-tweets, ratings and reviews, and any other feedback provided by the individual of a piece of content found in a social community.

Marketers who can understand the motivations needed to move an individual from consumption to conversation can significantly increase the value of their community to their members and to their brands. Because individuals in a community are looking for good content, regardless of whether it comes from other individuals or the marketer, increasing the quality of the content can help community participants to gain the most value out of the community quickly. Carefully profiling their community user-bases can help marketers determine which participants could be moved deeper in engagement and thereby provide value for the rest of the community.

Conversation is the dimension of the funnel where the consumer outwardly and actively engages with others. The conversation may be as simple as a post to another member, a comment on a picture, audio or video file, submitting a social bookmark on Digg (a popular social bookmarking site), applying a public tag on Technorati or launching a new topic in a discussion forum. It represents a fairly significant evolution in engagement, regardless of when it occurs. With so much online participation in a social community being passive—in the form of consumption only—the advent of the conversation is a sign that the marketer may have the right mix: the topic is engaging, the source of the content is credible, the engagement is appealing and the tactic to engage was within the scope of the user's capability and interest.

When a member moves to this level of engagement and begins to interact and converse, the reader (and now writer) believes that others will receive value from their action. The act of conversation indicates that the reader has even further trust in their membership in the community and that it warrants their exposure of an opinion, and signals their giving permission to have an interaction with others. Not only does the member expect to receive value through the submission of content, but often they are hoping to receive further value or validation through feedback to their contributions.

There is an indirect correlation between the level of conversation and the level of consumption. The better the conversation, the more value the remaining members will be able to glean from their membership and consumption of the materials on the site. In some cases, especially early on in the life of a community, the brand has to insert or seed value for the community to thrive. Once the community begins to thrive, the marketers can reduce their level of involvement and let the conversers take over the delivery of value to the community.

The correlation between conversation and consumption may also not be linear. Early on in the life of a community, there may be a lot of conversation, but few members and comparatively little consumption. As the number of submissions and conversations increases, consumption can soar. This acceleration in consumption can come from having reached critical mass in the membership, in the submitted materials, in the awareness of the site and finally in its ability to have gone viral.

In a successful community or social media campaign, and as illustrated in the 90-9-1 rule of thumb (see box in Chapter 2), the level of conversation and invitation activity is usually only derived from a small proportion of the total number of members. For example, A1 Steak Sauce hosted a video contest on YouTube, "Sing for Your Beef," where contestants were to submit a video and the winner would be entitled to a cash reward. In the YouTube A1 Steak Sauce contest (www.youtube.com/A1, November, 2009)," there were more than 500,000 views of submitted videos, but only 1,000 subscriptions and contestant videos.

To deliver on objectives for the contest campaign, for example, marketers must make certain that a critical mass is met for the number of submissions, as well as generate awareness of the campaign to drive higher viewership once the submissions have been made. In order to increase the chances of a successful social media campaign, it is critical to deliver as many contest submissions as possible. In the A1 Steak Sauce contest, A1 marketers needed to market with two separate objectives in mind—one to drive incremental contestants and one to drive contest awareness and viewership.

An analysis done based on the YouTube contests executed through June 2009 determined that there was a positive correlation of the number of submissions versus the number of views. Also, there was a significantly higher coefficient as the number of submissions grew from zero to about 750 submissions. As more submissions were made, though, it follows a typical diminishing returns curve (Figure 6.3.)

With the A1 Contest at this level of viewership (=consumption), with an assumed high level of engagement with each of the viewers, this campaign can now be compared with the value of a traditional TV campaign. How this will be done is discussed in Chapter 5.

Conversation is also critical to drive search engine results. As the content of a social community grows and continues to change, the search engine bots will index the community website and deliver higher and higher rankings. These rankings will drive awareness through more highly

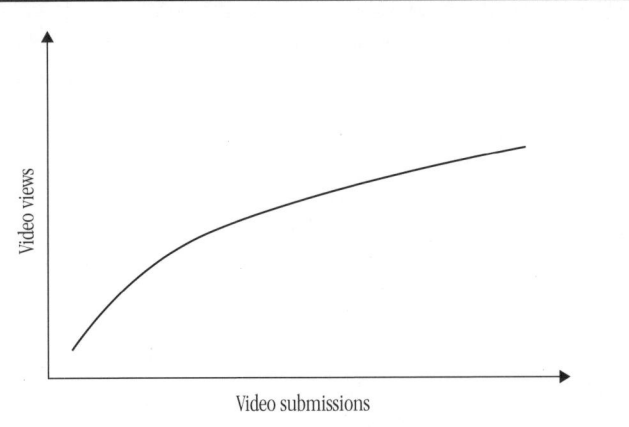

Figure 6.3 Diminishing returns relating video submissions to number of views

ranked search engine results. Tracking search engine rankings of key, community-related search terms will provide a metric of the quality of the conversation. By properly designing the community, marketers may be able to influence the desired results in their favor. For example, if Huggiesbabynetwork.com has determined, it can do better by attracting searchers of the terms relating to "pregnancy" versus "expectant," headings and discussions (that are index-able by the search engine bots) should be designed and written with the term "pregnant" as opposed to "expectant." Marketers should than submit content for discussion using the preferred "pregnant" term.

A second dimension of conversation includes sentimentality. It has two dimensions: positive/negative tonality and emotional tonality.

Positive/Negative Tonality Tonality represents whether the post is positive, negative or neutral toward the brand. Monitoring this trend can be very helpful in determining whether something may be brewing in the blogosphere about the brand. A rash of negative posts may indicate bad service levels, software bugs or other operational anomalies. By monitoring the tonality, crises may be averted, or at least mitigated, based on the type and speed of response. As we'll see, 1-800-FLOWERS. COM successfully improved their tonality surrounding the Mother's Day holiday. Comcast was also able to use this method to quickly respond to individuals posting negative comments about their service.

Net tonality is the average tonality of all posts over a given time period. Net tonality can also provide an indication of how a marketing message may be being received by consumers. If the tonality starts trending either up or down, the marketer can potentially start to correlate the trend with messages being otherwise inserted into the marketplace. The change could be due to their own marketing or operations or it could be due to competitive advertising or actions.

SENTIMENTALITY

Sentimentality is made up of two dimensions: *Positive/negative tonality and emotional tonality*.

Positive/negative tonality

Tonality measures the positive, negative or neutral tone of a post.

Emotional tonality

Sentiment measures the emotions behind messages.

Emotional Tonality Emotional tonality, on the other hand, measures the emotional components contained in a post. Measurement tools, such as Alterian's SM2, measure emotional tone across a number of emotional dimensions. These are:[3]

Anger	Sadness	Social
Family	Friend	Anxiety
Bio	Body	Sexual
Ingest	Achieve	Home
Money	Religious	Death
Leisure-related		

Measuring tonality can then help the marketer to determine whether the marketing messages inserted into the marketplace are being interpreted in the desired way to enhance the brand image. By monitoring and tracking the brand's image against competitive images, marketers can then potentially adjust the message in order to make certain the desired emotional image is being generated amongst their social followers.

Both sentimentality and tonality can be measured, with mixed success, using an automated process. Many of the automated tools are only able to measure sentimentality accurately from 30 to 50 percent of the time. With manual intervention (and significantly higher cost), this can easily be raised to about 90 percent. As web 3.0 comes to fruition, the automated measurement of sentimentality may get even better.

A third very important component of social media and conversation in the CEF is advocacy.

Advocacy Advocacy is when an individual speaks about a brand because they are so enamored with the brand experience that they are willing to tell others about their experiences. They will advocate the purchase of the brand to their friends, acquaintances and contacts. Marketers can influence this by asking for referrals (especially in B2B) and testimonials that can be quoted to amplify the value of these advocating messages.

Advocacy also takes place when a message is forwarded. The conversation is perceived to be so valuable that the individual adds value to it and forwards it to his or her chosen followers. The advocate may add a preface to the message or may just forward it without a preface, simply leveraging the weight of his or her reputation to the forwarded message.

On the other hand, if consumers have a negative experience, or if the messaging delivers expectations that can't be met by the experience with the brand, then it is possible that marketing may deliver negative advocacy. On the Internet in general, and now in social media, it is very easy for dissatisfied customers to voice their opinions to their friends, acquaintances and the world in general. Of paramount concern for the brand is that the memory of the web (see below) causes these messages to exist and appear in search engine results for a very long time.

SUBSCRIPTION

Subscription is a one-way, opt-in permission from the individual indicating their agreement to formally participate in the community. Subscription or membership may be free or paid for by the individual. Depending on the site, individuals may join before they review its content or they may visit the site, consume content but never become members. They may be invited to participate in a free trial membership, allowing the individuals either partial or full access to the content during the trial period.

As discussed above, single sign-on is a growing trend that makes it very easy to join multiple communities without having to enter a lot of redundant profile information.

Once members join the social community (used here to include communities, blogs, discussion forums and ratings and reviews) they can fill in their profiles. Subscription then has three or more dimensions for a marketer to measure their recruitment success:

- membership level
- profile completion
- visibility level.

Membership level

With social communities, there are a number of types of membership:

- free with no obligation to provide personal information, other than maybe an email address
- free with opt-in, where the member must enter some personal information
- free-mium, where offer is initially free, as part of a trial, then paid thereafter
- paid premium only, where the member must begin paying immediately.

Generally, consumers will move from one level to the next as they reap value in the community and wish to partake at a higher level.

Brand marketers can use this membership depth as a gauge to determine the success of their marketing. Both traditional and social media marketing can drive increased community membership. Communities offering exclusive content (e.g., Forrester for Consulting at www.forrester.com, IToolbox.com for technical info, the Official NASCAR Membership Club for NASCAR at onmc.com), or value-added offerings (such as special access to products or coupons) can even charge for their membership.

Depending on the type of community, the number of members and its growth or decline is a relevant metric to understand how a brand's awareness activities are turning into conversion (or abandon). With steady monitoring, marketers can track to see how their membership marketing activities are succeeding. Marketers can use the profile demographics, combined with membership conversion and abandon rates, to determine whether the marketing activities are attracting the desired demographic.

Profile completion

Profile completion is a relevant metric for marketers to measure because it symbolizes the trust and value a member receives from their community membership and how much trust they have in the community's brand.

For most social communities, profiles can be created upon registration and can be added to throughout the term of the membership. As members learn to trust the site more and gain more value from the site, they are more inclined to complete their profiles.

Sometimes a little encouragement is all that is needed, such as a "degree of completion" thermometer to move members to add to their profiles. LinkedIn and Plaxo both have degrees of completion gauges supporting their communities. In other cases, marketers can provide incentives to add information to a profile. These can be made up of points, status level or monetary incentives (e.g., coupons). Lastly, the member may receive value from the community through a fully completed profile in order to be more easily found or contacted by other members.

Depending on the information provided to the community through the member profile, marketers can use that information to selectively target specific offers, build look-alike models to drive membership or analyze behavior in order to minimize churn, build retention and drive participation, thus fulfilling its promise to its members. Marketers can then use profile completeness as a great performance indicator to determine their marketing effectiveness at this level in the CEF.

PROFILE VISIBILITY LEVEL

Often communities allow the limitation of the publishing of profile information to other members in the community. Typical levels include fully public, partially public and fully private. In some countries, and in some demographics, certain levels of privacy are mandated. Children under certain ages may not make their profiles public. In some parts of the world, the religious leadership in the country imposes yet another set of constraints that online marketers may need to respect and consider in their social media presence. All these situations may affect the level of visibility afforded to an individual or their online profile.

The level of profile visibility indicates the trust that the individual has with other members in the community and the community's brand. It is also an indication of how fully the individual will be able to participate in the community to reap the benefits he or she signed up for.

LinkedIn is an example of building on all three of these subscription levels. Free members have access to just about all of the features within the community. They can join groups, send messages to contacts and build their own communities. However, to take advantage of sending a larger number of unsolicited emails to prospects or join a larger number of groups, LinkedIn members are asked to upgrade to Business, Business Pro or Pro, ranging in price from $25 to $500 per month.[4]

Members are also reminded of their profile "completeness" every time they visit the site. The LinkedIn profile includes:

- current employment
- past employment
- education
- recommendations
- connections
- websites
- Twitter handle.

LinkedIn also allows the designation of the level of publicity for their profiles. They can either be fully public, partially public or private.

Facebook, on the other hand, allows brands to establish fans within the larger Facebook community. Branded "fan pages" are public, indexed by search engines and can use existing templates. The pages can include videos, pictures and discussions, or a brand can create and upload customized pages to enhance the fan page experience. To build awareness among Facebook members, brands often use in network ads, promotions such as sweepstakes or contests or they can attempt to build awareness solely through the social graph of their members.

In the case of the Dove brand, the Facebook fan page is an extension of the "Campaign for Real Beauty." It includes videos from the brand, as well as members posting their own videos, pictures, discussions and other activities. Because this community is a sub-community of the larger Facebook community, the branded Facebook page has limited access to certain information.[5] Demographic information is available and can be used by marketers to help target look-alike segments to those that are most active and most likely to gain value from the website. At this time with Facebook, marketers have little control over the gathered profile information that may be otherwise afforded a branded community such as Huggiesbabynetwork.com.

Conversely, in the rare case of a member reducing the amount of information in his or her profile or level of visibility, the marketer should immediately investigate the trigger for this event. A reduction in profile completeness may be a trigger for negative messages within or outside of the community. It may also be an indicator of upcoming churn in membership. Monitoring profile completeness may assist the marketer in delivering early warning signs of disenchantment with the community.

MEMBERSHIP LIFETIME VALUE

When consumers become members in a Facebook fan page, it drives value for the brand in two ways. In the short term, it is a direct measure of the success of a marketing program to drive membership. The activity taking place upon membership then is the result for that marketing activity. There is a long-term component to this value such that once an individual joins a community, the likelihood they would unsubscribe is relatively low. Therefore, all future marketing activities are able to leverage the memberships gained as part of earlier marketing activities. With good creative content, the marketer can continue to market to those members to continue to reap ongoing value from them over the life of their memberships.

INVITATION

The social media space is partially defined by the reputation of the individuals participating in the ecosphere. The reputation of the individual, as seen by their peers within the online social community, is the element of exchange within the community. It is this reputation that will take an individual and propel them to influencer status or relegate them to the rank and file of online users, known only to their direct community. The reputation is drawn from the community's perception drawn from the cumulative tweets, posts, comments or entries made by the individual in the various social platforms that he or she frequents. It is developed over time and built as others consume their content and share the content within their communities.

For example, a behavior that in the long term does not enhance reputation is the constant re-tweeting or re-posting of content developed and posted by others. This type of user is not generating any new content, but tries to build a reputation by merely re-posting the content that was developed and posted elsewhere. The behavior will be noticed by others and, while it may produce short-term results, it will not produce a result that allows the individual to extend an invitation to others that will be noticed or acknowledged.

The highest level of engagement with a site comes when a member invites others to participate in the community and thus becomes an unpaid advocate of the brand. With a personal invitation to become a part of the community comes a level of endorsement and trust for the community and for the message behind the community. These members trust the community enough to lend their reputation to the community by inviting non-members to engage in the conversation and join them in their community activity.

For branded communities, the individual has firmly identified with the brand, uses your product and invites others to do so as well. Although recent rulings from the FCC requiring bloggers to disclose any posts-for-pay or in-kind compensation, advocates will invite friends to a community because they identify with the brand promise: the brand has displayed enough appeal to draw them in and lend their reputations.

ADVOCATES VERSUS INFLUENCERS

Although these two terms may be used synonymously, they have clearly different meanings. An advocate is someone that actively promotes a specific cause or brand. They may not be successful at it and therefore may not be an influencer.

Influencers, on the other hand, are successful at persuading others. They may or may not be an advocate for a brand and, in some cases, may actually influence others not to engage with a brand. In an ideal world, marketers need to find influencers who are also brand advocates.

Influencers are defined as acting at both of these levels in the CEF: invitation and conversation. Influencers can be identified as individuals in a community with high levels of conversation. When a marketer can identify influencers who also make recommendations about the brand, these influencers become advocates.

An advocates program (or a champion or hero program) is made up of people who will invite their friends to your social media presence, post pictures of their own, provide peer-to-peer product support or create videos extolling your product or service. If the invitations are not done to excess, they will be trusted enough by their peers that the invitation will not be ignored: they may not be acted on, but they will not be ignored.

In many branded communities the number of invitations can be directly measured. In Facebook and other mainstream public communities, metrics concerning the number of invitations are not directly available; however, when this metric is in place in a private community, marketers can determine which member profiles have a high propensity to invitation and develop marketing plans to incite them to invite their friends. Look-alike models can be used to analyze member behavior in order to find others with a similar profile and then market to them to potentially improve this valuable result.

As marketers understand how their actions drive consumer activity in each of the levels in the CEF—realizing the interdependencies between the different levels—marketers can determine whether actions at one level deliver the overall community goals versus actions at another level in the funnel. As we saw with the 90-9-1 rule, the number of invitations with most communities is generally relatively small. Because of this, marketing may not be as effective driving incremental invitations as it is at driving higher awareness and subscription or driving more consumption or conversation. With the right metrics in place, the relative success of marketing actions along each level in the CEF can be determined to make certain that the marketing tactics related to community growth are properly allocated and that the right growth at the right level is driving the most revenue, profit, brand and share.

In 2008, the Travel Channel launched the "Kidnap!" game where users can virtually kidnap their friends. Kidnap victims are held in a hideout until they can answer questions about their hideout location. Clues are offered in a cheat sheet linked to TravelChannel.com and the Facebook application. The application was able to successfully garner invitations through the kidnapping function, quickly driving high traffic volume. "During the first six weeks, the game registered 225,521 monthly active users and 23,034 daily active users, with 1,711,300 kidnap requests."[6] Traffic to the TravelChannel.com website also grew significantly, increasing over 28 percent during the same time period compared with the six weeks prior to the launch. In this case, the Travel Channel was able to increase web traffic and exposure significantly through a simple game designed to increase invitation through a Facebook application game.

Here is an example of how a software company developed a highly successful proprietary community available to all of their business users. Anyone with Internet access could participate in the community. No membership requirement was necessary to access any content on the site. The key component of this valuable community was the provision of highly valuable application-related articles and examples submitted by domain experts across a wide range of industries. Domain experts were solicited (and paid) to develop custom value pieces illustrating how the brand's software could help business users apply the software to specific problems they might have. Hundreds of value pieces were submitted and made available for download. Visitors to the site could visit anywhere throughout the site, they could download the value pieces, comment on them and/or vote on them.

Just over a million unique visitors visited the site every month, with a larger proportion of them being returning visitors. Thus, total awareness could be measured using the proxy of total number of unique monthly visitors. Members were defined as the number of returning visitors. Although, in this case, there were no membership requirements, marketing actions that drove higher or lower returning visitors was a good indication of the mix of visitors delivered by the marketing action.

To measure consumption, two metrics were used: time on site and download count per month. This was further subdivided across vertical segments of each industry. Marketing actions targeted toward a certain vertical were measured to determine whether those actions delivered corresponding increased levels of downloads in the targeted vertical.

To measure conversation, the level of comments and votes were counted by vertical. A proxy for invitation was measured through a "forward-to-a-friend" function, although this clearly was not an accurate indicator of the total level of invitations made.

In order to validate the structure of the funnel, an exit survey was carried out asking visitors about their level of purchase intent for the software and intent to recommend to the IT team to make it available for the company. Based on the exit survey, the relative values of each of the actions relative to the funnel were measured. The lowest value action was simply time-on-site as determined by the level of purchase intent for these visitors. High-value activities were downloads, with the highest value visitors having submitted comments and votes.[7] Analytics were run to correlate stated purchase intent and intent to recommend to actual purchases. It was found that the model—classifying low, medium and high-value activities—was predictive in its ability to accurately model past purchases and predict future response to upcoming marketing activities. This allowed the calculation of ROMI factors[8] for each of the marketing activities and to gauge what worked best at least cost to directly drive web activities, and thereby indirectly purchase intent and finally software purchase and upgrade.

CONCLUSION

The CEF has proven itself in many other cases, as well as across many industries, illustrating the level of value a brand receives based on the level of engagement in the community. Depending on your community structure, the engagement funnel may vary. As in the software example above, each of the high-value activities were able to be linked to marketing's success in driving value for the community and for the brand.

In the past, websites have often incorporated certain functions to capture interim metrics that could be used as a proxy for conversion. This was especially important for brands that could only realize revenue offline. Some of these functions included store locators, e-newsletter subscription pages or e-coupons. In a similar way, social community marketers must now build in functionality into their communities so they can make concrete measurements in order to measure and manage the success of their marketing across all levels of the engagement funnel. In the case study, downloads and votes were measured to differentiate low-, medium- and high-value activities. Once the marketer begins measuring these, they will be able to determine what drives more versus less value for their community and their brands and take appropriate steps to choose the right mix of activities that will drive overall value.

The CEF provides a series of interim metrics that can be easily linked to marketing success. Now that we have the key interim results to measure, we can start to work through how we connect these interim measures to increased revenue, profit, brand and share.

Individuals may be consumers or influencers, both a consumer or influencer or neither. The CEF provides a framework to design a pattern for repeatable, manageable interactions that can create awareness, drive community activity and encourage members to invite others to share the experience. Marketers can use this construct to develop and measure programs that can deliver the highest value for the brand and community.

Endnotes

1. http://www.recordholders.org/en/list/hulahoop.html, February, 2010.

2. Facebook Success Stories: How 21 Companies are using the social network to connect with customers. MarketingProfs, LLC. 2009. http://www.marketwire.com/press-release/Traction-Corporation-925678.html, December, 2009. The game can still be found at http://www.adobe.com/education/students/GroundswellAwards2009/. See if you can beat the authors 50 percent success rate.

3. http://blog.techrigy.com/category/sentiment-and-tone, December, 2009.

4. Price structure as of November 2009.

5. This may change as Facebook changes its privacy policies.

6. This was from the MarketingProfs document previously cited.

7. The number of measurable invitations made by survey respondents was too low to make any conclusive recommendation.

8. See Chapter 8 for more on ROMI factors and modeling.

7

The Competitive Set—Vying for Attention

The competitive set dimension in the MEF represents the competing elements the marketer must work against to obtain awareness, time and attention of the various personas. Each persona has a different competitive set, so the marketer must have a clearly delineated strategy and metric for each persona.

Endorsement share as the competitive set for influencers

Important to the success of an influencer strategy is the level of endorsement—the share of endorsement—the marketer has with a particular influencer and set of influencers. Although the primary goal of a social marketing campaign is to drive engagement at the community level among the target audience, one valuable interim success metric for marketers is to track the share of endorsement the marketer has with each influencer and influencer segment. Because the influencer's post frequency, audience size and post quality are out of direct control of the marketer, a key top-level metric for success can be defined as the share of posts achieved by the marketer.

Endorsement with influencers is defined as the public support for a brand that an influencer exhibits when writing about an endorsed brand. Because influencers can also post about many other related issues, marketers must measure their relationship with the influencers based on their share of endorsement with them. Endorsement metrics with influencers can be broken down into share of posts at each level in the conversation hierarchy. KPIs can be set to achieve a certain share of posts at each level and from each influencer or influencer segment.

A related metric could also include the penetration percentage—the number of influencers who have written about the brand—among each of the influencers belonging to a certain target segment of influencers.

For example, Mommy Bloggers are an ideal target segment because of their influence in the baby diaper category. Because Mommy Bloggers are often active influencers across many consumer categories, diaper marketers compete with marketers from many other categories. They have to offer a high value to the Mommy Blogger in order for them to blog about the diaper category versus other consumer categories.

Although Pampers competes against Huggies for time at the consumer persona level, at the individual persona level, Pampers will find itself competing against TheFoodNetwork channel and Walmart (see "ElevenMoms" on page 107) or anyone else who feels the influencers' audience represents a substantial segment of their market. Because of this, a Mommy Blogger will only be able to endorse a limited set of brands vying for their attention.

MOMMY BLOGGERS

"Mommy Bloggers" refer to the blog websites produced by mothers (and fathers) that represent topics common in family life. The sites are so popular with other parents that brands such as Johnson & Johnson and Graco are reaching out to advertise on them.

BRAND AS THE COMPETITIVE SET FOR CONSUMERS

Marketers must compete against different competitors at the consumer persona in the MEF. When consumers make a purchase decision or choice, they make it based on the perceived net utility of each of the brands and products offered in the distribution channel at the time of purchase. The net utility is made up of the sum of four primary dimensions:

1. the accumulated purchase intent from the consumer purchase funnel
2. the brand equity, based on a function of the value of the brand attributes multiplied[1] by the brand preferences a consumer segment has for those attributes across the category
3. the market utility[2] of the offer provided at the point of contact
4. the disutility of price—with the exception of luxury goods, the higher the net price paid the lower the utility.

One brand may provide higher utility, but may also be sold at a higher price. Another brand may also deliver a high utility, but its price is lower. This may then be the brand chosen because the net perceived utility across all the brands in the category offered for sale at that time is higher for the lower priced brand than for the higher priced brand. Competitors at this level in the MEF are those offering products and services in the specific category. Marketers are competing, just as they have done in the past, but they are no longer competing for time, as they are with individuals in general, or endorsement, as they are with influencers.

CASE STUDY

COMPETING DEMANDS FOR TIME— HOW MUCH ZOO CAN YOU USE?

In this era of real-time Internet and mobile access for work, family and home, the average consumer is inundated with messages and opportunities for conversation. How can a brand break through and get its message heard? What if that message is not about

(continued)

buying something, but rather about saving the habitats for polar bears and pandas?

The World-Famous San Diego Zoo and the San Diego Zoo's Wild Animal Park

Five million people per year pass through the gates of the various parks that the Zoological Society of San Diego owns and runs. Adding social media to the marketing effort is the next big opportunity for the society, and they are working very hard to make it a reality.

Ted Molter, Corporate Director of Marketing, and his Online Design Manager, Damian Lasseter have produced an integrated marketing effort for the organization that includes, print, TV, digital and social media. The online and social media presence emerged about 11 years ago, with a live "panda-cam" at the zoo trained on the zoo's pandas, Bai Yun and Gao Gao. The nascent online presence gave people the ability to watch the birth and growth of the five pandas that had been born in captivity. Prior to the panda-cam, an impatient public couldn't see the panda babies for nearly six months. The panda-cam solved that problem, and did so for a global audience.

The zoo's social media presence today is sizable, with an active presence on Facebook, YouTube, Twitter, and privately branded sites that use social media components, such as Facebook Connect and FourSquare in a custom mobile app. They have a very active blog presence, with regular content posts from a variety of authors who generates a wide variety of visitor comments and participation. A recent post on one of the pandas gathered over 188 comments in less than a week.

Facebook Connect and the Polar Bear Plunge

As part of the effort to understand more about their visitors, the zoo has begun utilizing Facebook Connect for their private-labeled Polar Bear Plunge website, which allows visitors to log in using their Facebook credentials. Visitors to the site can have a very personalized experience and the website allows visitors to make a pledge to help protect the polar bear habitat. Visitors can make a Facebook post to their Wall pledging support of protecting the polar bear habitat in the wild with just a few mouse clicks. For Ted and Damien, the use

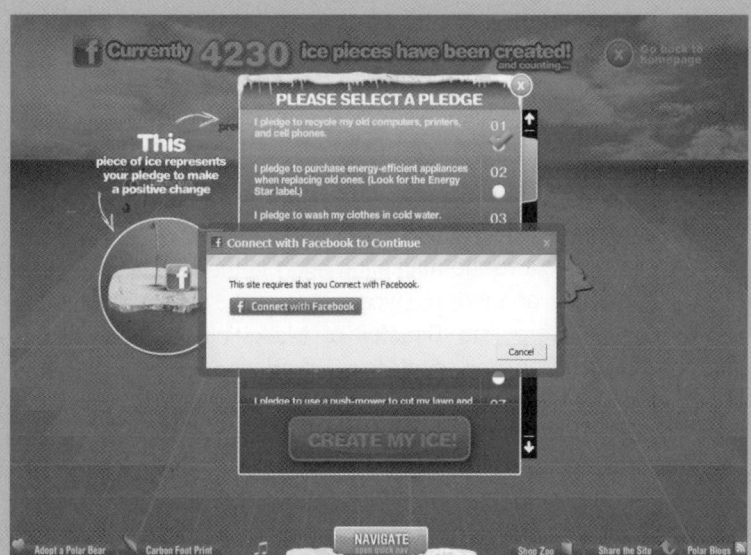

Figure 7.1 Polar Bear Plunge log in screen

of Facebook Connect provides them access to demographic information they would not have otherwise been able to collect.

Metrics other than revenue

Traffic to the site is generated though awareness campaigns that include advertising the games found on the site in venues such as the Cartoon Network. What they have noticed is that although visitors come to the site and play a game, they frequently stay and take in more of the site and some visits translate into ticket purchases. Ticket sales, however, are just one of the objectives for the marketing campaign Ted and his team is responsible for—with the non-profit roots of the organisation, they also have a charter for providing education to the public and a good deal of what they do is to educate people with entertaining and creative websites that help people to learn about the mission of the Zoological Society, the zoo's inhabitants and the zoo itself.

If visitors do decide to share information, Ted recognizes that it comes from a desire to connect with friends around a topic, and

(continued)

the zoo is committed to helping to make that process easy and the experience enjoyable.

Competitive set issues—time

With all the elements competing for the time of the target audience, the zoo recognizes that expanding engagement between the brand and the consumer will have to be something more than just increasing the number of visitors. Ted and the team recognize that they can make a difference and influence consumer behavior by making the visit to the social marketing properties fun and educational, which is important when you consider all the other things competing for the attention of the consumer.

Source: Interview with Ted Molter, Director of Marketing, and Damian Lasseter, Online Design Manager, World-Famous San Diego Zoo and San Diego Zoo's Wild Animal on March 29, 2010. Published with permission. All rights reserved.

TIME AS THE COMPETITIVE SET

There are two elements individuals have to exchange in the pursuit of happiness—time and money. If you have sufficient money (capital), you can essentially create more time for your endeavors by hiring others who will trade their time for your money. This is not groundbreaking or amazing in any way, but it does point out the only irreplaceable commodity that all marketers and marketing efforts are trying to wrestle from the individual is their *time*.

Individuals have an over-abundance of activities to which they can allocate their time. Steve Rubel states that there is a "crisis of attention"[3] facing individuals. A second spent on activities unrelated to the brand is a second that could have been spent engaging with the brand. When it comes to time, marketers have to compete against other online options, not to mention other enticing offline activities.

As part of their strategy, savvy marketers will try to increase engagement for the limited time and attention of individuals. In social media, where an individual can easily move from one activity to another, the marketer's strategy must appeal to the individual's desire to spend valuable time engaged with the marketer's social media offering over some other activity. As we've seen with many of the case studies, to measure the level of success in garnering time, marketers can use time on site as a good indicator. This can be compared against other popular competing activities to determine whether the marketer is improving the relative value of their social media offering by determining whether they are garnering more time on site relative to competitive offerings.

CONCLUSION

When marketers put together their social marketing plans, they must always be cognizant who their competitors are at each of the levels in the MEF. With this three-tiered structure in place, marketers can now develop effective strategies to make certain their social media activities off high value compared with each competitive tier. Whether it's traditional or social media, marketers must now realize that they aren't competing just at the brand level. They are competing at two new levels within the MEF, within which they must also be successful.

ENDNOTES

1. This is a simplification of the brand equity formula.

2. Market utility represents the emotional value of a deal offered in the retail channel at the point of purchase. For more information, see *Marketing Calculator* op cit.

3. Podcast interview and transcript posted at http://www.SocialMarketingConversations.com and included in the case studies in Chapter 10.

8

THE BRAND IMAGE

BRAND IMAGE ACROSS THE MEF

The perceived brand image by each of the MEF personas is involved in virtually all the dimensions making up the MEF. The influencer, the individual and the consumer will each have differing perceptions of the brand influencing their actions relative to the brand.

BRAND IMAGERY

Marketers spend a significant amount of time, brainpower and investment defining, refining and protecting their brand image in order to generate the highest perceived value among their target audience. The brand image represents the emotional image a consumer holds in their mind about a brand. A brand image is made up of a set of emotional attributes that describe the emotions associated with that brand in a consumer's mind. Brand images could include attributes such as, ". . . this brand is good value for the money," ". . . this brand is eco-friendly" or " . . . this is a healthy brand." Brand attributes are emotional and driven by both the advertising and physical experience with the brand.

For social media-active individuals, this also includes the virtual experience with the brand. Brand attributes can also represent the perceptions a consumer may have about the physical attributes of a brand. For example, the brand attribute "...this brand is low fat" is different from the physical attribute "...this brand contains 1 percent fat."

All advertising, regardless of the source of the message—whether its traditional or social media—will have some impact on the brand image and the perception that consumers have on the attributes considered to be important in the category. As consumers receive more persuasive messages along a certain attribute, that attribute associated with that brand will be strengthened. Negative messages will weaken the attribute.

ASSOCIATION SCORE

Brand imagery is typically measured through association scores (see box opposite), where the respondents are asked whether they associate each of the attributes defined for the category to a particular brand. If many consumers associate a particular attribute with a brand, the attribute has a high association score. Brand imagery and brand-tracking studies measure the attribute association scores for the major brands in a category. The association scores can be strengthened based on the messages in the creative, brand use and continued viewing of the advertising. Association scores can also decay if the brand attributes aren't reinforced through advertising, physical consumption or virtual engagement. If the consumer receives no further messages about the brand, or doesn't engage with or use the brand, the image of the brand will begin to decay. Fewer consumers will associate these attributes with the brand and fewer consumers will choose the brand. The association scores will decrease.

Brand imagery typically has a long decay period. This is good for existing brands, but poses challenges for new brands. For existing brands, it means less advertising will be required to maintain their association scores. On the other hand, it is difficult to make major changes to a brand's position relative to the association scores for competitive brands. It requires either much more advertising or much more use. For new brands, it means that marketers must either insert a large amount of advertising into the market, or make it easy to try the brand (e.g., samples, free trials, or high discount value coupons) in order to build up the brand image quickly in the minds of the consumer. Without either of these effects, the brand image will not grow quickly among consumers and marketers will have trouble reaching critical mass in market share. Without this share, the retail trade may then not be as willing to carry the brand and the brand may falter.

ASSOCIATION SCORE DEFINED

The association score represents the score a particular category emotional attribute achieves when fielding a brand image survey. If a survey of 1,000 respondents is fielded, each of them will associate a particular attribute with a brand. For example, "this brand is eco-friendly" could receive 725 respondents associating this brand with that attribute. This brand therefore has a brand association score with this attribute of 72.5 (72.5 percent of the respondents).

With traditional media, the brand is in full control of the messages inserted into the market and therefore has a reasonable expectation of the resulting brand image developed in the mind of the consumer through advertising and marketing efforts. With the advent of social media, the brand is no longer in full control of the messages received about the brand. If certain consumer segments receive most of their messages through social media, they may hold a significantly different brand image in their minds when compared with those consumers who only receive messages from traditional, one-way sources. The brand imagery received by social media- and non-social media-active consumers through brand use and experience, however, will be the same for consumers in either group. The net result of these brand messages and brand experiences will deliver brand imagery that is different between the two groups. Marketers now need to determine whether the differences in imagery between the two groups warrant any need for messaging changes to move the social media-active consumers closer to the imagery perceptions of the non-social media-active consumers.

Social media is also more engaging than traditional media and can spread faster than traditional media. Because of this, brand marketers may see a different overall brand image immediately after launch from the image that develops as traditional media starts to take hold. This has enormous implications for marketers as they launch their communications in both social and traditional media.

BRAND PREFERENCES

Brand images, as measured through brand tracking studies or other market research, represent only one component of brand equity. Brand equity is determined by the brand preferences consumers have for each of the brand attributes. Although it is more complex than this, it can be considered that the brand equity is the sum of the brand preferences multiplied by the brand association scores. This then provides a relative weight a consumer has for one brand versus another. For example, a younger consumer segment may prefer the attribute "... this is a luxury brand" over an attribute "... this brand is good value for the money." By evaluating each brand preference against the relative brand association scores, a calculation of the brand equity can now be made for a consumer or consumer segment.

Understanding the relative brand preferences for a specific segment is critical to developing the right kinds of messages for a marketer to insert into a market. If the social media-active segment has different relative preferences from a non-social media-active segment, the messages and conversation in social media need to be different from those in traditional media in order to take advantage of the two different media channels to deliver the highest brand equity for both segments.

All else being equal, those brands having higher brand equity can generally sell for a higher price than those having lower brand equity.

Brand preferences and association scores typically differ for different persona in the community engagement funnel. What may be important to an influencer may not be as important to an individual or consumer.

CASE STUDY

AUDIENCE SEGMENTATION AROUND A TOPIC

Joan Koerber-Walker—CorePurpose

Joan Koerber-Walker is the CEO and principal of CorePurpose and has a background in the practical application of social media in a small to medium business setting and its use in branding on a personal and a business level.

CorePurpose was founded in 2002 to support organizations with resources that they need to make their efforts more successful. Joan works with medium to large organizations around the globe. Her journey in social media has been one that questions the time that is needed—from her beginning a single blog, a single Twitter account and a LinkedIn profile, she has found positive ways to connect with customers and prospects and realize solid business from it using a variety of Twitter IDs and multiple locations for blog content.

Joan long ago accepted the challenge of developing her own content for her social media presence and it led her to develop the #BeOriginal blog, overcoming the challenge of developing meaningful content for a worldwide social presence. The global reach is a key reason for CorePurpose's use of social media: to be able to reach out and connect with other thought leaders, regardless of their location. For CorePurpose, social media was an expansion of the thought leadership, visibility and publicity programs she already had under way supporting her presence as on the globe as a business leader, writer and public speaker.

Joan cites how social media as an institutional advertising tactic is quickly emerging and how CorePurpose have transitioned their traditional advertising to an online, social marketing model and expanded it to include a long-term "word-of-mouth" campaign. The various KPIs they monitor are pretty straightforward:

- Where was the resource accessed?
- Where was the connection made that was directly related to their social media presence?
- Did they get a customer that came from a social network?
- Were they able to find a piece of information for a client or research project that the social media presence provided?

CorePurpose also considers the number of hits a blog post receives and how many comments were made by visitors. From these indicators, they get a sense of what people are looking for in terms of the online content they post.

Regardless of the ease with which a social presence can be created, Joan suggests that you still need to go through many of the same questions you have to go through using traditional media, which are:

- Who is my audience?
- What are they looking for?
- Where will I access them?
- How will I interact?

CorePurpose is a small company with a big vision and executive capability. Social media has led them to many client engagements and she maintains a very active profile on LinkedIn, Facebook and Twitter.

Source: Interview with Joan Koerber-Walker, CEO, CorePurpose on December 15, 2009. Published with permission. All rights reserved.

INFLUENCERS AND THE BRAND

Influencers are more likely than not to endorse a brand that, in their eyes, has a high equity. Influencers would be more likely to write positive things about Coca Cola—a brand that competes on brand value—than a private-label store brand that competes on price and otherwise may have a low brand value. For example, Guy Kawasaki's posts on the Audi R8 test drive may have had a different tone from posts he may have written had he been asked to test drive a less luxurious vehicle. He most likely would not have test driven it, unless it was some sort of spoof.

CONSUMERS AND THE BRAND

As marketers vie for attention in the minds of the consumer, they promote their brands with various messages that marketers believe will deliver the highest association scores and brand equity with their target consumer set. Prior to the introduction of social marketing, the desired attributes were defined well in advance of the campaign. The creative and advertising team would develop messages and creative concepts that would promote the desired attributes. Social media has changed that model such that the attributes the marketer may desire can now be commented on and made visible by the community. This may cause social media-active consumers to have a different perspective on the messages inserted by the marketer into the marketplace.

It may also be that the set of attributes may be different for those consumers in social media from the set of attributes for non-social media-active consumers. The attributes and preferences in social media may be tainted by the conversation and comments provided by individuals who aren't consumers in the category. As we illustrated in the Unilever Dove Greenpeace Onslaught(er) campaign, a group of individuals and influencers were able to hijack the conversation and move it in a totally new direction. This illustrates how individuals and influencers who may not be consumers have different preferences associated with attributes that may not be part of the set of desired attributes on which the marketer wants to compete. In this case, the new attribute inserted into the category may be "... this brand destroys the rainforest."

Some experts say that, through social media, marketers have lost control of their brands—we disagree. They may have lost an element or degree of control, but the marketer and the creative team still can exert considerable sway over the message that gets talked about in the social media ecosphere. In some categories, this sway may still be large; in others, it may be small. Looking at it in reverse, if the marketer had absolutely no control—as some social media experts claim—then why would any marketer waste valuable marketing resources engaging in social media?

INDIVIDUALS AND THE BRAND

The brand image is also important for individuals who are non-consumers and non-influencers. Because social media hits a wide swath of social media-active individuals, the value of a social media activity is enhanced for the brand by having all individuals (non-consumers, consumers, non-influencers and influencers) participate in the social media activity. An individual's participation in a brand experience is partially driven by the brand image, along with the other value an individual can receive when using the social media property.

TRACKING ATTRIBUTE SCORES IN SOCIAL MEDIA

Capturing attribute scores is traditionally done through a quantitative research process, recruiting participants either over the phone or through email. The survey itself can be done through a website or a one-on-one telephone interview. In a social media presence, similar research can capture the perceptions of the participants using an exit survey or some other online mechanism prompting the visitor to participate in the survey. In this way, the marketer can determine the brand image in an ongoing fashion, based on those participants who participate in the online survey. This has been used to great success by the authors, and can help the marketer gain a better understanding of brand perceptions of the individuals participating in their social media properties. As these brand imagery values change over time, these changes can potentially be correlated to marketing activities or other external factors. In that way, marketers can keep their finger on the pulse of what drives consumer perceptions in their category in social media.

CONCLUSION

The brand image influences all participants in social media. The brand image is typically associated with consumers in the category, but, because there are now many other non-consumers participating in a social media activity who can provide value for the brand, the marketer must determine how these differences affect each of these groups whether they are social media-active or not.

The brand image is made up of brand attributes and preferences that may differ for each of these segments. Understanding these differences and the impact marketing can have on them will help marketers to be more successful when approaching influencers, individuals and consumers.

9

SEARCH–BEING FOUND IN SOCIAL MEDIA

BEING VISIBLE IN SOCIAL MEDIA

A well-laid-out plan in social marketing must take into consideration the entire experience for the influencer, consumer and individual, including search. Of the billions of web pages extant today, one of the big online tasks of the marketer relates to when individuals search for brand-related terms. When the consumer has an intention to purchase, and there is a computer available, the search engine is the very first place they will go. In addition to its inherent value to a consumer, social media also has a high impact on search results.

Generating content that is "link-able"—that is, content that has high value and is likely to be linked to by other websites—will affect the page ranking of a listing in the search engines. Because of the high activity and use of high-value, link-able content, social media can have a strong impact on search engine results and page rankings. Other methods to increase rankings include search engine marketing and the mention of a social media presence in traditional media, such as through the use of chicklets as discussed in Chapter 6. Because of the strong connection between social media and search, search must also be included in the discussion of the ROI of social media.

SOCIAL MEDIA AND SEARCH

Social media activities taking place on the web related to a brand increase due to many factors. As consumers and other interested parties discuss a brand, they write both positive and negative comments that build up over time and may exist for a very long time, if not forever. These comments form a persistent cloud of references to the brand. Both traditional advertising and social marketing belong to the set of drivers that can produce increased social media activity.

If no further advertising were undertaken, these search and social media effects would also decay over time.

Search results provide a strong "glue" between the impact social media can provide and the response in traditional media. Search is where the consumer will go first when they have questions about a brand, product or service. An anecdotal study of 50 consumers illustrates the power of search. When asked "What is a browser?", the study showed that people equate a browser with the search engine they use—only 8 percent of the study respondents could make the distinction between the browser and the search engine.[1]

This suggests that searching has become so synonymous with the online experience that unsophisticated users no longer make the distinction between the Internet and the tools used to find content on it. Combine this finding with the number one search term "Facebook" and you get a pretty fair sense of where things are headed.

When it comes to search, there are two aspects for the marketer to consider:

1. The ranking of a site in the "organic" search result
2. The ads that show up alongside the organic results.

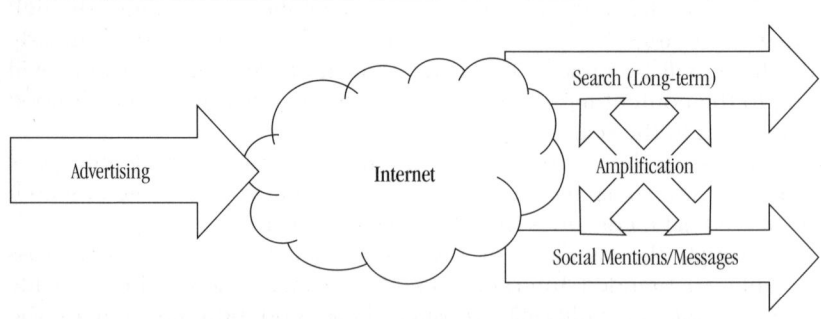

Figure 9.1 The effect of advertising on the Internet

The over-arching process in improving a result for a site on the web during a search is called "search engine optimization" (SEO), whereas the presence of an advertisement that appears in a search result is called "search engine marketing" (SEM). Figure 9.1 shows the amplification of effects of search engine optimization on social mentions and messages and the effect of social mentions and messages on organic search engine results. Each feeds back on each other to drive accelerated results for the brand in both areas of traditional search and social media.

ORGANIC SEARCH

The placement of a listing in the organic search result is a result of a myriad of factors, expressed as algorithms, that the search engines employ as soon as the enter key is pressed by the users. Some of the factors include: frequent activity, inbound links (links to the website), outbound links (where the website links to) and the connections between the content on the site, the headlines, and many other factors.

LEGITIMATE AND ILLEGITIMATE SEARCH

There are a wide variety of ways to achieve highly ranked organic placement and they fall under three major categories: "black hat," "white hat" and "gray hat." Black hat tactics seek to uncover flaws in the algorithms and then employ tactics that misrepresent the appropriate relative rank of a page. White hat tactics are those that seek to follow the rules laid out for effective linking from one site to another and user content. Gray hat tactics employ aspects of both.

Social media embodies a "natural" capability to accomplish high organic rankings. By virtue of good, pertinent content posted regularly, the links will be created by visitors and more and more visitors will link to the content more often via the various social sites. *Voila!* A good placement in the search engine ranking!

Because of the algorithms search engines employ to rank and index a specific site, social media can have a strong impact on branded search results. Social media does this in a number of ways:

- Through the rankings of the social media sites providing cross links to branded Internet sites. When social media sites provide cross links to traditional websites, these inbound links increase the score a particular traditional website achieves. If a site is mentioned in many different blogs, each of these increases the ranking of the traditional website. If these sites are highly trafficked, this adds to the rankings in the search engines.

- Because of the high traffic volume a social media site generates, this scores higher with the search engines than sites with low traffic volume.
- Because social media sites are written with the voice of the consumer, they use different words from a marketing-written traditional website and therefore provide a wider portfolio of search terms that can rank better than a traditional, marketing-oriented website.
- Because content is frequently added, this also increases the rankings.

Because social media can improve the rankings of a traditional website, social media provides a strong synergy with traditional websites. This synergy is often overlooked when determining the value of a social media campaign.

Higher rankings increase the number of visitors to a branded website, and can increase the depth a user goes inside the website. Both of these are important metrics when measuring the response generated by organic search. Search results for social media pages represent a key metric for the success of a social media presence. Depending on the type of social media presence, these can be easily tracked and calculated.

PAID ADS ON THE SEARCH PAGES

When the consumer is presented with their search result, the search engine provider usually includes advertisements alongside the search result: these are carefully selected ads that complement the consumers search engine terms with a relative click-through rate (CTR) of about 4.5 percent of the total click-throughs according to comScore.

These ads, referred to as "search engine marketing" (SEM or "paid search") when tied to proper search terms can provide brands with another way to approach consumers and make them aware of their brand, their social media presences and specific value components of their social media presences.

SOCIAL MARKETING AND THE IMPACT ON SEM

Improving the result of a search engine optimization (SEO) campaign can be a dimension of social marketing due to the linking that a social media presence provides. The impact on SEM from social marketing is tenuous though. A study in late 2009 found that the CTR could increase 11.8 percent "when users were exposed to both influenced social media and paid search around a brand."[2] What this means is that a social presence can improve the success of other forms of online media by possibly more than doubling the CTR.

Let's compare two different marketing campaigns. The first campaign is a simple sponsorship of a promoted event with no specific social media component. In this case, the event takes place, brand impressions are made and the brand value is increased by the number of impressions and the association with that promoted event.

In the same case, if a social media component is added, the promoted event can generate traffic and subscription to a brand's community. This could consist of a Facebook page, a Twitter account or a branded community. Once those members visit the community, they become aware of the community, they may subscribe and they may consume and converse in the community. As individuals subscribe to the community and opt-in to membership, their length of engagement with the brand increases dramatically. Marketers can take advantage of this by adding value to the community through additional activities and opportunities for engagement. They can now reach out to these individuals in a more targeted fashion, providing them additional value through engagement with the community. This long period of decay of engagement can last significantly longer than the brand decay with a simple sponsored event. It may never decay. If the community is valuable enough, it could grow through subscriber invitation. This is especially true because in social media, it is very easy to subscribe to a community. Once subscribed, it takes a lot of negative engagement for the individual to decide to unsubscribe. Yet during the lifetime of participation in the social media community, the marketer can continue to reap benefits from the original awareness, subscription and other value generated by the community. The value of a social media membership can be looked at in terms of its membership or customer lifetime value.

THE "MEMORY" OF THE WEB

The Internet adds some new wrinkles to the value of advertising, especially in the long term, because of its persistence in storing web-related information (articles, cross-links and other brand mentions) about a brand. Content posted on the web has an indefinite life to it. The useful life is finite but, once the campaign is over, there is a residual value of this old content and related links.

As discussed above, once a fan page has been "friended," the un-friending of the fan page may take place a long time into the future, if ever. Therefore the base of subscribers a marketer can bring to their branded social media properties has a long-term value that is often overlooked when evaluating short-term results from a social marketing activity.

WEB PAGE ARCHIVING AND STORAGE

Imagine that a global campaign is wound down, the initial value is realized and then the campaign comes to a close. The effort was, by all measures, a success: more product was sold, the influencer community posted article after article about the brand and the campaign; individuals opted in to receive ongoing messages about the brand and a strong community connection was made. Now that the campaign is over, content can be taken down, or left to be available or allowed to be archived in some of the online archival services.

The Internet Archive (http://www.archive.org) is building a digital library of Internet sites and other cultural artifacts in digital form. Like a paper library, it provides free access to researchers, historians, scholars and the general public. Part of the initiative is a function referred to as the "WayBack Machine" where visitors can browse through over 150 billion web pages archived from 1996 to as recently as a few months ago. Versions of the author's web presences can be viewed as far back as December 2005, providing a sometimes painful reminder of just how much we did not know then about an online presence.

The obligation to the social community and influencers weighs in after the campaign as well. The links created by the community are expected to be valid and useful after the fact—indefinitely. If the brand team repurposes a contest URL for any reason, this can be perceived as disingenuous and may negatively affect the brand. The cost of leaving the content and links in place is negligible, but the value to the social community is high enough to make sure that the planned exit from the campaign includes an intention to update the campaign pages to indicate that the effort has concluded, but not to modify the substance of the content of the pages.

CONCLUSION

Social media and search—whether it's SEO or SEM—are very closely intertwined with each other. More social media activity drives better search results. Better search results drive more social media traffic. With this in mind, both search and social media must be measured to determine the true impact each has on the overall marketing mix.

Marketers must also make certain that as they build and conclude marketing campaigns they don't neglect to take into consideration these effects can have on their brands. Maintaining and archiving old versions of a web and social media presence can continue to provide value for a long time.

ENDNOTES

1. YouTube Video; "What is a browser"; http://www.youtube.com/watch?v=o4MwTvtyrUQ

2. Chris Copeland, *The Influenced: Social Media, Search, and the Interplay of Consideration and Consumption*. (GroupM Search, October 2009).

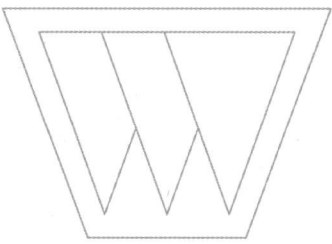

SECTION 3
PRACTICAL APPLICATIONS OF SOCIAL MEDIA ROI

10

PUTTING VALUES TO THE "R" AND "I" OF ROI IN SOCIAL MEDIA

WHY ROI?

There are a number of dimensions of ROI. Sometimes, we need to look backward to determine how successful our marketing was. Sometimes we need to look forward to determine what the estimated or planned ROI could be in the future. Both of these calculations are important for organizations in general, and marketing specifically. Although marketing is usually more interested in allocating marketing investments properly in the face of uncertainty for the future, they also must look in the rearview mirror to see how they've done and how they might improve.

Although the past isn't always a perfect indicator of the future, it does help to understand what worked in the past and how to glean insights in order to improve the future. Secondly, it is important to know how successful the marketing results were in the past in order to survive the internal decision-making and budgeting process. Unfortunately, many marketers often focus on the wrong measures when trying to justify their budgets and results, but without a hard and fast connection to the lifeblood of the company—revenue and profit—the eyes of the non-marketer glaze over and at the end of the discussion marketing budgets are simply cut. Marketers must show and prove their connection to revenue and profit or they will lose control of their fates when they come to the budget.

PUT MARKETING IN THE CRITICAL PATH TO CORPORATE SUCCESS

With hard numbers, with solid analytics and with valid data sources, marketers can win the budget battle and come out better than unscathed. They can win the battle, make the numbers and win their bonuses. They will finally become a critical component of corporate success and being in the critical path to corporate success will make it much more difficult to cut a marketing budget. Regardless of any arguments put forth by any other department to defend its budget, all companies want improved revenue and profit generated by successful marketing. This is what drives executive bonuses and is what the CEO and shareholders are looking for.

MARKETING ROI FOR THE SHORT AND LONG TERM

Marketers need to work for both short-term and long-term success. In the short term, they must help the company make the numbers for this week, this month and this quarter. In the long term, they must put the company in a position to make the numbers next quarter and next year. This can be done only with a valid foundation of marketing ROI—there is no other method.

Marketing ROI applies to the entire marketing budget. Whether it's traditional media or social media, marketing must make decisions based on the estimated ROI of the future and they must show how well their efforts delivered ROI in the past. In this book, we talk specifically about marketing ROI as it relates to social marketing. In this chapter we will discuss how best to calculate these numbers so that they will be defensible and actionable.

REVENUE, PROFIT, BRAND AND SHARE

When making decisions for the short and long term, marketers must trade off investments that will drive sales revenue and profit now versus sales revenue and profit in the future. ROI, which is calculated by determining the sum of the expected profits due to a specific investment, should be a reasonable estimate of the expected success of the social marketing effort based on the marketer's projection of the short- and long-term future. Another method is based on net present value, although few firms have the financial rigor in place to perform these calculations with more accuracy than a simple estimate of future profits. Depending on the data availability, a pseudo-ROI estimation can be made based on many key variables such as the net cost per incremental dollar of revenue over a certain period in the future, the net cost to win a new lead or new account, the cost to win one more million dollars in invested assets, one additional vote or the cost to increase brand imagery attributes by 1 percent.

Setting the company up for the future can be measured by understanding the brand position—its image, the level of awareness and purchase intent—and its share—how well the brand is doing relative to the other competitors in the category. These measures are more indicative of expected future revenue and profit flows. When looking into the future, it is never certain: the competition may increase or halve their advertising; they may come out with a new product or discontinue operations; distribution channel partners may grow their presences or decrease them; and other external factors may take place that may affect the category—or not. In an ideal world, marketers would know exactly what the impact of these factors might be on their sales volume. Knowing these effects, they can then weigh the risks of possible scenarios and take the path based on their expectations of the future that will have the highest probability of delivering the highest returns—revenue and profit—and in the worst case still deliver good returns. With this in mind, investing in the future can be measured by proxies for the position of the brand and these are "brand" and "share." In parallel with this, marketers must then make a determination of what actions will support making the numbers now and optimizing the position of the brand for the future in terms of brand and share.

Optimization: Approachable through Continuous Improvement

This chapter will discuss how to evaluate the numbers so that the marketing effort can be optimized based on hard and fast financial numbers. Marketers need to weigh the cost of the analysis, and of the data, against the possible improved future outcomes of their creative thinking. When looking into the future, there is no single optimum. Marketers can only develop plans that approach it more and more closely. Because of this, marketers must always be on the quest for better data and analytics, with the goal of continuously improving results and reducing risk. This has wide ranging implications for the company in terms of revenue and profit and for the marketer in terms of career and bonus.

Optimization needs to be thought of as the best of all imagined options. Marketers can never analyze and estimate the outcomes of *all* possible scenarios to find a single optimal solution. They can only analyze and optimize a set of scenarios that they can think of and have time to evaluate. This means there may be a better option lying just around the corner, but if they never look around the corner, they won't be able to find it. However, with the right framework in place, they can make significantly better decisions to approach that optimum, and the media engagement framework is that framework when optimizing social marketing.

With this in mind, the following discussion describes a framework to capture and calculate the ROI for social marketing in the past and estimate the ROI for the future.

CASE STUDY

SOCIAL MARKETING ROI: A FOCAL POINT FOR THE FINANCIAL SERVICES INDUSTRY

Financial services firms need to project an image of stability, honesty, confidentiality and a sense of responsibility to properly handle the money of consumers and businesses. Effectiveness in social media is achieved through a communication style of *laissez faire*, openness and transparency. Banks must be adept at all three in order to reap a return from their limited marketing investments in social media.

First Tennessee Bank

First Tennessee Bank (FTB) is one of the top 50 largest banks (First Horizon National is the holding company) in the US, with a history going back to 1864. FTB is the leading bank in Tennessee and is committed to staying in contact with, and listening to, their customers.

Dan Marks, as the Chief Marketing Officer at FTB, is moving where it is likely that no bank or financial institution has even gone before. When Dan noticed that 11 percent or more of their consumer base was already involved in social media, Dan decided that the bank needed to be finding ways to connect with them online.

Dan cites the biggest obstacles for the use of social media in financial services as:

1. Conservative image—banking is typically fairly conservative, so any action that might be seen as risky might be hard to adopt.
2. Safety and security—"First Tennessee takes customers safety and security very seriously so any new area or channel needs careful thought to assess the risks in order to protect customers."

FTB are very sensitive to these challenges and are very careful in assessing what risks they're taking, but they are taking measured steps. Dan shares the key metrics they use to help focus their resources and actively measure the ROI of their social marketing. As they determine what works and what doesn't, Dan predicts that they will make larger investments in the tactics that work best. Dan says they are currently looking at how, or if, a Facebook ad campaign might increase and improve click through for Internet marketing.

FTB has also seen some crossover between social and traditional media. In one traditional media effort, they leveraged unsolicited online testimonials to build proof points for the brand in print ads. Consumers were invited to participate in the online conversation and the results of that conversation were fed back into the traditional media effort. From Dan's perspective, social marketing is not considered a separate channel from traditional media—they leverage one another.

The operational tactics Dan and his team focus on include an approach that acknowledges the difference in a long-term "let's-plan-this-out-to-forever" versus a more nimble, agile approach that allows experimentation and testing to see what works. Dan and his team acknowledge that while the thought of the potential for failure is a factor behind their experimental approach, it better suits the organization and, he thinks, the financial services industry at large.

Dan shared an example of one of their experimental approaches that did not work out. "The unsuccessful test was on a B2B campaign on LinkedIn where we learned that since most users were likely using it for job hunting, they were not necessarily in the buying frame of mind." So FTB discontinued the campaign. What they've learned is that if consumers sense an overt advertising and marketing campaign in a social setting, it will affect the ability of the marketer to adopt

(continued)

social media elements more deeply with that target segment. The lesson is to let the consumer come to you in his or her own way and in his or her own time.

According to Dan, advertising with social media is a leverage point about a brand. If the product is good, people will want to know about it; if the product is bad, people will want to know about it. Product flaws and operational errors in the organization will be discovered and commented on, and organizations need to embrace these comments and use them to improve the customer experience with their brand. The ability to hide from the conversations taking place in social media is no longer feasible.

Source: Interview with Dan Marks, Chief Marketing Officer, First Tennessee Bank on April 23, 2010. Published with permission. All rights reserved.

INTRODUCTION TO ROI

An effective ROI process should focus on capturing and evaluating all relevant investment costs. Marketers and business executives need to make certain that metrics connect to hard financial ROI, as opposed to some softer metric. Developing a social marketing ROI model is relatively straightforward. A valid ROI model has the power to quantitatively demonstrate the tangible benefits of your marketing activity. A valid model will show the direct correlation between revenue and the marketing activities being undertaken, and help the organization to allocate its resources more effectively and provide a competitive advantage.

The validity of any model doesn't come from complex formulae, but rather from the preparatory work and stakeholder management that must be carried out before actual calculation and analysis. Prior to developing an ROI model, an organization often conducts workshops and planning sessions to define the key drivers of success in its business overall and its marketing program in particular. These workshops help to support key concepts by assigning values to these drivers to make certain that there is broad agreement on the core methodologies and analytics framework. With the individual nature of a social media presence for a brand, it is

66 Plans are nothing; planning is everything. **99**
—General Dwight D. Eisenhower[1]

essential to have clearly stated business objectives and businesses benefits that will be measured and tracked. In this way, the team can be empowered to act according to the plan and provide periodic reports based upon agreed KPIs at appropriate intervals.

Once the business objectives and expected benefits from social marketing have been identified, the next step will be to develop the investment plan required to realize these benefits over the agreed timeframe. Because of the unique nature of social marketing, most of the costs are typically incurred upfront, while the returns are expected to accrue at some point in the future. For many organizations, a significant proportion of costs are incurred because personnel now have an additional duty in social marketing as well as their other roles. Important to the success of social marketing and to the acceptance of the associated ROI analysis, stakeholders from marketing, R&D, finance, HR and other groups within the organization must fully understand these social marketing investments and their expected impact on revenue, profit, brand and share.

The ROI equation itself isn't difficult to calculate. The calculation for ROI (in percent) is:

$$\text{Marketing ROI} = \left(\left(\frac{\text{Incremental revenue} \times \text{Contribution margin \%}}{\text{Marketing cost}} \right) - 1.00 \right) \times 100\%$$

But most marketers don't need to calculate the full ROI for their own internal purposes. ROI is necessary when speaking to executives outside of marketing. Internally, marketers can use a simpler equation based on ROMI (return on marketing investment). It is calculated as follows and represents a simple index that can be used to compare investments between different media channels:

$$\text{ROMI} = \frac{\text{Incremental revenue}}{\text{Marketing cost}}$$

Another calculation that can be used by marketers is the margin ROMI index, which uses incremental margin as opposed to the incremental revenue used in ROMI:

$$\text{mROMI} = \text{ROMI} \times \text{Contributing margin \%}$$

ROMI AND mROMI DEFINED

ROMI = The incremental revenue generated from a particular marketing activity, divided by the cost of that activity.
mROMI (margin ROMI) = The incremental contribution margin generated from a particular marketing activity, divided by the cost of that activity.

THE "I" SIDE OF THE ROI EQUATION

Investments for social marketing are incurred in a number of ways and must be evaluated against how a social marketing activity is designed. Care must be taken, though, to make certain that true marketing costs—with the objective of driving incremental revenue—are separated from other functions, such as customer service, operation, market research or product development. These are:
- one-time campaigns that lead to specific results
- ongoing campaigns with no foreseeable end
- add-on campaigns to support traditional media campaigns.

The *WOMMA Metrics Best Practices Guidebook*[2] sets out a list of elementary cost sources:
- technology and hosting fees
- advertising
- program investment costs
- creative and build costs
- hard product costs
- fulfillment
- loyalty programs
- staff costs.

To ensure completeness, costs should be considered across four dimensions:

1. *Set up and preparation of the infrastructure*—all initial set-up costs of the social presence for the company. These include either the internal or external agency costs, for example:
   - writing a formal set of social media guidelines
   - getting approval from the senior staff

- investing in the infrastructure technology
- investing in the creative design for the customer facing properties.

Many of these costs are relatively low. Facebook fan pages and Twitter accounts are free, but to make them look professional and incorporate the brand image, it makes sense to include some creative design effort. All of these costs fall under this dimension and the personnel costs associated with these efforts are often overlooked or ignored. These costs are more about the initial investment in a social media presence for the company; once the social media presence is in place, these costs decrease rapidly. These costs also should be applied against all future social media investments and should not be applied solely against the first social marketing activity.

2. ***Ongoing costs***—Ongoing costs are those costs that are required to keep a base of activity and presence going in social media. These could include hosting fees, but could also be a community platform or service and personnel related to it. It's not sufficient to have an online social media presence if there's no one from the firm monitoring activity and, where appropriate, contributing content, engaging with consumers, individuals and influencers, and providing administrative support where necessary on an ongoing basis. Typically, only the largest firms will purchase dedicated equipment and therefore need to worry about capital expenses and depreciation, while others will use cloud-based services, paying only for what they use. Marketers typically require help from the finance team in order to capture these costs properly and completely (including overheads and fixed costs).

   As mentioned above, ongoing costs must also include the "listening" functions *required* in social media. Individuals, software and workflow are required to perform the new listening function in a timely and accurate manner. The costs for a listening function need to be allocated to those departments assigned to engage to resolve the issues identified by the listening function. For example, if 55 percent of the mentions are customer-service related, 55 percent of the listening costs should be allocated to customer service.

   The cost of measurement tools must also be included as part of the ongoing costs. If these are used only for a particular campaign, then they must be partially allocated to that campaign to make certain that all costs are accurately tracked and allocated. Many measurement tools are free of charge, although larger organizations are investing heavily in tools such as Radian6 and Alterian, which offer web-based applications that provide ongoing listening support, tone and sentiment trend data and statistics for the accurate calculation of ROI.

3. *Campaign level*—At the campaign level, all costs need to be included associated with starting, designing, producing, executing and completing campaigns that have clear beginnings and an end. This includes any specific technology infrastructure, design and creative from the PR or ad agencies to get the campaign up and running. They need to include production and insertion costs of traditional media that are used to drive awareness of the social presence within the target audience and any costs associated with the recruiting and engagement with influencers. Care should be taken to keep campaign-related costs separate from other ongoing social marketing costs. For smaller companies, these might be allocated based on the level of effort spent on a particular social media campaign versus other social or traditional media campaigns.

4. *Risk factors*—With social media, individuals and influencers have easy access to the "virtual" bullhorn and there may be some chance of negative sentiment or social media campaign targeted at the brand in the social ecosphere. Dunkin' Donuts, Nestlé and Unilever Dove have all felt the impact of negative social media. Unilever's Dove Onslaught campaign was targeted by Greenpeace who stated that their use of palm oil was leading to the loss of the rainforests in Indonesia and Malaysia. Firms must now allocate some level of implied costs associated with the potential risk of negative social media. The overall cost of a negative social media campaign can be very high, especially if the company doesn't respond properly. Marketers are only now learning how best to respond and there may be a cost in terms of lost sales revenue and long-term diminished brand value.

With these types of costs properly captured and allocated and backed by the finance department, the marketer can now accurately measure and calculate the investment side of the ROI equation. These costs can be used to determine what the ROI was for past campaigns or they can be used to estimate the cost of future campaigns more accurately, based on actual costs that are not easily disputable.

In some cases, the management or oversight time by the marketing management may also need to be factored in, particularly for the portion of time the senior staff spends managing the personnel engaged in the social marketing effort. If there is a heavy amount of oversight on a social media campaign, then this represents an opportunity cost that must also be captured and allocated to the campaign.

THE COST OF A CEO BLOG

What is the cost for a corporate CEO blog? If the CEO spends time on writing and managing a blog, should the cost be calculated based on his imputed hourly rate or as an opportunity cost based on his hourly rate? If only the CEO's salary were charged, then what number would be appropriate for those who take a zero or one dollar per year salary? If the CEO were spending time doing something else, he or she would be developing value for the company. This opportunity value has a cost and it is this cost that must be applied against the investment side of the ROI equation. In this calculation, the CEO blog is very expensive in terms of the opportunity costs it represents. This is also true for any senior executive in the company writing a blog or participating in a social marketing activity. If the CEO's opportunity costs exceed their hourly salaries, then the costs associated with their efforts in social media must be the opportunity costs associated with their value to the company.

CASE STUDY

STRATIFYING RESPONSE TO DETERMINE EFFECTIVENESS

1800Flowers.com[1]

1800Flowers.com began in a unique way, with its roots growing out of a part-time vocation for the founder, Jim McCann, as he shouldered the responsibility as the overnight manager in a home for boys. To bring in money, Jim started working during the day in a flower shop. He was good at it and, within a few years, he built his own chain of 14 flower shops in the New York metropolitan area.

In 1986, he acquired the phone number "1800Flowers" (+1 (800) 356-9377) and built the national business based on an intimate knowledge of his consumers. The brand was built on a reputation of trust and reliability in providing a perishable product that arrived on time at the right location and was easily ordered.

(continued)

Lewis Goldman, SVP of Marketing for the company describes that special relationship they have with their customers by saying "We are about expressing and connecting with the important people in our lives and while no one has to send anybody flowers, they send them because they care about that person." In 1992, the company expanded beyond the typical retail channel to the online channel and, in 1995, built the 1800Flowers.com website, selling directly to consumers and through a number of online services including America Online, MSN and Yahoo!.

Customers can "call, click or come in" to shop for the 1800Flowers brand. 1800Flowers.com continued to look for new and innovative ways to connect to consumers and now they can also be found in a number of social media communities including Facebook, MySpace and Twitter; they even have had a virtual presence in Second Life offering virtual flowers through their virtual store. They also offer an application for SmartPhones, including the iPhone, Android and Blackberry.

"Tina"

1800Flowers.com targets their model consumer named "Tina," in an integrated media strategy across multiple platforms. Lewis tells us that "Tina enjoys giving just as much as receiving; she enjoys reaching out to friends and family through the gift of flowers, chocolate or cookies. Tina likes to give just 'because' she gets that same charge and excitement by making somebody's day by giving as others get through receiving. Tina is a big Facebook user and she wants to keep that connection going even if they are geographically far away from where she lives. She wants to cheer up a friend having a bad day, congratulate another because they got a promotion as well as the normal occasions of birthdays, and Mother's Days."

Spot-A-Mom

In 2009, 1800Flowers.com launched a campaign around Mother's Day named "Spot-A-Mom." The objective was to promote the gift of flowers to Mom's, Mom's-in-law or even sisters who might have recently became a new Mom. It was designed to make it easy to give a gift for Mother's Day so that "no Mom was left behind." The campaign began by identifying and reaching out to influential "Mommy Bloggers" six weeks before Mother's Day. Different Mom-types were defined, including the "Pet Mom," the "New Mom" and the "Mom of Moms." Through the social component of the campaign, they touched over six million different followers before the company's other traditional marketing activities even kicked in and, in the process, generated sales much earlier than they had seen in the past.

As the campaign progressed, they measured response along three types of metrics:

Sales—As an e-commerce business, the most important metric is direct revenue generated primarily measured through last-touch attribution (see below) through the use of promotion codes. Although this provided a good indication of response by source, there is always some "breakage," which is where purchases were made without a promotion code but was probably due to one of the Mommy Bloggers or other online efforts.

Traffic—Traffic through interactive, search and affiliate efforts can generally be directly measured through specific landing pages and promotion codes, but there is always a level of unattributed traffic. This "untapped traffic" increased, representing visitors coming to the site directly and spontaneously with no clear identification as to the source.

Share of discussion—1800Flowers.com tracked discussion volume and, during the campaign, the share of discussion increased, representing a real response to their social media campaign. During the campaign, 1800Flowers.com designated customer service agents to review and be available to respond to service issues appearing in social media channels. This campaign monitoring was successful in that they were able to quickly counteract delivery issues and negative sentiment as soon as it appeared.

After Mother's Day came and went, 1800Flowers.com was able to achieve a two-thirds *positive* sentiment versus the three-quarters *negative* sentiment for their leading competitor. The result was that the campaign was successful on many fronts, including enormous short- and long-term gains in improved loyalty and retention. Through their first responder customer service capability, they were able to enhance their relationship with existing customers through the quick mitigation of customer service issues and turn a potentially negative

(continued)

experience and resultant negative social message into a resolved
problem and positive social media sentiment.

Through their online, social marketing activities, 1800Flowers.com
is able to build engagement with customers and improve loyalty
and retention.

Once you have determined what types of costs you will capture, you
need to think about the ease of data collection, the data frequency and
interval, timeliness and format. Then, give consideration to what timeframe
you will capture costs over: it must be in line with the time period of the
returns. Finally, give some consideration to the disposal or shut-down costs.

MEASURING THE "R" OF ROI

The MEF provides the necessary tools to determine the value of social
marketing in driving revenue, profit, brand and share. Positive increases
in any of the three persona funnels deliver a framework-based metric
that can be used to determine their short- and long-term value for the
brand. These, however, need to be evaluated such that they represent
real increases in financial values. There are many methods that can be
used, and some are mentioned here with a short description of how
they apply to social marketing.

Critical to the measurement of returns is the understanding of
the levels of sophistication that can be applied. In many cases, it may
be that using a less sophisticated, less accurate approach may be sufficient to make the right decisions. As the capability grows, more can be
invested in data and metrics to improve accuracy and make even better
decisions.

As we discussed above, marketing ROI has three purposes: to make
better marketing investment allocation decisions; to diagnose and
improve the response to a particular marketing channel; and to communicate results back to the rest of the company. Here are four methods to achieve these purposes:

1. *Last-touch attribution (LTA)*—LTA assumes a direct connection
   to the last activity that created revenue or value for the brand as if
   it was the only factor that drove the action. There were no other

previous, concurrent or long-term values from any other source. So, for example, if the click-throughs were measured for those originating from Facebook to a revenue-generating conversion page, LTA would deliver an answer that said that all that revenue must be attributed to Facebook and that no other marketing activity can be attributed to those conversions. However, if there was a TV advertising campaign running concurrently with these conversions, and the rate of conversion was twice as high when the TV campaign was running versus when it wasn't, this would probably be considered an incorrect answer and usage of LTA. On the other hand, if it is assumed that the impact from any other marketing is relatively small, then this could provide a reasonable answer. Marketers should always test to make certain that they aren't violating those assumptions. LTA can also be used for interim values. For example, if a certain level of advertising drives new Facebook fans and, over the course of a year, all new Facebook fans visiting the fan page represent on average an incremental revenue of $1,000 per year per fan, then the advertising costs needed to drive a single new fan to the Facebook fan page can be applied against the $1,000 per year of incremental revenue, even though the Facebook fan page didn't directly drive the $1,000 of revenue. Instead, it drove the incremental fan count measured on an interim basis. Similarly, if it requires $5,000 of online advertising to drive 1 percent incremental purchase intent and, on average, 1 percent more purchase intent correlates with $45,000 in revenue, then the $5,000 investment in advertising can be applied against the incremental $45,000 in the ROI equation.

2. *Marketing mix modeling (MMM)*—MMM can be used to determine the incremental effects of each marketing activity in the face of many changes taking place concurrently. For example, if during the year, there are product price changes, TV advertising, print advertising, changes in the weather and competitive advertising, then MMM can determine the impact of each of these elements on incremental revenue. Price elasticity and ROMI factors can be determined for TV and print advertising and the same method can be used for social marketing. If the membership on Facebook grows due to traditional media, SEO and social marketing, MMM can be used to determine the incremental cost of each member due to each type of marketing. MMM, however, doesn't include the long-term value of marketing. It typically doesn't include the value of customer equity (i.e., the value of long-term revenue from a customer as opposed to the first purchase from that customer), and brand equity (i.e., the incremental awareness, purchase intent and imagery) that accrue from advertising and marketing.

3. ***Predictive modeling***—Predictive modeling uses past behavior, demographics and other customer or prospect information to determine the optimal segments to target in order to reduce churn or increase engagement. For example, F150online used a simple version of this to determine which members weren't engaging with their site. They then sent emails and other messages in order to influence them to become more active. In a similar way, marketers can use predictive modeling to determine the behaviors that have a higher propensity to lead to higher community engagement and then determine which marketing activities can increase that behavior or, for members starting to wane in engagement, determine which marketing actions can increase the propensity for the member to engage more and therefore drive more value for the community and the brand.

4. ***Agent-based modeling (ABM)***—ABM uses a method based on purchase intent, choice and other factors to take into account the cumulative impact of advertising on awareness and purchase impact; the impact of customer equity and the impact of brand preferences and attributes on choice. Bringing all of this together allows the marketer to make a more realistic calculation of the true short- and long-term impact of a marketing activity. ABM can factor in the impact of each media activity on the final purchase, whether it is from traditional media or social media. In this way, the impact from 1,000,000 views on YouTube can now be compared with the impact of 1,000 GRPs[2] of TV to determine the relative ROI of each. This technique has been used to determine the impact of influencers in a category and can demonstrate the long-term value of actions so that they can be evaluated for their impact on short-term as well as long-term revenue.

There are many other methods to calculate the value of social marketing response as defined by the MEF. By employing one or more of those methods, whether simply measuring the value by LTA or by using a sophisticated modeling technique such as MMM or ABM support, the marketer in making better ROI-based decisions.

All of these techniques can be used to determine the impact of marketing actions on interim, or on final, financial metrics. Before they are applied, however, clear objectives and constraints need to be determined. By using them to determine the impact on interim values, valuable KPIs can also be defined that can now be tracked and are meaningful to the success of the marketing activities and eventually of the company.

Marketing dashboards

Metrics can also be used to manage the business. With the MEF properly applied to your brands and company, KPIs can now be easily defined and targets can be set. With these KPIs in place, they can be monitored and tracked on a regular basis to determine whether marketing actions are driving them to meet and exceed their target levels. In social media relative to the MEF, these KPIs may include:

- Facebook fan counts for your brand and your competitors
- Facebook comments per week
- positive versus negative sentiment
- Twitter mentions per day
- the number of own brand and competitive brand mentions by your key influencers.

With these KPIs in place, marketing now has a tactical weapon that can help to make more timely decisions. Those companies that implement these KPIs in the MEF can track them on a regular basis and can respond to them. They will be more agile and be able to reap rewards over those competitors that haven't seen the value of sophisticated metrics, KPIs and dashboards on real-time response.

Marketing ROI applied

Imagine that a marketing activity costing $10,000 delivered 2,000 Facebook fans. Over the next 12 months, one out of 10 of those fans purchased on average $1,500 worth of product with a profit margin of 33.3 percent. With these numbers in place, the total investment was $10,000, and the total revenue generated from those customers over the next 12 months, (assuming no other marketing costs were applied to these customers) was 2,000 × 10% × $1,500 = $300,000. The total profit generated was $300,000 × 33.3% = $100,000. This comes out to a ROMI factor of 30 and an mROMI factor of 10 and an ROI of 900 percent.

The next question would be whether investing $100,000 could deliver 10 times that result. There are many factors that come into play in this estimate. These are the size of the total available market, diminishing returns and the ability of the marketing department to scale up an investment 10 times larger than the previous estimate.

Depending on the type of business, the objectives and calculations of the returns of the ROI equation will differ. Here are a few examples:

1. *Generating brand awareness*—(measured in the consumer purchase funnel) for a consumer brand. Incremental brand awareness

can lead quickly to revenue. This can be expressed as the amount of revenue attributed to each incremental percentage point increase in brand awareness.

2. *Lead generation*—For B2B marketers, leads of a certain quality generated by marketing are a good indicator of the success of a particular marketing campaign. If 30 percent of all the high-quality leads generated convert into a customer, the returns can be easily calculated. On the MEF, high-quality leads represent those that have some interest in purchasing the product. Therefore leads representing the purchase intent in the consumer purchase funnel could be measured as the number of high-quality leads generated in a given period of time. Also important is how these leads flow through the consumer purchase funnel from awareness of the brand to consideration set (i.e., being part of the bid process, to becoming one of the final contenders in the purchase process). The velocity with which leads move through the consumer purchase funnel can also be a good indicator of marketing success.

3. *Influencer engagement for a consumer brand*—Influencers can send out messages of value to a brand to their followers. These messages have a certain impact in terms of making those followers aware and then making them interested in purchase intent. The impact an influencer has on a brand can then be measured based on the number of individuals visiting a site (or landing page specific to the influencer) immediately following a branded post from the influencer. Additionally, the quality of those visits can be an indicator of incremental purchase intent. If the visitors' time on site was more or less than others, more pages were clicked on or more high-value activities were undertaken by those visitors, then that influencer delivered more value than other comparable marketing activities. Additionally, a second measure could be how many of these initial visitors returned within a certain period of time. With the exception of Facebook, many of these metrics can be captured using some of the currently available metrics tools. Because many of the metrics for Facebook pages cannot be captured through these tools, Facebook Insights can provide a proxy for incremental purchase intent and value.

CONCLUSION: THE ROI OF ROI

The investment in measuring marketing ROI as it relates to social media must also deliver an ROI. The investment must be high enough to justify itself to include the cost of data acquisition, infrastructure, analysis and internalization of the results. If it isn't, the investment in marketing ROI needs to be scaled back to make certain that it delivers significant value for the organization. Marketers shouldn't use the most sophisticated tools, requiring the capture of expensive data, to make simple decisions. The cost of the investment in ROI needs to be in line with the potential benefit in revenue and profit for both the short and the long term.

Before the investment is made, the costs and potential returns must be determined and estimated for each year moving forward. Once a decision is made to invest in marketing ROI and analytics, the results can be expected to repeat for each year thereafter. The first model typically embarked on by any marketing organization can have some enormous implications in terms of the re-allocations of marketing investments. The next time the model is repeated, the gains from the re-allocations can be analyzed and determined and the gains can be repeated moving into the future. As the ROI process moves forward, new questions are asked, requiring new data, and the investment can make even further gains in its ability to improve the overall marketing mix. Marketing ROI itself can be continuously improved to drive continuing improvements in marketing effectiveness *ad infinitum*.

As social media becomes a larger and larger component of the marketing mix, marketers will need to make certain that the investments in social marketing are done correctly and continue to be done correctly so that extraordinary returns can be achieved with this media compared with other media. However, the larger-than-average returns that early adopters are realizing are not sustainable: as more marketers invest in social media, the competition for a limited set of social media assets will naturally lead to diminishing returns. Marketers will compete at higher and higher costs for the same influencers, social media assets and eyeballs. Knowing the expected returns on those investments will be critical in helping the marketer make the best decisions possible with this new media.

ENDNOTES

1. http://www.brainyquote.com/quotes/quotes/d/dwightdei149111.html

2. WOMMA Metrics Best Practices Guidebook, presented by WOMMA Measurement and Research Council, November, 2009, Neal Beam's article, "ROI of Word of Mouth," pages 37 to 41. (http://dmabenchmarkshub.wikispaces.com/file/view/WOMMA+-Measurement+Toolkit.pdf Oct. 2010).

3. GRP = gross rating points

11

Eight-Step Process to Measuring Social Marketing Strategy and ROI

Building a culture of metrics in social media

Without a simple guide, outlining and executing a process to developing social marketing metrics and ROI can be a challenge for many organizations. The goal of this book is to help organizations establish a foundation and a defined process from which to improve the ROI for social marketing and many traditional marketing efforts. For organizations that already have a strong metrics and ROI culture, this process is made up of simple adjustments to their current infrastructure to accommodate the concepts identified in the previous chapters.

If there is no culture of metrics in the marketing organization, then developing a culture of metrics in social media alone can be difficult.

If there is no culture in the marketing organization of evaluating ROI, then an initiative to first develop the culture and a strategy for marketing metrics can have a big pay-off. It may be that after reading this book the marketing team will want to use social marketing metrics and ROI in a pilot program to understand and further develop these concepts for the rest of the marketing activities.

Even though social media offers many measurement options, choosing the right ones is critical to building a successful social marketing strategy, infrastructure and campaign. Developing links between social marketing activities and response in terms of revenue, profit, brand and share is the goal of social marketing metrics and ROI. Whether it's using interim metrics or direct financial results, marketers must work to identify the right metrics, and continue to test and refine those metrics, for their impact on driving revenue to the bottom line. Presented below is a social marketing campaign development process of which metrics is an integral part.

SOCIAL MARKETING METRICS INFRASTRUCTURE

Building a successful social marketing infrastructure in the organization requires activities and organizational changes in four primary dimensions: corporate and marketing infrastructure; social media channel; campaign; and ongoing metrics and flighting of messages.

CORPORATE AND MARKETING INFRASTRUCTURE

At the corporate level, there are metrics critical to all activities in marketing. The right metrics, infrastructure and culture must apply across all media, brands and channels. Corporate standards of measurement and performance need to be established across the company and across each business unit in order to ensure a common language between marketers. These standards provide an ability to roll up lower level metrics into higher level metrics and an ability to develop cross-organizational comparisons. There are many books and white papers written on marketing performance measurement (MPM), marketing resource management (MRM), marketing investment management (MIM) and return on marketing investment (ROMI). Once these concepts have been understood, implemented and embraced, they can easily be modified and enhanced to incorporate social marketing metrics and ROI concepts. A white paper from Laura Patterson,[1] President of VisionEdge, outlines six best practices to building an infrastructure of analytics at the corporate level:

1. Create a performance measurement system based on data and analytics.
2. Link marketing to business outcomes.
3. Adopt a metrics framework.
4. Improve measurement competency.
5. Add the right skills, systems and tools.
6. Monitor and report progress.

Corporate marketers endeavor to make the most profit for the company at least risk for the short and long term. Making better use of data and information allows the company to make significantly better fact-based decisions and reduce the risk associated with those decisions. Investments in better data have pay-offs in how marketing can support corporate objectives and become a critical component of corporate success. With a clear analytics-driven marketing organization in place, marketing can easily invest in experimental and emerging media channels to determine how to implement them for the company's benefit.

To drive ROI and metrics, the company requires a culture of accountability in marketing. This includes the ability and infrastructure to track costs, interim results and success. Key disciplines to invest in include modeling techniques such as direct response tracking, marketing mix modeling, predictive modeling, look-alike modeling, agent-based modeling and experimental design. With any or all of these in place, the company can deliver significant gains in marketing performance and overall profitability.

As it relates to social marketing, marketers must invest in tools that can be used by the organization to track and respond to conversations taking place in the social media universe. Tools such as Radian6 and Alterian SM2 implemented corporate wide provide a complete social media workflow processing application to deliver improved sales lead processing, customer service and operations support, as well as marketing response modeling.

Just as PR must prepare for potential negative events that might take place, so too must social marketers prepare for potential negative events that may drive detrimental conversations in the social media blogosphere. Investing in preparatory measures for these cases can deliver huge pay-offs if and when a crisis occurs. Many firms have already made many mistakes in their efforts to respond to negative online word of mouth. Being properly prepared can mitigate the detrimental effects and potentially lead to positive pay-offs once the crisis is over.

SOCIAL MEDIA CHANNEL

Just as the measurement and analysis of traditional media channels vary by media channel, so, too, must the measurement and analysis of each social marketing channel differ. Whether it's YouTube, Twitter, Facebook,

LinkedIn or a corporate blog, measurement and analysis require a nuanced approach to deliver the best results for the brand. This is especially true when measuring and translating results for these channels into the corporate measurement and tracking infrastructure.

As we saw above, social marketing investments can be further divided into ongoing, continuous efforts and one-time campaigns. For example, a corporate blog may be a channel of continuous information inserted into the market. Similarly, a Twitter channel can be used to deliver a certain set of messages to a certain target audience on an ongoing basis. In this case, these two social channels deliver ongoing conversation valuable to the brand. On the other hand, as we saw from Blendtec and Heineken, one-time campaigns might be run on YouTube or Facebook and the results for each specific campaign can be measured and analyzed, then the next campaign can be developed and executed with insights applied.

Lastly, for many brands there is often a certain baseline of conversation taking place in any social media channel. When either a traditional or social-based, a campaign is executed, the overall conversation may increase, but when the campaign is complete, the conversation decays back down to a baseline level. Differentiating campaign-specific conversation from the baseline conversation is important for each media channel in order to make certain that, as marketing campaigns are executed, only the incremental conversation from each campaign is properly attributed to that campaign.

CAMPAIGN

At the campaign level, marketers need to know how to integrate their social marketing tactics into their wider marketing efforts. Social marketing campaigns can either be a component of a larger integrated marketing campaign or simply stand alone. Un-integrated campaigns can develop value on their own. Even though social marketing campaigns often appear to be inexpensive relative to other traditional media, they still need to be measured and tracked based on valid data and analytics. Many of the modeling techniques mentioned above can provide valuable insights based on the gathered data to help marketers make better strategic and tactical marketing decisions supporting more appropriately allocations based on the relative success for each of the media channels.

ONGOING METRICS AND FLIGHTING OF MESSAGES

In contrast to many traditional media types, social media provides both campaign-specific activities and ongoing activities. Typically, a traditional media campaign has a clear start and end. Media flighting plans (the timing and sequencing of media insertions) are made and media buys are executed accordingly. With social marketing, once executed, the media doesn't necessarily end. The conversations persist indefinitely: stored on various servers and indexed by the search engines for future recall. In addition, ongoing activities take place: a blog, a Facebook fan Page or branded social community will usually live on even after the campaign concludes.

A social marketing campaign can include a membership base that persists and converses well past the end of the end of a campaign or event. In GAB's case for the Heineken brand in Malaysia, while each Green Room event delivered value to the members recruited during the event, each event also delivered value to members from previous Green Room events and provided a base for the next. Metrics should be designed to take this effect into account to understand fully the future value of any marketing activity.

EIGHT-STEP PROCESS TO MEASURE SOCIAL MARKETING STRATEGY AND ROI

The major steps in developing a successful social marketing measurement and ROI plan depend on the type of organization, the current measurement environment and the level of investment available to be made in metrics. Investment in metrics—and an infrastructure and culture to use these metrics in making better strategic and tactical marketing decisions—has a clear pay-off, but that doesn't mean that this investment can be too high. As discussed in above, the investment in calculating ROI must have a sufficiently high enough ROI commensurate with the risks of implementing the investment in tools, training and infrastructure. If not, the investment needs to be scaled to deliver the requisite ROI compared with any other investment made in the company. For many organizations, this investment is best made in a gradual, phased approach: investing initially in certain easy wins and then expanding from there.

For social marketing, similar considerations must be made. Once made, and the investments are justified, a marketer can follow the eight-step process outlined below to understand what is necessary to develop a measurement and analytics infrastructure to calculate social marketing ROI, to improve social marketing strategy, and know what tactics can deliver improved revenue, profit, brand and share.

1. DEVELOP STRATEGY AND SET GOALS

Many marketers will have different definitions for a strategy. At a high level, it is defining where to go and how to get there and how to get there in the face of competition and other exogenous factors:

- **Setting corporate goals and objectives**—Once the corporate goals and objectives are set, marketing must put in place plans to deliver their part to meet those objectives at least cost and risk. These include the short- and long-term objectives over which marketing has influence. In the short term, marketing must help the company make the numbers this week, this month and this quarter. For the long term, marketing must also set the company up to make the numbers, next quarter and next year.
- **Listening and market research**—For traditional media, market research is done to understand consumer behavior and attitudes to support the development of messages, needs and segments that marketing can address at least cost and risk. Use and attitude studies, focus groups, brand tracking studies and many other research tools make up the list of available market research tools to gather valuable information about consumers, the competition, the category and the distribution channel. It is similar for social media. In addition to the traditional tools, social media market research can be done by listening to the conversations in the social media ecosphere that are taking place about the brand, the category and other related trends. There are many tools to gather information in the social media space. They can be used to understand what is being said, how to use that information to build and refine a social media marketing strategy.
- **Goal setting in social marketing**—Goal setting for a social media campaign needs to fit corporate, campaign (for integrated marketing campaigns) and social media channel objectives, with clear objectives defined for each level of the community engagement funnel. Top-level goals can include building the brand, driving acquisition or retention or about improving service and reducing negative word of mouth (WOM). Goals along the community engagement funnel can include increasing community membership, consumption, conversation or invitation. Additional goals can include search engine marketing optimization, driving the brand image or other defined value for the brand.
- **Developing metrics and measurement objectives**—In order to determine the effectiveness of any marketing activity, marketers can evaluate them in a number of ways. Marketers can have as a goal to grow along each dimension in order to deliver continuous

improvement in overall marketing effectiveness. There are five levels discussed in *Marketing Calculator*, each with requirements on data collection and analytics:

- Activity trackers—Implement a framework of data collection.
- Campaign measurers—Use the available data to measure the effectiveness of each campaign based on last-touch attribution.
- Mix modelers—Measure across the entire marketing mix to determine which marketing channel is most or least effective.
- Consumer analyzers—Apply all consumer tracking and marketing data across the category to deliver optimal results for the short and long term.
- Brand optimizers—Look at the ROMI by brand to make informed strategic decisions as to the viability and dispositions of specific brands, each competing for corporate resources and funding.

Social media marketers can implement some or all of the methods to determine the effectiveness of each media channel, social media or social media compared with traditional media in order to allocate resources to drive revenue, profit, brand and share more effectively.

2. IDENTIFYING TARGET AUDIENCES

As we have seen in the MEF, target audiences are made up of three key personas: influencers, individuals and consumers.

- **Identifying the consumer audience**—Defining and identifying the target consumer audience is critical when implementing a media campaign, with or without social components. The case studies show how some marketers have used social media to segment the channel and the message. Just as with traditional media, the message has to deliver a clear benefit to the target consumer in order for the consumer to positively engage with the message and convert that message into brand awareness, preference and purchase intent.
- **Defining the brand image**—Brand attributes, and the preferences for those attributes, determine how influencers, individuals and consumers may derive value from the brand. For example, a brand with low brand equity in the mind of an influencer will more than likely not be endorsed by that influencer. Similarly, brands with low brand equity in the minds of the consumer will not be purchased. If they do write about them, they may write about them only in a derogatory manner. Brands with high brand equity will more likely not suffer as much negative word of mouth as those with low brand equity if a service incident occurs.

- **Developing and communicating the value proposition to the consumer and individual audience**—The value proposition for a marketer's social media activity must be such that it will be more valuable to the individual then spending their valuable time elsewhere in the social media space. The marketer isn't competing for a share of wallet, but a share of time.

- **Identifying competitors**—The target audience in the social media space has a different competitive set from those in the store where the marketer's product may be found. When competing in the social media space, marketers must offer enough value for the target consumers and individuals to be willing to invest their valuable time. This is different from the goal in the physical space where the marketer is competing for purchases against competitors in the category. Individuals may spend their time on games, viewing YouTube videos, commenting on friends' Facebook pages or on brand fan pages. The competitive set is now much wider than what can be found in a physical store.

- **Aligning the appropriate media channel to the audience**—Depending on your target audience, they may use different tools in the social media space. B2B decision makers may be more likely to be found in discussion groups on LinkedIn, while music lovers may likely be found on MySpace. Campaigns must target the audience and find out where they spend the most time and the types of behaviors they might exhibit in each of the different social media channels. Part of the campaign design needs to select the media channel most likely to deliver the desired message to the desired audience at the right time and place at least cost and risk.

- **Identifying the influencer audience**—One of the key advantages of social media is the ability to leverage influencers within the community who can forward a message and amplify its reach. They will also add credibility to the message if they've found the right level of value in it. With influencers, social marketers must not only develop a message delivering benefits for the consumers' use, but the marketers need to deliver a message that the influencers that will find valuable and forward on to their followers.

- **Developing and communicating the value proposition to influencers**—Marketers must make certain that their offer to their targeted influencers is competitive and valuable. The offer to the influencers will be compared with other such offers that the influencer receives. It must also be of high enough value such that it won't cause burn out (see box opposite) or diminish the reputation of the influencer.

- **Identifying competitors at the influencer level**—Many other brand marketers want to reach out to influencers. The influencer is

INFLUENCER BURN-OUT

When dealing with influencers, brand marketers would do well to assess whether or not the influencers' value doesn't get "burned out" due to the over promotion of sponsoring brands. If the influencer sends out too many messages, coupons or other promotions to their followers, they can quickly lose credibility with their audience and their level of influence and persuasiveness will fall.

If they are offered too many promotions, they will need to receive higher and higher value for their participation in your campaign and the price for their participation in your programs will go up. Although they have to disclose certain relationships with a brand according to FCC guidelines, compensation may need to be in the form of more valuable samples or other enticements in order to gain the influencers' support in your program.

being targeted by many categories and brands and a marketer must determine which other brands in the category and outside the category are targeting the same influencers.

3. DEVELOPING THE CAMPAIGN MESSAGE AND MONITORING CONVERSATION CONTENT

The campaign design must support the marketing plan in meeting overall corporate objectives. Content is the most important component in driving conversations within the target audiences: content is king in social marketing.

- **Listening**—Once the target audience has been defined, listening is the next most important step to understand what's taking place with the target influencers, individuals and consumers. Understanding the types of messages of interest to these groups will lay the groundwork to designing the right kinds of messages once the actual engagement campaign begins.
- **Developing message content**—Although marketers don't necessarily have full control over the conversation, they often have control over the initial phase of the conversation. BlendTec started their conversations by posting creative YouTube videos. Although

this book isn't about how to develop these messages, the immediate access to valuable, engaging and credible content is what makes social media so important for marketers. Tracking and monitoring how the conversation unfolds once the initial message is inserted into the social media ecosphere is critical to reaping the most value out of a social media activity.

- **Designing and monitoring the conversation**—Because the conversation in social media is interactive and two-way, the concept of campaign message design needs to be done very differently from in traditional one-way media. In social media, marketers have only a partial level of control over the content of the conversation so they need to be ready to step into a conversation to nudge it back on track, or to let it go where the conversation participants want to take it. In both cases, marketers must monitor how the conversation unfolds so that, if possible, they can work to move it in the desired direction.
- **Segmenting the message and conversation**—Messages in social media can be targeted using specific channels and tactics that put the message in front of specific audiences. Channels can be segmented such that specific accounts can have specific target audiences receiving specific types of messages and driving conversation around specific topics. Multiple Twitter and Facebook fan pages can easily be set up to deliver varying messages to each of the account followers. The content of a Facebook conversation on a fan page is different from the content found or designed into a Twitter message stream. Marketers must consider the type of conversation they want to moderate in a particular social media channel.

Because the conversation design and target audience are closely linked, and that the individuals have some control over where and how they want to interact with your brand, individuals may participate one day in one channel in one conversation and then move to another conversation in another channel the next. Monitoring the conversation by social media channel is imperative in order to make certain that the targeted audiences are receiving the planned messages.

4. Executing social marketing campaign tactics

Once the campaign content and target audiences have been specified, the campaign must be tactically executed and messages delivered to drive value and generate conversation. The following represent key elements in executing a successful social marketing campaign:

- **Integrated or stand-alone**—Many social media activities begin as separate, un-integrated activities. They are begun by teams in the digital marketing side (in the worst case in a "silo") of the company, which is also not integrated into the other traditional media marketing teams. This has advantages and disadvantages. It allows social marketing campaigns to easily be started without having to wade through all the organizational issues that can be associated with new marketing activities. It allows the campaign to start very quickly in order to gain a foothold by an internal social media marketing enthusiast. Once it starts and success is apparent, the other groups will start to take notice and the activity can be migrated to a more integrated place in the mainstream marketing process. The disadvantage is that social marketing campaigns can't reap the benefits of having them integrated into the overall marketing effort and synergies are lost. Mentions of branded social media properties, such as simply referencing a link or showing a Facebook or Twitter icon, are missing in powerful traditional media, impeding the awareness of the social media asset.

- **Production or experimental**—After the social media strategy has been set, but before the organization may be fully ready to invest heavily in social media, marketers may run experimental campaigns in order to test how the social media channel can be used to support the brand: quickly learning from successes and failures.
- **Call-to-action**—Calls-to-action (either explicitly stated through an offer or implicit through the inclusion of a link) are often key components of a social media campaign. Many social media campaigns have explicit calls-to-action. In Twitter, these will be via shortened links that have a high degree of track-ability. In Facebook, these might include the offer of coupons or the invitation to submit a contest entry. On a blog or elsewhere, they can include downloads, podcasts, videos or coupons and promotion codes.
- **Budget**—Any campaign effort must have some level of expected investment. This can include external costs with the agency, the cost of impressions purchased or the internal costs of personnel assigned to the project. Cost elements are discussed in detail in Chapter 10. Once the social marketing campaign activity has begun, actual costs need to be tracked to make certain the costs are in line with projections.
- **Sustaining or short term**—For long-term sustaining campaigns, dedicated resources need to be identified to maintain the social media activity. These resources can apply to the setup, maintenance and moderation of a Facebook fan page or a custom tab on the page, a Twitter account or a blog. Once the campaign has kicked off, a schedule of activity should be defined so that high-quality content continues to be delivered to the audience(s) to maintain engagement between the community and the brand. Short-term campaigns can be made up of a one-time event, such as a music or beer festival or they can be the social marketing component of an integrated marketing campaign.

- **Risk mitigation**—As opposed to social media, choosing a channel and campaign concept for traditional media has little risk associated with it. As we saw with the case study on the Dove onslaught social marketing campaign and the palm oil/rainforest protection protest campaign, marketers must now consider as part of their social media campaign planning a "what if" analysis of what could go wrong and develop contingency plans of how to deal with any negative eventuality.

5. DEFINING, MONITORING AND EVALUATING INTERIM AND SUCCESS METRICS; CHOOSING THE ANALYTICAL METHODOLOGY

The MEF is the key underlying concept to measuring the right things in social marketing and how your marketing actions drive value for the brand. If there isn't any prior social marketing experience with the brand, understanding how similar brands and similar campaigns performed in the past can be a good starting point for how a similar campaign may deliver in the future. These can be used to benchmark the success of the campaign as it unfolds.

Metrics development should also follow the SMART process:[2] they should be **s**pecific, **m**easureable, **a**chievable, **r**elevant and **t**ime-based. This helps to keep the number, scope and applicability of metrics to a minimum and makes certain that the organization is following metrics that are valuable and can help the marketing team make better strategic and tactical decisions.

- **Defining interim metrics**—Measuring interim metrics based on the MEF provides the marketer with the ability to determine ongoing success and, when necessary, take appropriate corrective actions to improve the likelihood of overall campaign success. The MEF provides interim metrics for each of the key personas: influencers, individuals and consumers. Often minor adjustments to a campaign, or to the design of a social community engagement plan, can help to deliver metrics otherwise not available during the execution of a social marketing campaign. By designing these metrics into the engagement or campaign, marketers can better monitor the campaign success and intervene when results are missing their targets or invest more when results are exceeding target and opportunities exist to scale the effort. Some of these designed in metrics can include the use of URL shorteners (such as bit.ly) that can provide precise statistics or promotion codes that can be tracked specifically to a social media channel.

- **Defining success metrics**—There are many types of success metrics that can be used to measure success based on the MEF, these can include click-through rates, increased awareness or purchase intent and incremental revenue or margin percentages. When planning a campaign, it is very useful to calculate an expected return on marketing investment factor also known as a budget or plan ROMI rate. ROMI represents the incremental revenue generated for each dollar of marketing invested.[3] If the plan ROMI rate isn't above some minimum hurdle rate for the estimated risk in the program, then it should be re-evaluated and diagnosed to make certain the investments aren't too high, the expected revenues (and margins) aren't too low or something else in the design needs to be altered to deliver better results.

    Similarly, the success metric must be one that can be measured in an accurate and timely basis and will help the marketing team make better decisions.

- **Choosing the analytical methodology**—As the metrics infrastructure gets more sophisticated, social marketing analysts can move from just measuring direct response to measuring the indirect response and then measuring long-term brand value based on the MEF. Direct effects can be measured through simple click-through and conversion rates to online sites or promotion code redemptions to on- and offline sales based on last-touch attribution. For many industries, a direct connection cannot be measured but can only be modeled or deduced using other methods. Experimental design or the tracking of promotion codes can also be used to determine the direct effects a particular campaign may have on short-term results. Indirect effects can be calculated through the use of marketing mix models based on statistical regression analysis and other methods. For example, the measurement of social marketing activities driving sales of soap in a store is often done using marketing mix modeling. Although direct response can be measured through coupon and promotion code redemptions, more accurate results are determined through modeling. These models are more accurate because they include components that are missing when only measuring the direct effects based on last-touch attribution. For example, synergies, halo and cannibalization are not counted when using last-touch attribution. In some circumstances, these statistical methods will also have difficulty measuring social marketing results. Compared with traditional media, the impact from social media can be very small and can be lost in the "noise." This will change as more and more marketing investments are allocated to social media. In the meantime, other methods need to be employed to measure the impact of social media marketing activities. The analytic method will likely also require other sources that include not only internal data, such as sales volumes and web statistics, but also external data, such as syndicated data from Nielsen, IRI or other sources, as well as public data, such as weather and other exogenous factors.

- **Determining long-term effects**—Measuring the long-term effects of social media requires the understanding of the key components of long-term brand value. The dimensions of long-term value include:
  - customer equity value
  - brand equity value
  - brand attribute
  - preference value.

In social media (as described in Chapter 2) these also include the long-term value of social marketing, such as search engine results and the increased engagement delivered by social media for the brand to its target consumers. Agent-based modeling is a great tool to determine the combined short- and long-term effects of social marketing campaigns.

6. MONITORING AND MANAGING THE EXECUTION OF SOCIAL MARKETING CAMPAIGNS

Social marketing campaigns take on a life of their own. As brands give up partial control of the brand message in favor of the two-way interactive conversation with the community, a social marketing campaign may not unfold exactly as planned. Marketers must carefully monitor a campaign as it unfolds to make certain any risks are managed as per the goals of the campaign plan.

- **Tracking short-term, interim metrics**—Because the conversation is being moderated and only periodically being engaged with by the marketer, it may tend to move in different directions from intended. The marketer may not find the traction as originally planned in order to meet campaign objectives. For example, if conversation starts to wane prematurely, the marketer may need to intervene to regain momentum. As opposed to the fire-and-forget method associated with traditional marketing campaigns, social marketers can, and must, now actively monitor the campaign metrics and intervene where, or if, necessary.
- **Moving the social marketing decision-making process to the edge of the organization**— Because of the interactive, high-speed nature of social media, the hierarchy of the marketing organization must now be turned upside down. In the past, multiple levels of approval were needed to design and make changes to campaigns.

Legal, regulatory, agency and marketing management workflows were developed to speed this process and remove bottlenecks. It was still a process and, even in a highly automated marketing workflow environment, the process requires time to move from project initiation to completion.

With social media, the marketer now needs to move trust closer to the edge of the organization, perhaps all the way to those on the front lines of interfacing with individuals and handling the conversation in the community. As we saw with PitneyBowes, the use of "loose governance" is an integral component of the social media marketing function.

- **Tracking plan versus actual**—When executing a campaign, different opportunities arise that can be taken advantage of in order to improve results. If one channel is delivering better results due to external or unplanned influences, then resources might be quickly shifted over to enhance and amplify response in that channel.
- **Responding to negative comments**—Negative comments and responses to a campaign can easily and unexpectedly take place in social media. Social media marketers must be prepared to respond based on a specific course of action. Negative comments can be classified in a number of different ways and each needs a specific response plan. Some comments don't require a response, others can be forwarded to customer service and others still can be forwarded to the PR team or to Investor Relations. Critical to delivering success is to be able to quickly respond when necessary and appropriate in order to mitigate any deleterious effects of negative WOM.
- **Engaging based on the life stage of the community**—As a community grows and builds, the dynamics change. Forrester Consulting illustrates this in his "Life Process of a Successful Community," showing the three stages of a community—conception, adolescence and maturity (Figure 11.1).

The tone and level of moderation by the marketer needs to evolve in line with these changes in dynamics to make certain that the community continues to thrive and engagement with the brand continues to grow.

7. MEASURING AND TRACKING ACTUAL COSTS, CALCULATING ROI

Many marketers believe that it is impossible to calculate the ROI on social marketing because there is no investment; they see it as just the effort of a few hours of an individual's time working in the marketing

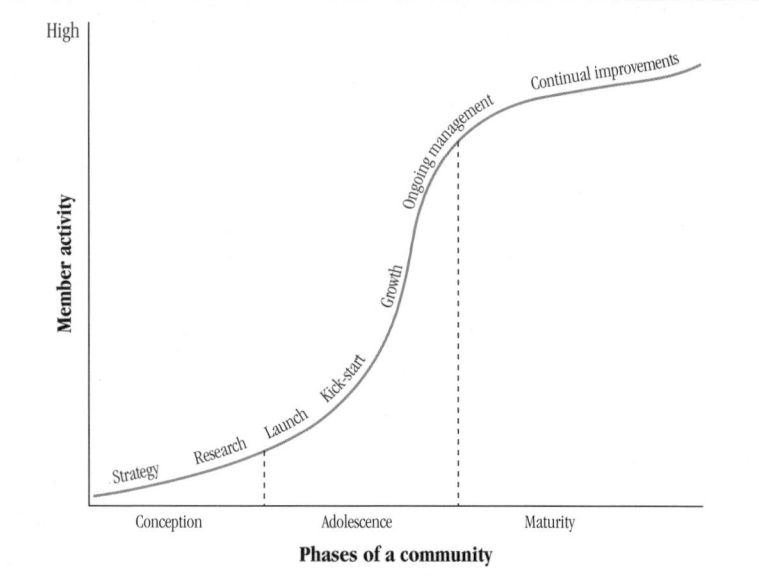

Figure 11.1 Life process of a successful community

Source: Online Community Best Practices, Forrester Research, Inc., February 13, 2008 http://www.forrester.com/rb/Research/online_community_best_practices/q/id/44795/t/2.

department responding to tweets or monitoring alerts. They reason that there have been no investments made in hard purchases of media, coupon redemptions or direct marketing pieces and therefore the investment is zero.

In reality, as with any labor-intensive campaign, it is this investment in people (and the equipment that they use) that must be measured and evaluated in order to calculate the total level of investment for a specific social marketing activity. The easiest way to determine the level of investment in personnel is to ask, "What would it take to double the effort currently being made?" Is it a few more hours, is it additional personnel? Whatever the incremental cost of doubling the effort, one of the major inputs is the level of investment, and the hard dollar investment represents a major component of the "I" in the ROI equation. Chapter 10 describes each of these cost elements associated with social marketing.

Working with the CFO or finance department to get the data and setting up accurate tracking and assigning costs to the appropriate social marketing campaign is important to make certain that all costs are captured and properly applied to the determination of the relative success of a social marketing channel or campaign compared with other campaigns or media channels.

- **Calculate the investment costs**—The finance team can help with these costs and see that they are captured and allocated to the right campaign or marketing activity.
- **Calculate the value of the returns**—This can be done either directly using last-touch attribution or using some level of modeling such as predictive modeling, marketing mix modeling or agent-based modeling.
- **Calculate the ROMI or ROI**—Depending on the requirements of the organization, it may be sensible to simply calculate the ROMI factor, especially if the results are to be consumed internally by the marketing department. However, if the results need to be communicated back to the rest of the organization, ROI is preferred.

8. REVIEWING SUCCESS OR FAILURE AND ITERATING

Upon completion of any campaign, especially a social marketing campaign, the results need to be studied for insights that can be shared with others in the organization and used for the development of the next campaign.

- **Knowledge transfer**—In many large organizations where there are multiple brands, it is often the case that insights gained from the successes and (especially) failures of different social media campaigns aren't shared across the brands. Marketers must establish a knowledge base of various campaigns and track their results so that all of the other brands can learn from these past activities. Because social media is evolving as quickly as it is, insights can be gleaned from what worked yesterday to make certain campaigns for tomorrow have the highest probability of success.
- **Risk taking**—Although no marketer wants to have failures in his or her career, with new media it may be impossible to avoid them. Marketers must be judged based on a portfolio of activities. What's critical for marketing using social marketing is to learn quickly from these mistakes in order to drive success in the future. With new media, marketers must think the way venture capitalists think—invest in 10 ventures, expecting one to be a super star, three to break even and the rest to be duds. Marketers must do their homework, but they must be willing to take risks and be in an organization that will allow risk taking and learning from failures in order to deliver that one super star that makes up for all the rest.

CONCLUSION

These eight steps have been defined to help marketers improve their execution and management of social marketing campaigns. They provide campaign- and media-level instruction, but they also touch on infrastructure requirements for the marketing organization as a whole. Depending on the sophistication of your marketing organization, these infrastructure requirements include:

- corporate-level, campaign-level and media-channel-level marketing planning
- a risk-taking environment
- knowledge management
- influencer and target audience strategy development
- negative WOM response planning
- cost tracking for both internal (personnel) and external (media) costs
- setting up social marketing guidelines for the edge of the organization
- campaign-execution tracking
- results tracking at the interim and financial (unit volume, revenue and profit) levels.

With this culture and process in place, marketers can stay ahead of the competition, develop exceedingly successful social marketing campaigns and deliver great results to their businesses.

ENDNOTES

1. Laura Patterson. *Winning with MPM: 6 Best Practices to Improve Marketing Effectiveness,* (Vision Edge Marketing, 2010).

2. Source: *5 Social Media Marketing Best Practices for B2B*, www .toolbox.com

3. For more information, please see Guy R. Powell, *Return on Marketing Investment: Demand More From Your Marketing and Sales Investments* (RPI Press, 2002) and *Marketing Calculator* (op cit).

12

SOCIAL MEDIA METRICS TOOLS PROVIDERS

EVALUATING METRICS TOOLS AND HOW TO SURVEY TOOL CAPABILITIES

Any effort to determine ROI needs some tactic or technology to gather the raw data and process it into useful information and statistics of some kind. Social media is not without several developers, tool manufacturers and vendors in this space. The computer-based nature of social media activity makes this process more measurable than its comparable traditional-media cousins and more cost-effective than a human clipping service. At the same time, this abundance of data makes it difficult to select the valuable data from the rest in order to deliver actionable insights: with the volume of data, it's like trying to take a drink from a fire hose.

In this chapter, we provide a framework for analysis of metrics tools, so marketers can make a prudent selection of the tool that will give them the best statistics for their marketing efforts and provide support in an effective ROI strategy. We accept that the tools themselves, the vendors and the manufactures will expand, contract and change as the market continues to unfold, so we will not attempt to publish a complete list here, but we will cover some of the concepts and tactics that fit into our measurement framework.

MONITORING VERSUS METRICS VERSUS INFLUENCE

Many of the tools mentioned are monitoring tools and not necessarily metrics tools. The primary difference between the two is that monitoring tools won't necessarily provide summary statistics.

As opposed to simple monitoring tools, we are defining metrics tools to provide:

1. a summary statistic, such as posts per week
2. some type of analysis, such as determine negative or positive sentiment, or a rating of some type relative to what level of influence they possess (e.g., Klout.com).

Many of the metrics tools also provide access to their statistics and analysis through an application program interface[1] (API) availability—APIs provide a valuable tool for access to key statistics that often aren't available in any other way, but there are challenges.

- If the API is available, it may be well documented or not. It may be subject to frequent updates, or the tool provider may not have the resources needed to produce, manage and work with a developer.
- Feature enhancements of the major social communities and platforms need to be reflected in the API. As these features change, the API also needs to change in order to incorporate the new feature set.
- The metrics tool provider must be successful and not at risk of going out of business. There may be some interesting applications available today, but, for many reasons, they may not survive.

A FRAMEWORK FOR EVALUATING TOOLS

We introduce the framework and explore it in detail below. Beyond that, we show how to apply a set of tools in a small to medium setting, using some of the free tools out there already and an overview of two popular tools: Radian6 and Alterian SM2.

This outline should be referenced to help you develop an assessment of tools in monitoring, metrics and management space for your own use:

- type of tool
  - monitoring, metric, influence or supporting
- listening capabilities
  - real-time or "message stream" oriented, search for past references in a stored warehouse of data, analytics, tonality or sentiment analysis
- platform orientation
  - blogs, micro-blogs, social networks—quality, quantity of data, online and offline
- scalability
  - Single user or team-oriented functionality
- metrics provided
  - summary statistics
  - historical time series data provided
  - analytics
  - dashboard.

The ROI of Social Media Facebook fan page will point to as many listings as we can identify. The purpose of this information is to provide a framework of understanding the evaluation characteristics and how you might fit into the MEF.

Marketers, listening platform providers and the social communities will be able to use this framework to support the conversation around them. With improved offerings, marketers will be able to evaluate multi-channel marketing initiatives in order to determine where and how best to invest their marketing budgets.

TOOL PRICING

There are many free services that will support an initial monitoring and metrics effort and many of them provide a path to upgrade to a more robust, fee-based premium service—this is often called a "free-mium" licensing model. Other tools have only limited time trials and permit no use past the trial period without a fee. If a particular tool is going to be incorporated into your marketing measurement infrastructure, it may be better to pay for it than to use the free version in order to make certain it supports your monitoring and measurement needs.

TOOL ASSESSMENT CHARACTERISTICS

TYPE OF TOOL

The type of tool required may be influenced by several factors. Here we suggest grouping them by one of four functional categories:
- monitoring
- metric
- influence
- supporting.

A monitoring tool will, at a minimum, provide a means of finding and presenting data from one or more social platforms, whereas a metrics tool will apply some assessment of the data collected for you. The assessment might be very simple, such as counting the number of mentions for you, all the way to giving a reading on the tone or sentiment of the posts it finds. Likewise, specialized tools exist that can provide some kind of ranking or rating of a participant relative to their ability to influence or reach others in the social media ecosphere. A "supporting" product will not necessarily add value or detract from the data being collected, but it may serve an otherwise innately useful function such as being an aggregator of content, facilitate publication or serve some other content management function.

LISTENING CAPABILITIES

Different social media monitoring packages and tools "listen" in different ways. Listening is also being enhanced through the use of semantic engines to get a sense of sentimentality and tonality.

Overall the aspects of listening fall into three areas:
- **Time value (real-time or delayed)**—Some listening tools are able to provide near real-time monitoring of the conversation taking place about the issues important to your brand. Others use a recurring, periodic search every few minutes.
- **Currency (live stream or searchable data for the past)**— Many tools provide a live stream of data, which can identify mentions when and where they occur. Many free tools do not store the data, so there is no capability for later processing. If the monitoring effort is not maintained around the clock, the ability to interact and engage with the audience may be lost.

- **Interpretation (analysis and information or just raw data)—** The social communities themselves are starting to offer some interpretations and statistics for their users. YouTube and Facebook fan pages deliver robust statistics for members or subscribers. This is not usually a tone or sentiment analysis, but rather presentation of the data in a meaningful format may be lost.

THE METRIC OF TONE AND SENTIMENT

It is in tone and sentiment assessment where we have found tools can offer significant value by taking the hundreds or thousands of mentions (millions of mentions for global brands) and processing them in some way to help the marketer make sense of the volumes of data being collected. Some tone and sentiment tools will leverage automated data collection with human assessment.

For large brands, it may be impossible to process each and every mention manually. In this case, an automated "first-pass" analysis can help the marketer sort the mentions into those that may require further processing from those that don't. When listening platform tool providers provide a "first-pass" analysis on the raw data and provide some analysis based on the captured information, the job of managing and monitoring a social media presence can be simplified and streamlined. This is an area that is sure to grow as semantic processing engines and the aspects of artificial intelligence are applied to social media listening.

Some tools also provide an ability to "educate" the listening tool and to build a library of phrases to improve their accuracy in ranking a message in either a positive, negative or neutral tone. The challenge is to do this with high accuracy without human intervention. At present, without the human intervention, the semantic processing functions provide an accuracy of only about 50 percent. With a hybrid approach this can reach about 90 percent. With the nuances of multiple dialects in each language, the use of jargon and the continuous emergence of new slang it may never be possible to achieve 100 percent accuracy. Several services are also now available that support the assessment of tone and sentiment with human intervention though. For large global brands, these providers have the task of trying to successfully scale a human-intensive process to encompass the bursting global adoption of not one or two but hundreds of social platforms.

The burgeoning need for a listening function within the enterprise means that organizations have developed social media listening post functions with full-time staffing within their marketing organizations to take advantage of the value that can be found within the social media conversation.

PLATFORM ORIENTATION

There are many places in the social media ecosphere a post or mention might occur: many marketers view "social media monitoring" as looking at the messages in Twitter and see that their function in social monitoring is complete. As a social marketer, Twitter is only one of the many platforms you need to monitor, and North America is only one of the geographies.

In a social ecosphere where there are billions of blogs, tens of thousands of social networks and hundreds of micro-blogging services around the world, identifying the platforms where your audience resides and being able to monitor them is the first priority. A monitoring function should include at a minimum: Facebook, Twitter and Google Blog Search. From this basic starting point, you can expand to other services and social platforms.

SCALABILITY

It is no real hard task to open a desktop program and build a single-screen, single-system monitoring capability to tracking Twitter, Facebook and LinkedIn messages like the one we assembled. Add to that an RSS aggregator and a few feeds of data and you have a pretty capable listening post for a small business or a single person.

For an enterprise, it is quite another task to put a team of people to work together to provide first-response customer service, lead management or an engaged integrated marketing and advertising presence. It also adds a very different dimension to the effort to attempt to include a segmented presence in social media and to capture and process a global stream of all relevant mentions and conversations.

Some of these tools have enterprise-class capabilities made up of the ability to support a team engaging in the conversation: listening, exploring, delegating and managing. Enterprise capabilities include the support and integration of workflow around the monitoring of social media sites and/or the integration with CRM platforms. Workflow integration includes the forwarding of posts to the right individual to respond, regardless of which department they belong to or what function they have.

METRICS PROVIDED

The tools have also been evaluated based on what they provide. Some provide a good listening and routing function, but may not provide historical time series data. Some may have built in analytics and yet others may have a dashboard so that the manager can quickly respond to trending events in order to scale up or down assigned resources.

EXAMPLES USING THE ROI OF SOCIAL MEDIA TOOL ANALYSIS FRAMEWORK

A sample analysis of a few key monitoring and listening tools is shown below. One presents a simple, low-cost option that an individual or small- to medium-sized business might start with. The others put popular enterprise tools (Radian6, Alterian SM2) though the evaluation framework:

- Free for SMB model
  - o SocialMention.com
  - o Google Alerts
  - o Twitter Search
- Radian6
- Alterian SM2.

There are many others that also deserve mention, but we limited the scope in this book to establish the framework and then publish ongoing results on our Facebook fan page community.

Sample analyses of a few social media metrics tools are provided in the appendix.

TOOL EVALUATION SUMMARY

Tools for monitoring, managing and supporting a social media presence are growing both in number, capability and investment. Marketers in the new $7 \times 24 \times 365$ social marketing arena must marry these tools with the implementation of their brand's strategy and tactics. The tools will continue to evolve, improve and merge over the next several years—marketers should expect more robust and capable tools to evolve. Having identified the evaluation criteria, marketers can now assess the type, the listening capability, the platform and scale of tool required.

VENDOR INTERVIEWS

As part of our work in being able to understand the tools and technologies out there, we conducted several interviews with select tool vendors, in particular Radian6, Alterian, Twitalyzer and Klout. Each of the conversations were captured and produced as podcasts and the podcasts and transcript are posted to our Facebook fan page (Facebook.com/ ROIofSocialMedia) and on our website at www.ROIofSocialMedia.com. Here are summaries of each of those conversations.

CASE STUDY

ANSWERING THE (SOCIAL) PHONE

The first step in any social presence is listening—if you're not listening, how can you possibly expect to respond and engage in a meaningful way, in context with your customer or a consumer?

Radian6

Radian6 was built around the idea that companies need to be listening to the social web in order to participate effectively. "Intelligence about online conversations is critical: companies need to know what's being said about their brand, industry, and competitors online." The Radian6 platform allows firms to listen to social media conversations, manage the workflow around the engagement in social media and measure the overall activity surrounding a brand or topic.

As Marcel LeBrun, CEO of Radian6, and the team began their work in 2006, the big issue was that social media was carrying and affecting the brand in an area outside traditional corporate control. Marcel said, "The definition of the brand was fast becoming the sum of all the conversations about it in what was an exploding number of platforms and sites. Corporate marketing managers began to see that the days were over where they sat inside a marketing room and determined 'what do we want our brand messages to mean?'" In our interview with Marcel, we talked about how the early focus of social marketing in the enterprise was an exercise in listening and understanding what a brand meant to a consumer.

Marcel also said that "the marketing organization could develop relationships with influencers in the social ecosphere." He added, "since those early days for social media-active brands and companies, social media has expanded and pushed its way into just about every business process in the company. It has become not just an enterprise application, but also a part of the enterprise's culture and companies recognize it as a vehicle to reach out to influencers and to hear and understand what the brand actually means."

"Radian6 initially targeted communications professionals, who were asking 'What are people saying about our brand?', 'Who are these people talking about us?' and 'How should we reach out to them?'" is how Marcel and his team moved to engage the industry. According to Marcel, marketers "have quickly moved to providing social media listening and management capabilities for a variety of business processes. One of the processes Radian6 has impacted is CRM or customer relationship management by providing integration with SalesForce.com. [Using Radian6 and Salesforce.com] a company representative can now reference a customer's social presence when they call in or an email is received into the sales and support organization from the customer. This provides the representative with a broad perspective for that customer and their interaction with the company; they can see the customers case history, what public conversations in social networks they've had and that this is their 'nth' complaint on the same issue. The company can now more effectively understand what needs to be resolved, along with any other prior issues the customer may have had. The customer or sales representative can respond with that context and act accordingly to maintain that conversation thread—this kind of intelligence can dramatically improve customer service."

The social phone cannot go unanswered

Marcel talked to us about how "The social media function is less like email and more like a telephone: a 'social phone'. Imagine that everybody has a phone and everybody uses it, but they use it for a whole variety of things. The social web is similar to that phone, more than it is similar to a television program or commercial. For example, a television commercial is interruption-based, the phone [metaphor] suggests that social media is more invitational; individuals are invited in and can choose whether to participate in the conversation."

"On the social phone, customers are talking, but many businesses are still not listening," Marcel says "a business person would say,

(continued)

'I'd never hang up on that customer or I'd never just completely ignore them,' yet how is that different in terms of what many companies are doing online with a proper monitoring technology or solution?" Marcel goes on to say that "Social media is now a mainstream communication channel that needs to be responded to and it is more like a party line, in the sense that everybody else on the line is listening."

Marcel says that there are several levels of involvement when it comes to corporate involvement in social marketing "The first level of involvement in social media is just listening. It's clear now that the social web is pervasive, it's growing and it can have a huge impact. Marketers have begun to get these 'ah-ha' moments where the inactivity and not listening hits them hard and they finally decide 'OK— yes, we definitely need to listen.'"

He says that he and his team are hearing "Marketers now saying we need to engage and respond directly when customers are talking. So when a consumer says 'Hey, I love this product,' a marketer needs to be able to you come back and say 'Thank you!' The consumer took the time to be an advocate and the very thing that marketers prize the most is happening—consumers are advocating the brand or product. Taking the time to say thank you is hugely powerful and it propagates and encourages a consumer advocacy behavior. Likewise, when someone complains, marketers or customer service must immediately address the issue in the venue or site that the consumer made the post in."

According to Marcel, the effort has to be able to scale for an enterprise, "In large organizations, one person can't listen to every conversation. The enterprise needs to be able to understand how to direct certain issues to certain people, who are the best people in the company to hear them and respond. The new listening business function needs to delegate the response to various conversations to the right individual or function within the organization."

"The brand is a sum of conversations between consumers and between consumers and companies—no one decided that's what a brand such as Dell should mean, but all of a sudden a consumer like Jeff Jarvis started to influence the perception of what a Dell Call Center experience is. Dell listened and they changed their call center procedures. They did so by first acknowledging the issues, by listening to consumers, by responding and then by putting a whole bunch of people out there on the front lines. These individuals would listen engage and where possible address the issues where they came up. This completely changed that experience for Dell's customers. **Now Dell gets something like 8,000 conversations a day that mentions their brand online.** Marcel concludes, "They are using tools like Radian6 to stay on top of the process 'History of social media—what history?'"

Marcel recalls that he once participated in a panel in 2009, and they were discussing how social media was so central to the (2008) presidential campaign and how US President Barak Obama used the social web so effectively. "Another participant on the panel made a comment and said, 'Do you realize that the last election we had, YouTube didn't exist.'" This put it in a perspective for him and Marcel said, "Yet, we can see how foundational it was to the communication strategy in the campaign."

Three steps in a successful social presence

According to Marcel, step one in a successful social presence is listening. He says that companies need to "listen to consumers for mentions of your brand, listen to what your competitors are doing, listen to what your customers are most passionate about and listen to what their needs are. Listen for the point of need. Everyone is expressing needs all the time and if you can listen to needs that your brand can relate to, then you can determine how you can add value."

"Step two is responding. Once you've determined where your consumer is found in social media, only then can you begin to understand the culture and what's appropriate and inappropriate in terms of how you as a brand representative should participate. Only then can you start to connect with individuals in a meaningful way and become a part of the conversation."

"Step three is engaging and connecting. Only after the connection is made should a marketer start telling the brand's story. They

(continued)

can start telling the story in the context of what they've heard their community say, in the context of relationships that have been built. It's like an 'old school' relationship and just like word of mouth, except that it happens in a much larger scale and much faster through social media."

Bread and water is on the menu

"What's interesting is the social web provides a far greater capability to gather data than anything we've had before." Marcel shares his thoughts around an analogy of gourmet cooking. "If all there is in the pantry is bread and water, then we know what we are going to have for dinner is bread and water; it's very easy to agree that bread and water is what we are going to have for dinner. What happens is, as soon as you have more ingredients, you now open things up to much more creative possibilities. Compare that metaphor to traditional media and let's take a print ad. A company says, 'What's the ROI of this print ad?' They've been building a relationship with a reporter at a trade magazine and trying to encourage them to cover the brand or the company. All of a sudden, it's done and what has typically happened there is that the PR person would determine that the article was a half-page, therefore the ad equivalency value of that half-page is $30,000, therefore that's worth $30,000; the PR person then says, 'I've spent this much time on it, here is my bill' "There's your ROI."

Marcel says that ROI is not that simple, however. "The funny part is that you really don't know what that article was worth. That's a kind of a manufactured formula that is really an intermediary number because you don't know who read the article. You know its circulation, so you know it goes to 300,000 people, but you don't know who dog-eared it, or forwarded it to their friends, who talked about it, who took action on it—you don't know any of those things. The powerful thing about the social web is that you can now determine who read a particular post and determine how they responded. You can now tie your social media initiatives to tangible business goals."

Source: Interview with Marcel LeBrun, CEO, Radian6 on October 21, 2009.
Published with permission. All rights reserved.

CASE STUDY

MEASUREMENT MAKES SENSE WHEN SOCIAL MEDIA HAS A CLEARLY DEFINED STRATEGY

The foundation for a successful social media implementation is a clearly defined strategy and an agreed upon model of what the ROI should look like. When you have that in place first, the monitoring and measurement make sense and allow the savvy marketer to show how their efforts support corporate revenue goals.

Alterian

"If social media is going to be a valid business process, we are going to have to measure ROI," said Aaron Newman, CTO of Alterian SM2 and co-founder of Techrigy, which was acquired by Alterian for its SM2 product. Aaron and Mike Talbot, co-founder and VP at Alterian, are working hard to provide one of the premier social media monitoring tools that supports the determination of ROI in the business application of social media.

Aaron says, "We clearly articulate the value of measurement in any business process, and certainly in the newly begun social media business process, and we see three areas of measurement critical to determining the ROI of social media:

1. **hard results**—in terms of incremental leads or revenue generated.
2. **soft results**—in terms of "relevancy, sentiment, influence and popularity.
3. **hard costs**—in terms of personnel and other related costs.

Because the technology is so inexpensive with social media implementations, the hard costs making up the investment side of the ROI equation are primarily made up of personnel costs."

He suggests that "Whether it amounts to just one half of an employee's time or five dedicated employees, the fixed and variable costs associated with these individuals represents the primary investment in social media activities. If we're going to invest time, money and resources in it, then I'm not going to be able to ramp it up without measuring and tracking the ROI."

(continued)

Jeff and Aaron told us that "Critical to any marketing activity is to understand and define the objectives. With the objectives clearly defined, the metrics can easily follow. We see a lot of people developing tactics without a strategy; Facebook is a tactic, not a strategy. A strategy must have clear objectives such as increasing engagement with clients, generating incremental revenue or generating qualified leads. These measurements need to be aligned with the strategy and objectives of the marketing action. This is true whether it is a social media action or a traditional media action. Many marketers forget this one key step in defining their media plans."

Two sides to ROI in social media

"One argument [against measurement] is that social media is developing like email—do we measure the ROI of email? No, businesses just do it and there's definitely a group out there in social media that thinks that it should just be engrained in everything, and we don't necessarily have to measure the ROI," said Mike Talbot. He goes on to say, "The other camp believes strongly that if we're going to invest money in this, we're going to invest time, invest resources, then there has to be a way to measure it. If there is no measurement, it gets to be difficult to justify the budget for it and marketing can't begin to improve the value of what it adds there. If there isn't a way to measure it, then an organization doesn't have a way to try to do it better next year."

"It is understandable that individuals and early adopter organizations don't necessarily want to try to measure ROI and many feel that measuring ROI in social media is too much an art form. That it's not at all a science. Measurement of social media is definitely an art form of trying to guess at what or how much the value of the social media mention is. The thought is that a lot of people say they don't want to measure social media ROI because they think it won't show a good return because it's hard to calculate, therefore the budget for it will be cut or it won't be done." Mike would say that in many cases, the entire opposite is true. "A successful social media strategy is also about identifying the audience you want to engage with, valuing the engagement in that audience, valuing what a particular level of engagement gives you in terms of increased brand awareness or increased sales or increased visibility and that's a more complicated thing that is harder to measure. That doesn't mean you shouldn't measure it."

Examining the value of a message in social marketing

Aaron observed that "When you look at a social media message or mention, there are several aspects of the mention that need to be examined: How many subscribers or eyeballs saw the post? What's the authority of the person saying it? What's the discoverability? What's the lifetime of it and then what's the sentiment of the post?"

Mike went on to say that "The more subscribers for instance to a blog, the more value it's going to be assuming the author has the authority for it. For instance, if it's somebody blogging about a heart valve and he or she is a cardiologist, that's going to have a lot more authority than me who has no idea about it, but I may have more subscribers, so authority is important around that as well."

"As to discoverability, this is something that considers that a Twitter post after an hour or two gets lost in a stream and can't easily be searched on or found later; the Twitter post is less valuable and that ties into lifetime of the mention or post. On the other hand, if it is a Wikipedia page that's going to be there for the next five years, the discoverability is much more important than a Twitter post," said Aaron.

Trending for sentiment and tone

Getting an accurate reading on tone and sentiment is still ahead of us says Aaron, "For sentiment, if it's positive sentiment, the value around that is positive. If it's negative sentiment, then the value is negative. So you can start to form these types of calculations and value scores to try to come up with 'I got this many mentions this month and it's worth this.' In SM2, we provide a high-level theme of the direction of tonality. Companies still have to understand what consumers are actually trying to discover to make sure that they are getting accurate results. You have to involve the staff in the effort, but even then with humans making assessments, it's very hard to determine what's negative and what's positive. SM2 can do some analysis at a macro level and you can do it reasonably well at that

(continued)

level, but a micro-level computer with the technology that is available today doesn't understand sarcasm, double entendre, or wry humor."

He goes on to say that "the perspective gained in a social monitoring process is a real value; what better focus group is there in the world for understanding how your message is being received and accepted than having the ability to read an individual's unguarded comments to each other about those products and those campaigns. It's vital to measure not just social media campaigns on social media—it's where the smart marketers are really seeing the value of social media."

Mike looks at how social media is evolving and observes that "For all the power social media provides and wields, it is not going to be on its own long term; it really needs to become a part of everything else you're doing, whether it's your email campaigns or your database analytics." It all "needs to be tied together. What Alterian sees is that social media is going to evolve and not to be its own entity, [it will be] integrated into all these other existing platforms and media efforts that we are already doing."

Source: Interview with Mike Talbot, Co-Founder and VP, and Aaron Newman, CTO, Alterian on November 30, 2009. Published with permission. All rights reserved.

TWITTER CAN BE ANALYZED

Twitalyzer

Twitalyzer is a social media analytics application focusing on short-messaging media. Headed by Eric Peterson and Jeff Katz, as the Product Manager for Twitalyzer, "Twitalyzer delivers great analytics and dashboard to understand how Twitter can be optimized for increased value and ROI."

According to Jeff, "Twitalyzer is betting on a shift in social analysis away from individuals focused on sometimes meaningless ratings and scores toward what they see as companies signing up for the Twitter service to connect with their consumers and customers." While there are some broad-based social monitoring tools out, Twitalyzer is focused specifically on the Twitter platform.

Jeff says that the genesis for the product was when Eric first set up his account on Twitter. Jeff shared that "Eric tried to figure out whether there was a worthwhile business in tweeting for a business. He surveyed most of the tools that were out there at the time and he felt that the content they gave him didn't reflect how he wanted to use Twitter." He continued, "The product was a side project for a couple months and then at an ad:tech conference in San Francisco, Guy Kawasaki said, 'If you're serious about measuring Twitter, you should use Twitalyzer.'" After that commentary, Eric realized that Twitter was here to stay and decided to move forward to finish the work on the product as a platform for both companies and individuals alike.

After they put out a second version of Twitalyzer in January 2010, Jeff says, "We started seeing that companies started to use more of the dashboard features which allowed them to set goals for certain metrics they wanted to measure themselves against, goals for their organization. Now Twitalyzer users could understand who is talking about them negatively or positively from an informed analysis point of view." To support the use of their data by developers, Twitalyzer built an application program interface (API) to get the information that Twitalyzer delivers from the raw data they access from Twitter.

Source: Interview with Jeff Katz, Product Lead, Twitalyzer on January 19, 2010. Published with permission. All rights reserved.

CASE STUDY

CHECK THE CLOUT OF INFLUENCERS IN YOUR MARKET

The influencer is a significant element in the MEF, but hours and days can be wasted on bloggers and other social personalities before you can actually determine which of the social digerati are worth spending time on.

(continued)

Klout

Based in San Francisco, CA, Klout believes that everyone publishing content to the social web has some level of influence; it is what Klout tries to assess. According to Joe Fernandez, founder and CEO of Klout, "Klout allows you to track the impact of your opinions, links and recommendations across your social graph. We collect data about the content you create, how people interact with that content and the size and composition of your network and from there, we analyze the data to find indicators of influence and then provide you with innovative tools to interact with and interpret the data."

"Klout measures influence across the social media ecosphere. We track over five million individuals, looking at all the content they create, digging into that content, running it again for semantic analysis and understanding what the content is about and then saying who the most influential people are on a particular set of topics. Klout then provides a numerical rating suggesting an overall influence score of a particular person. It suggests how influential a social media content creator might be on a scale of one to 100."

"Klout is not alone in their effort to assess the influence of the influencer: a lot of people are looking at influence from a lot of different angles." Joe suggests that "Now that the data is out there in the social web and companies can see how we're all connected, they can see whose content travels the furthest whether we tweet or comment or share on Facebook. The amount of data there is the semantic angle of digging in, and figuring out what specifically somebody is talking about. We really are trying to push the envelope here for data analytic sample."

To support the ability of other developers to leverage the information the Klout algorithm offers, Joe has a bead on that too. "Klout also offers an API that over 200 different companies have signed up for. They are using this data to power a CRM tool or an analytics tool in marketing, sales or product development. Hotel chains can integrate Klout into their reservation system, so when a guest checks in, they know who they are and how influential they are in social media. This kind of data is not a license to give less influential people bad customer service, but potentially their opportunity to give somebody great customer service, like send them to a show or something like that so at the end of the week, those people might tweet or blog about what a great time they had with the establishment or at a movie."

Measuring Klout—what matters?

When Joe talks about the way the Klout algorithm works, he says, "When measuring influence, Klout tries to be very transparent on how we create the ranking. There are three main components on how they calculate influence."

"First, Klout uses what they believe is a truer measure of the 'reach' somebody has, as opposed to their followers count. Klout has already allowed for inflated follower counts. The follow-follower tactic needs to be adjusted to capture an attention measurement. For example, with a following of 10,000 individuals, a Twitter user can never interact with them all and therefore their messages have significantly less impact than their follower count would lead you to believe. Klout goes beyond the follower count and measures the engagement with each node of the individual's social graph. It measures how much attention each node pays to the Twitterer." Joes says that they call this their "True Reach." Joe says that "'True Reach' defines the possible level of an individual's influence and they look at it on a message-by-message basis, what the likelihood is of this person being able to drive action."

"Secondly, there are re-tweets, replies, comments, re-comments, favorites and the types of actions that driving further actions which Klout calls the "Amplification Probability" of the influencer. The third factor is how influential are those nodes performing those actions." Joe says that "Klout borrowed from Google's and Amazon's theory of how important a page is linking to another page. A message being re-tweeted is an important show of clout on the social web. They have applied these analyses to the individual's social graph, weighing the value of the nodes who are interacting with you or following you, which then can increase your score further. Altogether there are about 30 factors that go into the calculation of the Klout score which is a number between 1 and 100."

They currently work with Twitter and are adding Facebook, MySpace and other online properties with the plan to move across all the social platforms as quickly as possible.

CONCLUSION

Other criteria will also be needed to evaluate a particular metrics tool especially as the type, capability and platforms continue to evolve. Our commitment to our readers is to facilitate the open discussion of the strategies, tactics and tools used to measure and monitor social media. The content presented here will continue to evolve and, through our online presence, we will provide an ongoing discussion to help social marketers implement and improve their efforts.

This is a very important area of activity in social marketing and one that should continue to change and improve as vendors innovate and leapfrog one another with new enhancements and improvements. These tools will continue to change and the tactics will continue to be improved and new strategies will emerge to support improvements in process and tactics. Nevertheless, implementing the right measurement tools will help the marketing to continue to prove and improve their effectiveness in social media.

ENDNOTE

1. An application programming interface (API) is an interface implemented by a software program to enable interaction with other software, much in the same way that a user interface facilitates interaction between humans and computers. http://www.computerworld. com/s/article/43487/Application_Programming_Interface

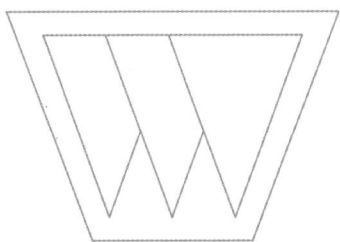

SECTION 4
WHERE DOES SOCIAL MEDIA GO FROM HERE?

13

THE FUTURE OF SOCIAL MEDIA AND ROI

It's an understatement to say that social media is maturing rapidly. The core technology, the adoption by consumers around the world and the strategy of how it fits into an online business marketing effort are all progressing at break-neck speed.

These trends are forcing businesses and marketers to invest in and operate in a 7×24×365, "always-on" marketing and customer service function that can respond to influencers, consumers and individuals who are always tweeting, always posting and always checking-in to their social media presences.

Social media will continue to play an ever-increasing part in the lives of individuals and the Internet will continue to become a more and more indispensible part of our global culture. Whether they are B2B or consumer, large or small, local or global, marketers will need to make their own assessments of how the future will unfold and based on that assessment develop the social media strategies and tactics that they can manage, measure and profit from.

The results of these assessments will be a complex evolution of consumer behavior, technology, economics and business processes, many of which do not exist today. The emergence of "conversational marketing" will focus on the consumer, the conversation and the ability to listen and engage effectively.

Even as we write this book, billions of individuals and consumers will join the conversations. Social media will become a part of their lives and can no longer be ignored by businesses, brands or marketers. With this in mind, we've put together our thoughts on what we see emerging on the social marketing horizon and how marketers can respond in order to drive more revenue, profit, brand and share—all at lower cost and risk.

CASE STUDY

BEING SOCIAL BEFORE THE ADVENT OF SOCIAL MEDIA

How do you create the largest, most highly visited food site on the Internet? By making the technology behind the site transparent, by supporting the needs of the consumer to get the information they want, when they want it—and by beginning 13 years ago.

Allrecipes.com

AllRecipes.com is the world's largest social network of food and entertaining, receiving over 390 million annual visitors. It is a website for cooks who want to "share and download recipes, reviews, photos, personal profiles and meal ideas." With over 44,000 recipes, AllRecipes.com has never been marketed anywhere, other than by word of mouth of its 3.6 million home cook members.

According to Esmee Williams, Vice President of Brand Marketing for AllRecipes.com, they don't focus on gourmet recipes fixed by culinary celebrities, but rather on everyday recipes that working parents could use to feed their family with whatever they had in the pantry or refrigerator. Although not initially begun as a social networking site, the adoption of social media has evolved to meet the needs of members. AllRecipes.com has evolved a marriage of social activity with tools that provide utility and permitted the processing that met the needs of their members.

Early on in the life of the site, the most important metric was based on the number of unique visitors, but that's becoming less relevant due to the use of multiple platforms. Now a better indication of success is the number of non-unique visitors and recurring visitors who come to the site every week for meal planning. Now, they try to measure the quality of the interaction and whether or not the members are being authentic and genuine in the interaction and they have adopted a "slow road" process that builds relationships that are more sustainable. The best relationship they can build is one that gives the consumer what he or she wants from their brand: great everyday recipes.

At the AllRecipes.com site, consumer brands that have a high degree of relevance to the content on the site are real winners when they make an effort to connect with members, especially when they adopt a more peer-to-peer approach with the AllRecipes.com audience. Esmee says it is "because people do not want to be spoken to, they wanted to be spoken with."

Consumers seemed to be willing to connect with a brand and have a dialog. The consumers are excited about it and those dialogs seem to increase purchase intent. As brands tiptoe into the AllRecipes.com community, they gain confidence and they do more and more as they find they can connect with consumers and can provide value in the relationship.

The future of social media for AllRecipes

Esmee and the marketing team see tactics and revenue growth as opportunities and threats. One concern is that with a good percentage of traffic generated from search engines, changes in the search algorithm are a possible threat. Outside of the awareness and traffic, new devices are attractive and interesting, but not at the expense of alienating their current audience. It's imperative for AllRecipes to provide an easy-to-use interface; it's a balancing act between high- and low-tech capability and serving users with the content they came to the site for: great recipes.

AllRecipes.com has begun expanding overseas, now reaching 15 different countries in their native languages and offering recipes reflecting local food cultures. The upcoming opportunity as Esmee sees it is to begin knitting them all together and begin some more exotic combinations for cooks all over the world.

Source: Interview with Esmee Williams, Vice President, Brand Marketing, AllRecipes.com on April 13, 2010. Published with permission. All rights reserved.

GREATLY EXPANDED BUSINESS ADOPTION OF SOCIAL MEDIA

Social media has begun the migration from the early adopter geek and student audience and has quickly become a necessary activity for many individuals. For business, this new behavior represents a new channel to reach out and engage with their consumers and is quickly becoming a fundamental new tool in the marketer's toolkit. This transition represents a fundamental change in the expectations of consumers and the type of relationship that they want to have with a brand.

More marketers from more businesses will get involved, and millions of new consumers will become a part of the audience that can be effectively reached with social media. It will, however, become increasingly more difficult to get your message heard by your target audience: the extraordinary ROI made by the early adopters will be harder and harder to achieve as more content from more sources comes online. The drive to achieve better and better results from social media will require more and more effort as the space matures and it becomes further integrated into the marketing activities of more and more brands.

THE DEATH OF SOCIAL MEDIA AND THE EMERGENCE OF A NEW SOCIAL PARADIGM

One of the most controversial topics presented in the last year is the almost heretical comment that social media is dying. The mental imagery the statement evokes suggests that social media is nothing but a fad and that, like the hula hoop, it will shrink into the background as a niche or specialty that is brought out to entertain future generations. Nothing could be further from the truth. Social media will expand to become a fundamental connector of individuals in our society: just about everyone on the planet will have an opportunity to find a place in the social media ecosphere where they can find other like-minded individuals. Those online connections can, do and will transcend the virtual world and extend to the offline "real" world. Already, meetings and events are occurring offline around users of the technology (Tweetups) or brands (Dell Swarm and Mashable Meetups). Social behavior does not stop at the keyboard. The keyboard is now becoming the jumping-off point for virtual connections and physical connections that start in the virtual world.

Social media will transform from its current form not because it will wane in popularity but because the opposite will be true. It is its popularity that will be its demise. We'll still have Facebook, Twitter and many countless other social media technologies, but smart marketers will work very hard to integrate them fully into their marketing activities, merged seamlessly with other traditional media. The reference to social media from the marketer's perspective will diminish as social media becomes an essential element to virtually all marketing campaigns. The social elements of a campaign will feed offline activities and the offline activities will be synergistic with social marketing activities. The objective of the overall campaign will be to drive individuals, consumers and influencers further down their respective funnels.

The change in the brand's relationship with consumers was succinctly characterized in our interview with Andrew Pickup, Chief Marketing Officer of Microsoft Asia Pacific, where he cited three phases of marketing tactics that businesses have deployed over the last several decades:

- **transactional marketing**—the model of the 60–70s marketer
- **relational marketing**—80–90s were an evolution that led to a strong one-to-one relationship
- **collaborative marketing**—the model for the 00s and beyond.

Because of social media, consumers will begin to expect conversations and collaboration with marketers in order to connect them with the brand and the organizations that wish to sell products and services to them. They will expect a human and genuine response presented in context to the issues at hand and the commentary they are producing.

NOISE

Because of the nature of social media, there is a lot of noise that marketers and consumers need to filter through. With the growing volume of conversations about so many topics, the automated search tools pick up conversations that aren't necessarily related to the brand or the category. Because of this, it is becoming increasingly more difficult and expensive to implement an effective social media listening post.

On the other hand, consumers are receiving more and more messages from their newly active social media friends, as well as from newly active social media marketers. With all these messages being received, consumers are simply tuning out this noise and only responding to a certain limited cross section of those messages that appear to be of interest. This makes it increasingly more difficult for marketers to rise above the noise with their social media messages. Although subscribers opt in to messages from many sources, it is often easier to receive them and ignore them rather than simply unsubscribing. And, as interests change, opt-in message sources that were interesting last month may no longer seem that interesting. As Steven Rubel of Edelman Digital predicts, individuals will suffer a "crisis of attention," making social media more difficult and more expensive for businesses to employ, thereby reducing overall ROI.

This creates frustration on both sides—brands will become increasingly frustrated with not being able to get the same ROI that the early adopters got (and are still getting) and consumers will become frustrated because they are not getting the quality of content they want.

For the marketer and the listening post, the response will be the emergence of better and better filtering capabilities. Some will be based on human intervention and others on an evolving artificial intelligence (AI) capability that develops a much clearer understanding of proper expressions and then learns how to better interpret slang, innuendo and sarcasm as it is taught by a host of human operators. For the foreseeable future, we expect that human interpretation and intervention will be required to achieve high accuracy (in the 90 percent range) in this function.

These types of listening capabilities will be deployed on both sides of the marketing equation: consumers will listen for items that better meet their interests and marketers will deploy them to identify the influencers and consumers who are talking about their brands, and determine where to focus their online marketing efforts to get the best results from individuals in their target markets.

Consumer expectations of understanding who they are

Social media will merge into the enterprise and influence sales via integration into customer relationship management (CRM) software packages: a core software component for medium to large organizations' sales, support, marketing and customer service functions. This will leverage the valuable consumer information found in the data that marketers collect.

Representatives will be able to open a contact form that includes the customer's past history with the organization and, potentially, their activity in general in social media. With the quality of information soon to be available, the customer service representative can determine how best to handle an inquiry, complaint or other issue. With this information, corporate representatives will be able to customize their interaction with that individual in order to deliver them an even more personalized brand experience. For example, with the implementation of social CRM, a hotel chain could determine if an individual is an influencer and, if so, to make certain that their experience exceeds their expectations in hopes that the influencer may blog about or, at a minimum, to avoid a negative experience that might also get blogged about. Consumers who are avid about social media will expect fully social media-integrated companies to understand their preferences and to assist them in making decisions about their products—they might take offense that the company did not take the time to connect to their public online profiles before offering to assist in a purchase.

A GLOBAL MARKET THAT NEVER CLOSES

Consumer adoption of social media is broad in the Western countries and it will get not just broader, in terms of technology application, but it'll also get deeper: more people will adopt social media tools as a regular part of their interaction with friends. Universal McCann produces a regular "Wave" report, detailing social media adoption and usage around the globe. In their Wave 4 report,[1] they estimated that there were approximately 625 million Internet users. The Earth's population is about 6.8 billion, so about 9.1 percent of the global population were on the Internet.

There is still a long way to go before Internet saturation, let alone social media saturation, will occur. The numbers change fast. As we write this book, Facebook is approaching almost 500 million users and a similar number of people are signing on regularly to QQ/QZone in China. Current estimates are that this number will plateau at about 50 percent of the world's population in about 10 years or so.

Global brands are already functioning in a never-stop market, but we'll see second and third tier vendors enter the mix from other countries. This will be a boon to them because they will be able to reach significantly larger audiences at significantly lower costs. Brands not seen before on one continent will now become available as marketers behind those brands find that a social media-savvy consumer will be able to engage with them anywhere and at any time.

CONSUMER PRIVACY, IDENTITY, LOCATION AND PORTABILITY

Scott McNealy, then CEO of Sun Microsystems, was quoted in a widely panned article in *PC Week* in 1999, that on the Internet "you have zero privacy, now, get over it". That was not to say you had no capability of keeping your information out of the public eye, but that the content you put on the web was, and is even more so now, very findable. In 2010, Facebook has over 400 million users in over 180 countries and, by and large, these people join to intentionally share their weekly, daily and sometimes hourly activities, and, once shared, the information is now available to all friends and acquaintances as well as prospective employers and others who might have an interest.

PRIVACY AND IDENTITY IN SOCIAL MEDIA

As one of the most visible properties in social media, Facebook's efforts in this area have gained them a good deal of press. As the Facebook platform has evolved, the company has evolved its privacy policies. These changes will become important as Facebook works to monetize their user base, providing highly targeted advertising opportunities to marketers. Facebook already gathers consumer information that is highly valued by marketers. It is now a question of how Facebook provides marketers access to that information without abrogating the trust the individual has with Facebook. The marketer will be willing to pay significantly higher rates for this highly valuable, highly targetable consumer information.

Privacy concerns will have a generational, geographic and a *quid pro quo* aspect to them. Younger consumers appear to have fewer concerns about online privacy than older consumers. US-based consumers appear to have a greater concern than their counterparts elsewhere around the world and yet other consumers are willing to trade some of their privacy for unfettered and low-cost access to popular social marketing services. The trade-off, or *quid pro quo* in the form of free services, has been a widely used tactic with traditional media, so it is not unrealistic to expect consumers to allow the same trade-off of reduced privacy in exchange for an offer of some intrinsic value.

A function of the privacy question is the loss of anonymity online. In the early stages of online culture, anonymous handles and identities permitted ranting and railing against products and people with no repercussion against the individual because their screen name did not permit a connection to the offline, real-world person. In the age of social media, a social presence is only believable when the consumer can somehow trust the person behind the presence. They have a social graph that connects them to real individuals, thereby tacitly authenticating the individual and lending them trust. Rants can no longer be done in an anonymous way, making them significantly more valuable when they do occur because they are done by real people with real identities and real friends.

When a consumer presents himself or herself as "RedHead9266" on MySpace, his or her comments (good or bad) on other pages will likely be ignored because they do not equate to the real user's identity. On the other hand, when Ashton Kutcher presents himself as "@APlusK" on Twitter, he wants you to know it's him.

PHYSICAL LOCATION IN A VIRTUAL WORLD

Many smartphones use GPS or GPS-like capabilities to determine the location of the phone and, by association, its owner. Participants of location-based, social games such as FourSquare and Gowalla, publish their locations as a part of the game. They earn virtual "badges" and mayorships that further encourage their engagement. Although there is value for the consumer in these types of games, there are also downsides. Consumers will want the benefits derived from the location-based marketing model (discounts, promotions and price specials tied to geo-fence capabilities), but security issues will have them wish to have that data guarded from general public view.

SINGLE SIGN-ON

The consumer's offline identity, and often their real world location, is a part of their social identity, but the requirement to repeatedly fill in a login screen and profile with the same information time after time is already a burden. Consumers will want to have their identity validated quickly and easily so they can move from one social network to another. This single sign-on functionality has additional benefits over and above the reduction in logins. It also significantly reduces the probability of mistakenly granting access to spammers or robots, because Facebook, Twitter and other accounts are authenticated through their user profiles.

The development of Facebook Open Graph and Facebook Connect is an application programming interface (API) offered by Facebook to application developers to use the consumer's existing Facebook login credentials to log in to third party sites. Facebook is providing incentives to platform developers by offering certain, limited data on the consumer. Twitter also has an identity management API (OAuth) and the Yahoo!–Microsoft conglomerate have theirs (LiveID based on OpenID and Passport), and others still are just starting up. Meebo recently opened "XAuth" as yet another service offering "an open platform for extending authenticated user services across the web," which is being jointly promoted by Google, Microsoft, MySpace, Yahoo!, Gigya, DISQUS and Janrain.[2]

Consumer identity is critical to help marketers better target their messages, offers and timing. If marketers can utilize and combine an individual's past behavior across social media platforms with their user profiles, marketers can more easily segment their audiences and provide them the right message with the right offer at the right time. Marketers' conversion rates improve and they are more willing to pay higher advertising rates for this highly targeted information. Developers, such as the San Diego Zoo, already use the single sign-on functionality of Facebook Connect to access their visitor's profiles so they can tailor the experience for their visitors, providing them with higher value and hopefully a higher likelihood of them engaging further with the brand.

TRUST AND REPUTATION-BASED ECONOMY

Access to personal information is less an issue for the consumer if he or she know and trust the party requesting access. The network of friends on Facebook is likely to be focused on people the consumer actually knows or are part of his or her extended network. Brands, however, represent a nameless, faceless entity: a group of people who have banded together to socialize with one another for a purpose—to sell something.

Consumers expect that they can trust their friends to handle their data confidentially and, by extension, the brands and companies they opt-in to connect to. Opt-in relationships will be the norm, and marketers will rely more and more on influencers to help develop a base of attentive consumers. The consumer is listening to the marketer's interactions in the social media ecosphere almost as intently as the marketer is listening to them. Marketers who violate the trust of the consumer by improper use of the data entrusted to them will not fare well.

Consumers will permit access to certain personal data, only so long as the brand relationship serves them. If marketers can argue that access to the data helps them better serve their fans, the fan will permit access to more intimate data. This can include their online friendships, their past social behavior and even where they are right now.

SEMANTICS

Semantics is a word meaning "the science or study of meaning in language." On the Internet, semantics are important in two ways: search and analysis of consumer-generated content.

As computers become more sophisticated, they will be able to not only see words but to understand their intended meaning. In social media, with the oceans of content generated by individuals, marketers will need to be able to aggregate that content into manageable and usable statistics. This will only be able to be done in a cost-effective manner through the use of automated searches where computers try and understand and interpret user generated content as it applies to a brand.

SEMANTIC ENGINES GET SMARTER

A key component of semantic search is the concept of "disambiguation"— or making something less ambiguous, thus clearer in the mind of the recipient.

With the enormous amount of content being generated and published on the web, it is becoming increasingly difficult to find a particular piece of information out of the millions of search results provided by existing search engines. The search engines continue to progress in their capabilities, but their ability to understand our search query and provide results that match it will continue to require improvement if they are to provide us with meaningful results. They need to evolve to provide more targeted results that encompass not only what we say, but, even more importantly, what we mean when we enter a search word or phrase.

A great deal of content is already out there and even more is being generated every day by marketers wanting to get their message in front of an audience. Content written by marketers and professional writers is now competing for attention with articles being written in social media by individuals in their own style, and with their own ability to use the written language. The search engine has yet to interpret fully what users want when they search for things. Search engines provide numerous links on a myriad of pages of results, but few of these results are relevant or meaningful. Semantic search can help the searcher to obtain a more relevant answer.

The difficulty facing the search engines is illustrated in the box on page 266. For example, the word "bark" has a number of meanings depending on whether it is a noun, verb or used idiomatically. All of these combinations can easily be found in content written by professional communicators or individuals in a social network.

SEMANTIC ANALYSIS OF CONSUMER GENERATED CONTENT

Semantic search is also critical for marketers to understand the net value of all conversations taking place about a brand. With any campaign— whether it uses traditional or social media—marketers want to know how consumers are responding and conversing. Are they conversing in a more positive or more negative way? Are they speaking in a way emphasizing one brand attribute or another? How are they speaking about the competition?

We've found that most automated semantic analysis is only correct about half the time. With a hybrid approach—combining computer and human analysis—at a much higher cost, that accuracy can be increased to about 90 percent. Even with human intervention, the sentiment and tonality of some messages simply can't be deduced. For example, is the following statement positively or negatively toned relative to Brand X?

"The new Brand X has some good features, but I like Brand Y better."

With the ability to monitor the sentiment and tonality of messages surrounding their brands accurately, marketers can use this interim metric to start to determine whether their marketing campaigns are delivering the desired effect in the social conversation. Even with the inaccuracies of automated sentiment analysis, trends can indicate how a particular brand is faring in social media. With these indicators in hand, marketers can begin to develop campaigns that are more effective at driving more positive conversations and reduce the level of negative comments. In this way, marketers can monitor these interim metrics to improve the effectiveness of their campaigns. If the campaign is not delivering the desired tonality and sentimentality, marketers can now react more quickly than having to wait for an eventual purchase, or lack thereof.

MEANINGS OF THE WORD "BARK"

Noun

1. the abrupt, harsh, explosive cry of a dog
2. a similar sound made by another animal, as a fox or seal
3. a short, explosive sound, as of firearms: *the bark of a revolver*
4. a brusque order, reply, etc.: *The foreman's bark sent the idlers back to their machines*
5. a cough
6. The outside covering of the trunk or branch of a tree or bush

Verb

1. (of a dog or other animal) to utter an abrupt, explosive cry or a series of such cries
2. to make a similar sound: *The big guns barked*
3. to speak or cry out sharply or gruffly: *a man who barks at his children*

4. Informal. To advertise a theater performance, carnival side-show, or the like, by standing at the entrance and calling out to passersby
5. to cough

Verb (used with object)

1. to utter in a harsh, shouting tone: *barking orders at her sub-ordinates.*

Idioms

1. bark at the moon, to protest in vain: *Telling her that she's mis-informed is barking at the moon.*
2. bark up the wrong tree, to assail or pursue the wrong person or object; misdirect one's efforts: *If he expects me to get him a job, he's barking up the wrong tree.*

Source: http://dictionary.reference.com/browse/bark, February 2010.

NETWORK ACCESS AND MOBILE

Access to the Internet is changing, especially in emerging countries. In advanced countries, and in the office environments of many emerging countries, the predominant method of accessing the Internet is through a laptop or desktop computer. With the emergence of new hand-held devices and wireless connectivity infrastructure, the Smartphone (e.g., the iPhone, iPad or Google Android-powered smartphone) is becoming the access mode of choice, especially in emerging countries. Soon, both the desktop and mobile devices will deliver different applications that will be used in different ways by the user. Social media will benefit greatly from this access trend. Marketers will need to monitor this trend in order to make certain they can provide the best interface for their social media applications for both modes of access.[3]

Besides mobile devices being more convenient, the wired infrastructure needed to support a wired desktop-based network as found in advanced countries, may never be built in emerging countries. Users in China and many emerging countries are already connecting to the

Internet primarily through mobile devices. Telecommunications providers in emerging countries can invest in a single cell tower that will connect thousands of users, compared with a wired connection that may only connect a single building or a single user in a single location.

THE MICRO SCALE ECONOMICS OF SOCIAL MEDIA

Economics and monetary transactions will be a driving force in the uptake by business of the Internet and the use of social media. Making payments easily and effectively will go a long way in making it beneficial for businesses to offer valuable services that can deliver profits.

Consumers have indicated that they do not mind the idea of paying for online content. Publishers will uncover ways to provide low-cost, high-value content and support 7×24 access to rich media to which consumers can opt-in. They will be able to access just the content they want: instead of having to purchase the entire issue, they will be able to consume content one article at a time. Micro-payments will make this possible, such that publishers will be paid only a few cents for each article, but be able to sell millions of articles at a time. Just as the model for buying complete music albums was affected by iTunes, so too will the payment for complete newspapers be replaced by payments for specific articles or sections. Once micro-payments are in place, marketers will be able to implement look-alike modeling in order to further enhance their sales, along the lines of what Amazon offers in terms of "people who bought X also bought Y" technology.

A consumer friendly, pay-per-access model that monetizes news gathering will emerge alongside the free citizen-journalist model. Although a 2010 Nielsen study suggested that consumers are not opposed to paying for quality content, what three out of four of them *are* opposed to is paying multiple times for content they already subscribed to in another media channel. If they already get the *New York Times* delivered to their doorstep in print, they are asking why they should pay an additional fee to get it delivered electronically.

The devices will change for content delivery and consumption too. Easy to use, full-color reader devices capable of providing rich content media with intuitive user interfaces will allow people access to publisher stores and subscribe to rich content quickly, easily and cheaply. The Apple iPad is considered to be the first of its kind in this category, providing immediate access to the iTunes Store containing a wide variety of digital content. Google and Amazon are not far behind in updating their devices to compete with the design and engineering of the iPad.

THE SOCIAL MEDIA BUBBLE AND GLOBAL PLATFORM CONSOLIDATION

In the US, a few platforms dominate their category, but in BRIC markets (Brazil, Russia, India, China), consumers can choose from a variety of platforms, each as large as and as well funded as Facebook or Twitter. A sign of market maturation is the swallowing up of smaller players by larger, more profitable ones. Google, Microsoft and Facebook are standing ready to do just that as they identify the winner and loser companies in the next tier down. Acquisitions will be determined based on the technology, consumer base or advertising networks each of them controls or manages.

Social media has been a fast-growing segment and, finally, revenue models are emerging showing how social media can deliver profitable business models. Comparisons to the dot.com growth and bubble are not inappropriate. Mergers and acquisitions will initially accelerate and then, after a period of time, slow down. At that point, social media will have fully matured into a business model that can deliver strong profits and large returns for investors.

Social media is now no longer local: it is global, and international merger and acquisition activity is underway. China's Tencent is flexing its 800 million plus strong user base by acquiring technologies and other social media platforms to add to its portfolio. As China continues to open its markets and remove constraints to its population's Internet access, the pace will quicken even more. As individuals hop from one social media platform to the next, marketers will be able to take advantage of this consolidation by gathering integrated information from the individual across a number of properties, which can lead to more highly targeted advertising and campaign development.

CHINA AND SOCIAL MEDIA

China and Western social media worlds haven't as yet overlapped. From within China, most of the major social media platforms are blocked; from without, language is still a barrier and sign-ups are constrained. Within China, there are a handful of social media properties led by QQ which is owned by Tencent. Across all the Tencent properties there are over 800 million users reported. Already QQ and QZone vie with Facebook for the largest number of users overall. With only one-third of the Chinese population online, QQ could easily surpass Facebook as more of China's population comes online.

UNFORESEEN APPLICATIONS OF SOCIAL TECHNOLOGY

Just as the television had uncertain beginnings and telephone technology was never foreseen to be used to connect to the Internet and cell-phone technology was never foreseen to replace the wired telephone, so too will social media deliver many unforeseen applications that are only now in the minds of a handful of software application developers.

The 140 characters in a Twitter message might take on an entirely different meaning if the characters used are not from the Western alphabet; imagine if the character set is the 1,000 plus Chinese character set, many of which represent entire words? The conversation can become much richer and more meaningful.

QR Codes (or quick response codes designed to allow consumers to immediately link to some webpage without having to enter the text) might take on an entirely different usage model when combined with location-based services that serve up incentives to purchase one product or service versus another, based on time, location and consumption patterns, all mined from the data consumers elect to post to their public profiles and social network.

CONCLUSION

Social media is in a maturation phase: business adoption of social media is growing and accelerating. With the use of social media for marketing, businesses will still demand results that show on the bottom line. Social marketing ROI for each of social marketing must be measured and calculated based on a valid framework. Regardless of how the future unfolds, metrics and measurement in social media will improve and the business results from social marketing will be monitored, tracked, diagnosed and improved.

Social media is a great opportunity to differentiate a brand message today, but its impact will begin to diminish as more marketers innovate and deliver better social marketing programs, improving their access to the individual's time and wallets. Those marketers who enter early will be able to reap both short-term rewards, in terms of significantly higher ROIs versus other traditional media, and will generate a potential critical mass that will be difficult for late-entering competitors to overcome.

ENDNOTES

1. http://www.slideshare.net/Olivier.mermet/universal-mc-cann-wave4, October, 2010.

2. YouTube Video; "Meebo pushes xAuth.org as solution to social network toolbar clutter problem"; Posted April 18, 2010 by Robert Scoble; http://www.youtube.com/watch?v=-UjXswWs7xg; collected June 7, 2010.

3. Aaron Smith Mobile Access 2010 report;/ Pew Internet &American Life Project; http://www.pewinternet.org/Reports/2010/Mobile-Access-2010.aspx?r=1; collected August 5, 2010.

AFTERWORD

Social media offers some excellent new ways for marketers to identify and engage with their target audiences. With social media, marketers have a way to respond directly to unvarnished, real-time comments from consumers. They can now openly thank brand advocates who make complimentary comments about the brand and they can directly intervene with a customer who has a service issue.

Social media doesn't come without its risks though—a brand's presence can be hijacked and virtual bullhorn-wielding protest groups can generate a storm of negative conversation around a brand or a company's business practices. Nevertheless, marketers must seek to engage with consumers, individuals and influencers in social media and endeavor to drive positive value for their brands using these tactic and tools in strategic initiatives. The risks need to be weighed against the positive value that can be had from social media marketing, and we think the benefits will usually outweigh the risks. We also see that social media will have far-reaching impact on a company in the way it interacts with all stakeholders in their sphere: customers, prospects, employees, past and future employees, as well as stockholders and investors.

The MEF is a foundation concept underlying a prudent, thrifty and managed social *and* traditional media strategy. To support a successful social marketing presence, the MEF provides a way to deliver value to the brand using integrated campaign tactics. The three personas—individuals, influencers and consumers—represent the main actors in social media. Marketers need to consider how they engage and win endorsement from influencers. They further need to realize that individuals only have limited time so that if marketers don't provide them lasting value, they will find other venues to occupy their time. Lastly, marketers must deliver more customers for their brand to drive more revenue at greater profit: growing the brand value and their share in the category. To that end, social marketing must still drive awareness, purchase intent and brand image, so that when the consumer makes a purchase decision, the marketer's brand is chosen over and above any other brand.

Data sources relating to each level in this framework may not exist directly, but good proxies are available. As social marketing matures, existing tools will improve and more will become available. Some of them were shown in this book and others are available at our Facebook fan page, (Facebook.com/ROIofSocialMedia) and at www.ROIofSocialMedia.com.

Now that you've read this book, we hope you will start to implement these concepts in your organization, recognizing that nothing that is worthwhile comes easy. We've found that marketers who invest that little bit extra now in metrics and analytics will reap benefits both in the short term and the long term. Those marketers who implement these concepts first and best will win. Those marketers who don't will be left wondering what happened. Don't just build a social media presence. Build a social media strategy centered on metrics and ROI to win market share and new customers from your competition in the short term and deliver value in the long term.

Can you really afford not to?

There are many other tool vendors that also deserve mention, but we limited the scope in this book to establish the framework and then publish ongoing results on our Facebook fan page community. Here are a few examples:

Tool	Where to find it on the Web	Investment
Google Reader	http://reader.google.com	**Free**

Google Reader is an aggregator, or collector, of RSS[1] feeds.
As a component of a monitoring implementation, it represents the collector of the data generated by the other tools so you can go to one place, not three, to view the data feeds generated by sites that do the actual searching and presentation of the data.

Type	Listening capability	Platforms	Scalability
☐ Monitoring ☐ Metric ☐ Influence ☑ Supporting	☑ real-time / stream oriented ☑ search / past reference ☐ analytics ☐ tonality / sentiment	☑ blogs (built-in) ☐ microblog ☐ social networks (limited) ☑ quality / quantity of data ☐ online / offline	☑ single user ☐ team-oriented functionality ☐ repeatable

Tool	Where to find it on the Web	Investment
SocialMention.com	http://www.SocialMention.com	**Free**

Social Mention is a social media search and analysis platform that aggregates user-generated content from a broad group of social media platforms into a single stream of data. The sites it has access to include Ask, Bing, Bloglines, Delic.io.us, Digg, Facebook, Friendfeed, Friendster, Google search (blog, news, video), hi5, Identi.ca, LinkedIn, MSN (social, video), Myspace, Ning, Prweb, Reddit, Slideshare, Stumbleupon, Techmeme, Technorati, Twitpic, Twitter, Wordpress, Yahoo, YouTube and several more.

SocialMention.com can provide an RSS stream that feeds the Google Reader automatically.

Type	Listening capability	Platforms	Scalability
☐ Monitoring ☑ Metric ☐ Influence ☐ Supporting	☑ real-time / stream oriented ☑ search / past reference ☑ analytics (limited) ☐ tonality / sentiment	☑ blogs (Built-in) ☑ microblog ☑ social networks (limited) ☑ quality / quantity of data ☐ online / offline	☑ single user ☐ team-oriented functionality ☐ repeatable

Tool	Where to find it on the Web	Investment
Google Alerts	http://alerts.google.com	**Free**

Google Alerts will tirelessly scour the web for mentions of whatever search phrase you provide it. You can select to have the data feed sent to an email address or a Google Reader account as they occur, once a day, or once a week.

The phrase can be as simple as the company name, a product or a person's name. It can also accept a more complex search term using Boolean expressions.

Google Alerts can provide an RSS stream that feeds the Google Reader automatically.

Type	Listening capability	Platforms	Scalability
☑ Monitoring ☐ Metric ☐ Influence ☐ Supporting	☑ real-time / stream oriented ☐ search / past reference ☐ analytics (limited) ☐ tonality / sentiment	☑ blogs (built-in) ☑ microblog ☑ social networks (limited) ☑ quality / quantity of data ☐ online / offline	☑ single user ☐ team-oriented functionality ☐ repeatable

Tool	Where to find it on the Web	Investment
Twitter Search	http://Search.Twitter.com	**Free**

Twitter Search provides a continuous and recurring search of the Twitter public message stream delivered in real-time.

Twitter Search can provide an RSS stream that feeds the Google Reader automatically.

Type	Listening capability	Platforms	Scalability
☑ Monitoring ☐ Metric ☐ Influence ☐ Supporting	☑ real-time / stream oriented ☐ search / past reference ☐ analytics (limited) ☐ tonality / sentiment	☐ blogs ☑ microblog ☐ social networks ☑ quality / quantity of data ☐ online / offline	☑ single user ☐ team-oriented functionality ☐ repeatable

Tool	Where to find it on the Web	Investment
Radian6	http://www.Radian6.com	Fee-based

"The Radian6 dashboard is a flexible, web-based social media monitoring and engagement platform that lets you view relevant conversations happening around your brand and products in real time. We aggregate those conversations—saving you lots of legwork—and put them into visuals that make analysis and measurement meaningful and actionable."[2]

Type	Listening capability	Platforms	Scalability
☑ Monitoring ☑ Metric ☐ Influence ☐ Supporting	☑ real-time / stream oriented ☑ search / past reference ☑ analytic ☑ tonality / sentiment	☑ blogs ☑ microblog ☑ social networks ☑ quality / quantity of data ☐ online / offline	☑ single user ☑ team-oriented functionality ☑ repeatable

Tool	Where to find it on the Web	Investment
Alterian SM2	http://www.Alterian.com/SM2	Free-mium

"Since 2007, SM2 has provided visibility into social media for anyone managing brands and reputations online. SM2 combines a massive data warehouse of online conversations with state of the art search, analysis and reporting tools. Marketers are now able to harness the power of the consumer's voice within social media as an integral part of their online and offline marketing strategy."

SM2 also provides a "Proprietary Social Media Warehouse with over 3.5 billion conversations stored since October 2007." Access to the Social Media Warehouse allows SM2 to perform an historical analysis of brands in social media as well as perform real-time alerting.[3]

Type	Listening capability	Platforms	Scalability
☑ Monitoring ☑ Metric ☐ Influence ☐ Supporting	☑ real-time / stream oriented ☑ search / past reference ☑ analytic ☑ tonality / sentiment	☑ blogs ☑ microblog ☑ social networks ☑ quality / quantity of data ☑ online / offline (when combined w/ other Alterian offerings)	☑ Single user ☑ team-oriented functionality ☑ repeatable

ENDNOTES

1. "RSS" stands for really simple syndication; RSS is an easy way to get data on one site, such as a blog or search result from one place to another on the Internet.

2. Product description culled from Radian6 website / www.Radian6.com; collected August 2010.

3. Product description culled from Alterian website / www.Alterian.com; collected August 2010.

BIBLIOGRAPHY

Larreche, J.C., *The Momentum Effect*. 1st ed. New, Jersey: Wharton School Publishing, 2009.

Li, Charlene and Josh, Bernoff., *Groundswell: Winning in a World Transformed by Social Technologies*. 1st ed. Boston: Harvard Business School Press, 2008.

Powell, Guy R., *Marketing Calculator*. Singapore: John Wiley & Sons, 2008.

Roeder, Linda, "14 Reasons You Should Join a Social Network." Former About.com Guide, http://personalweb.about.com/od/easyblogsandweb pages/a/whatsocialnetwo.htm, December 2009.

Safko, Lon and David K. Brake., *The Social Media Bible: Tactics, Tools, and Strategies for Business Success*. New Jersey: John Wiley & Sons, 2009.

#BeOriginal, 181
@AplusK, 68
@Comcastcares, 24, 25
@StevenGroves, 68
@TheRealShaq, 68
8-Step process for measuring social marketing strategy and ROI, 215–232
90 percent of all word of mouth conversations about a brand still take place off-line, 2
90-9-1
   90-9-1 rule, 43, 156, 164
   90-9-1 rule of thumb, 156
1800Flowers, 1800Flowers.com, 205–208
2008 presidential campaign, 59, 253

A

A1 Steak Sauce, 127, 129, 156
Acknowledgements, 12, 59
Activity trackers, 221
Adobe Creative Suite, 153
Adobe® Systems, Inc., 153
Advocacy. *See* Purchase Funnel
Advocates, 53, 159, 164
Agent-Based Modeling, 210, 228
Aided awareness, 126–127, 127
Allrecipes.com, 256–257
Alterian, 245
Alterian SM2, 277
Amazon.com, 17, 65–66
American Red Cross, 82
Amplifying the Effect of Offline With Online Social, 120–123
Association Score, 178–179

Attention metric. *See* Pitney Bowes
Audi Motor cars, 105
Audience segmentation around a topic authenticated presence, 180–181
Awareness, 126–129, 150
   Purchase Funnel, 34, 88, 124, 212

B

B2B marketing in social media, 133–139
Bai Yun and Gao Gao
   Panda's at the San Diego Zoo, 172
Baseline conversation, 32
Behavioral markers, 64–65
Behavioral targeting, 65–72
Ben & Jerry's Ice Cream, 35–36
Berry, John, 101
Biz Stone, 19
Black Hat
   SEO, 187
Blackeyed Peas. *See* Guinness Anchor Berhad
Blendtec, 13–15
Boycott of French wines, 109
Brake, David K., 40
Brand
   as the competitive set of the consumer, 171–174
Brand image, Brand imagery, 90–92, 177–179
Brand loyalty, 132
Brand optimizers, 221

Brand related. *See* Influencer stratification

Branded communities, 18, 163, 164

Brands in the MEF. *See* Competitive Set

Brandtology, 37

Bravo badge and FourSquare, 30

Bravo Networks, 29–31

Bravo Talk Bubble
    example of media engagement, 30–31

Bravolebrities, 30–31

Briggs, Rex, 39

Brogan, Chris, 81

Buck, Michael, 134, 137

Business Mashup Composer, 136

BzzAgent, 21, 59

C

CakeCentral, CakeCentral.com, 58

Call deflection, 83

Call-to-action, 225

Campaign for Real Beauty, 150–152

Campaign Measurers, 221

Canadian Marketing Association, 42

Category related. *See* Influencer stratification

CEF. *See* Community Engagement Funnel

Celebrity, 86, 105

CEO involvement
    in social media, 18, 205

Chappell, Scott, 62

Click Through Rate, 188

"Chicklet", 151, 152

ClickZ, 143

Co-creating a Brand, 87–88

Comcast, 24–26

Community engagement, 90

Community engagement funnel, 93, 146
    See also Measurement Set described

Compensating influencers, 106

Competing Demands for Time, 171–174

Competitive brand related. *See* Influencer stratification

Competitive Set in the MEF, 92

Connectedness, 64

Consideration set. *See* Purchase Funnel

Consumer Analyzers, 221

Consumer and the MEF Explained, 123–133

Consumer Packaged Goods, 126

Consumer Reports, 148

Consumers
    as a subset of individuals, 123–124

Consumption. *See* CEF

Content Quality, 112–113

Continuous efforts. *See* Social marketing investments

Conversation. *See* CEF

Conversation design, 224

Conversation hierarchy, 44–45

CorePurpose, 180–181

Costs in ROI, 22, 200, 202–204, 229–231

Cox Target Media, Inc., 39

CPM, 40

CPM (cost per thousand), 145

Credentialing system, 68

Crisis of Attention, 36

"Cross pollination" between social and traditional marketing, 187
CTR. *See* Click Through Rate
Culture of accountability in marketing, 217
Customer lifetime value, 138
Cyworld, 46

D

Decay period of brand image, 178
Defining, monitoring and evaluating interim and success metrics. *See* 8-Step process
Definition of social media, 2
Degree of completion, 161
Dell, 32
Dell-branded Community. *See* IdeaStorm.com
Dell Computers, Inc./EMEA, 136–139
Dell.com, 137
Delta Airlines, 87–88
Demographic markers, 64
Develop strategy and set goals. *See* 8-Step process
Developing a social marketing ROI model, 200
Developing campaign message and monitoring conversation content. *See* 8-Step process
Dickson, Tom, 13–15
Digg, 155
Discovery Channel. *See* BlendTec
Discussion forum, 16
Distribution channel related. *See* Influencer stratification
Dorsey, Jack, 19
Dove onslaught, 60, 204

Driving Value and Users in the Community Engagement Funnel, 142–146
Drucker, Peter, 37, 40
Dumping content, 122
Dynamic segmentation, 70–72

E

Edelman Digital, 35–36
Effect due to social influence, 49–50
Elder celebrity in the YouTube universe. *See* Tom Dickson
Eliason, Frank, 24–26
Eliminating the noise from the signal, 38
Endorsement, 86
Engagement Share. *See* Competitive Set
Eppinger, Steve, 144–146
Explained as part of the Influencer Competitive Set, 92, 169–170
Evaluating Influence, 99–100
Executing social marketing campaign tactics. *See* 8-Step process
External factors. *See* Influencer stratification

F

F150Online.com, 144–147
Facebook, 13, 18, 26, 54, 152, 162–163, 209, 261, 262, 263
Facebook Connect, 68, 172–173
  See also Polar bear Plunge
False Measures of ROI, 34
Fan Pages, 162–163
Farmville, 54–55
Forrester Research, Inc., 229

Fast Moving Consumer Goods (FMCG), 126
FastPitchNetwork.com, 19, 142
Federal Trade Commission, 59
Fire and forget, 28
First Tennessee Bank, 198–200
Fishville, 55
Four pillars of the Dell online presence, 137
FourSquare, 30
Frequency, 111–113
FTC, 59
FTC guidelines, 106
FTC guidelines on product endorsements, 113
Fulfill sense of belonging, 52–54

G

GAB. See Guinness Anchor Berhad
Gaming
    in social media, 54–56
General influencers, 100–101
Generating awareness, 211–212
Goldman, Lewis, 206
Grant, Amy, 83
Gray Hat
    SEO, 187
Green Room, 120–121
Greenpeace, 60
Gross rating points, 90
Groundswell, 83
Groups of participants, 50
GRPs, 90
Guides by Bravo, 30
Guinness, Arthur, 121–122
Guinness Anchor Berhad, 33, 120–123
Guinness beer, 120
Guy Kawasaki and the Audi R8, 105

H

Hall, Aneta, 81–83
Heineken, 33, 80, 218, 219
Heineken "Green Room," 120–121
Heineken beer, 120
History Channel. See BlendTec
Huggies, 44, 132, 157, 170

I

IdeaStorm. See Dell
Identifying target audiences. See 8-Step process
Impact on SEM of social media, 188–189
The Individual and the MEF, 141–167
Individual motivators, 48–51
Influence. See Pitney Bowes
The Influencer and the MEF, 95–96
Influencer Audience, 111–112
Influencer burn-out, 45–46, 110, 223
Influencer Communities, 106–108
Influencer funnel. See Measurement Set Explained
Influencer marketing agencies, 108
Influencer motivators, 57–61
Influencer segmentation, 86, 100, 110
Influencer stratification, 108–110
Inmail, 60, 135
Intel, 106, 107, 114
Internet Archive, 190
Intuit, 16, 35, 91
Invitation. See CEF

iPad & iPhone on WillItBlend.com, 14, 110, 267, 268

J

Jalichandra, Richard, 39
Jenner, Mark, 33, 120
Jive, 19
Just @#$% IT Campaign, 136

K

Keller, Ed, 4, 101, 114, 115
Koerber-Walker, Joan, 133, 180–181
Key Performance Indicators, 93, 149, 170, 201, 210, 211
Key social identities, 52
KickApps.com, 20
Kit-Kat, 59
klout.com, 72, 105–106, 115, 250–251
Knowledge transfer, 231

L

Lasseter, Damian, 172
Last Touch Attribution, 28
Lead Generation, 212
Life Process of a Successful Community. *See* Owyang, Jeremiah
Linkedin, 8, 51, 59–60, 61, 62, 63, 110, 135, 142, 161–162, 180, 181, 218, 222, 238
Listening, 114, 137, 203, 220, 223, 236–237
Look-alike
  Look-alike influencers, 104
  Look-alike modeling, 65–66, 268
  Look-alike models, 161, 164
Losing control of your brand, 22–23
Loyalty. *See* Purchase Funnel

M

Mafia Wars, 54–55
Mail for Heroes, 82–83
Malaysia, 33, 44–45, 80, 120, 121, 204, 219
Management costs factored in social marketing, 22, 229–231
Marketing and innovation quote by Peter Drucker, 37
Marketing investment management, 216
Marketing is The New Finance, 136–139
Marketing Mix Modeling, 209
  Marketing mix models, 227
Marketing performance measurement, 216
Marketing Process Diagram, 9–10
Marketing resource management, 216
Marks, Dan, 198–200
Maslow's Hierarchy of Needs, 3, 52–54
Master Brand, 109
Mazon, Ivana, 75
McCann, Jim, 205
Measurement set in the MEF, 80, 88, 93, 96, 201, 208, 226
Measurements to assess the success of a social campaign, 36
Measuring and tracking actual costs. *See* 8-Step process
Media channel agnostic, 83, 84
Media Engagement Framework, 9–10, 11, 13, 21, 24, 28, 45, 62, 79–93, 95–115, 117–140, 141–167

Media flighting, 219
Meebo, 68, 263, 271
Memory of the web, 159
Metrics Other Than Revenue, 173
Metrics that correlate to the value drivers. See Dell
Microsoft, 107
Microsoft LiveID, 66
Microsoft Most Valuable Professional, 107
Miller, Jennifer, 87
MIM, 216
Mix Modelers, 221
MMM, 209-210
Molter, Ted, 172
The Momentum Effect, 277
Mommy Blogger, 44, 45, 112, 170, 206-207
Monitoring and managing the execution of social marketing campaigns. See 8-Step process
Moving marketing decision making process to the edge of the organization, 228-229
MPM, 216
MRM, 216
MySpace, 19, 28, 29, 49, 51, 68, 206, 222, 251, 262, 263
Mzinga, 19

N
NASCAR, 86, 160
Near celebrity, 104-105
Near celebrity influencers, 104-105
Nestle/Kit-Kat brand, 59
Nielsen, 37, 228, 268
Nielsen BuzzMetrics, 37
Ning.com, 20

O
O'Reilly, Bill, 109
Obama, Barrack Hussein, 59, 243
One time campaigns. See Social marketing investments
Ongoing. See Social marketing investments
Oprah as an influencer in traditional media, 10, 105
Organic search, 187-188
Orkut, 8, 19

P
Paid Search, 188, 189
Palm oil, 44-45, 59, 60, 204, 226
Pampers, 44, 170
"Panda-cam" at the San Diego Zoo, 172
Papworth, Laurel, 73
Participation and engagement metric. See Pitney Bowes
Patterson, Laura, 216, 232
Peer influencer, 102-103
Peer Influencer Profiling, 102
Perceived net utility, 171
Pitney Bowes, 81-82, 229
Plaxo, 135, 161
Polar Bear Plunge, 131, 171, 172
Predictive modeling, 210, 217
Price elasticity, 209
Privacy & Demographic Markers, 64
Profile completeness, 161, 162
Profile visibility, 161
Purchase. See Purchase Funnel
Purchase committee, 132-133, 134-135, 136
Purchase Funnel. See Measurement Set explained as part of the Consumer Persona

Purchase intent. *See* Purchase
    Funnel
Purpose of ROI, 39

Q

Quenqua, Douglas, 143
QZone, 19, 261, 269

R

Radian6, 32, 37, 112, 203, 217, 235,
    239, 240–241, 243
Ratings and reviews, 17, 57, 80,
    129, 155, 160
Reach, 72, 80, 111–112
Reputation, 73, 110–111,
    115, 264
Responding to negative
    comments, 229–231
Return on marketing investment,
    216, 227
Reviewing success or failure and
    iterating. *See* 8-Step process
Rich Media, 19, 268
Risk taking, 231, 232
ROMI, 168, 201, 202, 209, 211,
    216, 231
Rubel, Steve, 35–36, 174, 260

S

Safko, Lon, 40
San Diego Zoo, 131, 264
San Diego Zoo's Wild Animal Park,
    172–174
Scoutlabs, 37
Search and social media, 186, 190
Search Engine Marketing, 120,
    187, 188, 220
Search Engine Optimization. *See*
    Tom Dickson

Seed value, 156
Segmentation, 32, 61, 63–65, 67,
    70–72, 86, 96, 100, 110, 113,
    124, 180–181
Segmentation criterion for
    consumers, 88–89
Segmenting Messages by Social
    Community, 62–63
Self-identified influencers, 104
SEM. *See* Search Engine Marketing
Sentimentality, 157, 158, 159,
    236, 266
SEO. *See* Search Engine
    Optimization
Serena Software, 135–136
Sessions College for Professional
    Design, 62–63
Sing for Your Beef, 156
Single sign-on, 66–67, 99, 159,
    263–264
SIRC, 52
SMART, 226
Smith, Julian, 81
Social as fourth leg of the
    marketing communications
    infrastructure. *See* Pitney
    Bowes
Social Before Social Was,
    256–257
Social graph, 66, 67, 250
Social Issues Research Centre, 52
Social marketing, 1, 2, 7, 8, 15, 21,
    32, 37, 89, 122–123, 188–189,
    198, 215, 224, 225, 226, 227,
    228, 247
Social marketing investments, 1–2,
    8, 12, 201, 218
Social media and customer
    support. *See* Comcast
The Social Media Bible, 23, 40

Social media campaign, 74, 156, 188, 204, 207, 220, 225, 227, 231, 248
Social media purists, 12
Social media switchboard, 38
Social media traffic cop, 38
Social media triage, 38
Social media workflow processing, 217
Social networking brand, 57, 58
Social presence as nothing more than a gimmick, 139
Society for New Communications Research, 107
Spontaneous awareness, 126-127, 129
Spontaneous retail therapy, 3
Spot-A-Mom. See 1800Flowers
Statistical regression analysis, 227
Stone, Ellen, 29-31
Stratification of Engagement, 80-83
Strunk & White, 113
Stuart, Greg, 8
Subscription. See CEF
Successful influencer program, 113-114
Swarm ad-hoc group buying event, 57

T

Tag, 155
Target audiences of this book, 221-223, 224
Technorati, 18, 155
Telligent Systems, 19
Tencent, 8, 269
TheFoodNetwork Channel, 170
Time, 47, 51, 62, 129, 141, 149, 151, 162, 169, 213, 218, 222, 225, 236, 243, 251, 263, 264, 266, 268
as the competitive set of the Individual, 92, 174-175
in the MEF. See Competitive Set
"Tina"
Model consumer for 1800Flowers, 206
Tonality, 157-158, 235, 266
TopChef. See Bravo Networks
Traditional and social media differ, 3, 23-31
Table comparison, 69-70
Traditional metrics in social marketing, 35-36
Travel Channel, 165
Tremor, 20, 59, 107, 108
Trust, 34, 73, 138, 161, 164, 205, 262, 264
Trust Agents, 81
Twitter, 9, 11, 13, 19, 20, 21, 24, 26, 30, 32, 36, 62, 63, 66, 72, 84, 105, 106, 106, 110, 112, 119, 133, 135, 142, 143-146, 172, 181, 189, 203, 206, 217, 224, 225, 238, 248-249, 251, 263, 169, 270
Twitter OAuth, 66

V

Valpak, 10, 39
Viral Videos, 13-15
Visible Technologies, 87
VisionEdge, 216

W

Wal-Mart's Elevenmoms, 44-45, 107, 170
Wanamaker, John, 8
WayBack Machine, 190

What Sticks: Why Most Advertising Fails and How to Guarantee Yours Succeeds, 8, 39
White Hat, 187
  SEO, 188, 190, 209
WIIFM, 27, 40
Williams, Esmee, 256–257
Williams, Evan, 19
WillItBlend.com, 14, 104, 124
Wilton, 58, 75
WOM. *See* Word of Mouth
WOMMA Metrics Best Practices Guidebook, 202
Word of mouth, 1, 2, 20–21, 26, 32, 64, 91, 217, 220, 221, 256
Wright, George, 14

X

XAuth, 68, 263

Y

Yahoo! as a platform for social gaming, 54–55, 68, 206, 263
YouTube, 8, 9, 10, 14, 15, 20, 26, 54, 56, 84, 87, 119, 124, 127, 136, 150, 156, 172, 210, 217–218, 222, 223, 237
YouTube categories, 56

Z

Zynga, 54, 55